D0216381

ARMY OF MANIFEST DESTINY

The American Social Experience Series

GENERAL EDITOR: JAMES KIRBY MARTIN

EDITORS: PAULA S. FASS, STEVEN H. MINTZ,

CARL PRINCE, JAMES W. REED & PETER N. STEARNS

ARMY OF MANIFEST DESTINY

*The American Soldier in
the Mexican War, 1846-1848*

JAMES M. McCAFFREY

NEW YORK UNIVERSITY PRESS
NEW YORK AND LONDON
1992

Copyright © 1992 by James M. McCaffrey
All rights reserved
Manufactured in the United States of America

Library of Congress Cataloging-in-Publication Data
McCaffrey, James M.
Army of Manifest Destiny : the American soldier in the Mexican
War, 1846–1848 / James M. McCaffrey.
    p.   cm.—(The American social experience series ; 23)
Includes bibliographical references and index.
ISBN 0-8147-5468-6 (acid-free)
1. United States.   Army—History—Mexican War, 1846–1848.
2. Mexican War, 1846–1848.   I. Title.   II. Series
E409.2.M35   1992
973.6'2—dc20   91-33517
                          CIP

New York University Press books are printed on acid-free paper,
and their binding materials are chosen for strength and durability.

LIBRARY
ALMA COLLEGE
ALMA, MICHIGAN

For my wife Ellen

LIBRARY
ALMA COLLEGE
ALMA, MICHIGAN

Contents

Preface

The impetus for this study began on a movie set outside of Natchez, Mississippi, in May 1985, when I and other history enthusiasts spent a week camping and working as extras during the filming of the television miniseries "North and South." The particular scenes in which we worked were those portraying a battle in the Mexican War, and I quickly realized how little I knew about that encounter. A year later I signed up for a directed readings course at the University of Houston and chose the Mexican War as my topic.

The number of books available in the local municipal and university libraries did not begin to equal the volume of work on the Civil War, which had been an early passion of mine, but there was enough material that I at least became familiar with the basic reasons for the war and the strategy and major personalities involved. But I wanted more. I wanted to find out about the soldiers who fought in this war. I wanted to understand their social history.

Then I stumbled upon Norman E. Tutorow's *The Mexican-American War: An Annotated Bibliography*. This book, just as the title suggests, contains an almost overwhelming listing of several thousand sources, both primary and secondary, published and unpublished. I spent the next two years completing course work for my M.A. and Ph.D. and poring over Tutorow's book. I identified what seemed to be the best collections of soldiers' letters and diaries and planned research trips around the resultant listing. And before delving into the various libraries and archives on my list, I read as much published primary material as I could. I then began traveling and visiting various repositories and gathering information.

The purpose of the present work, then, is to look at the war from the viewpoint of the common soldiers' experiences. What prompted them to enlist in the first place? What did they think of the Mexican people with whom they came in contact? How did they feel toward their officers? Were they adequately supported with food, clothing, shelter, and medical care by their government? How did they spend spare time? If they broke any rules, how were they punished? What did the regular soldiers think of these temporary volunteers, and vice versa? And finally, having answered these questions, how did the American soldiers in the Mexican War measure up to their counterparts of earlier and later conflicts?

This is not a new concept, getting at the social history of the military. Bell Wiley was one of the early practitioners, with his *Life of Johnny Reb* and *Life of Billy Yank* back in the 1940s and 1950s. In fact, the Civil War has probably drawn more interest from military historians than any other American war, and Wiley's success has led others to follow in his path. Notable among these later historians are James I. Robertson, a former student of Wiley, with his *Soldiers Blue and Gray;* Gerald F. Linderman, who wrote *Embattled Courage;* Reid Mitchell, author of *Civil War Soldiers;* Joseph Allan Frank and George A. Reaves, who focused on one particular battle in their *"Seeing the Elephant": Raw Recruits at the Battle of Shiloh;* and Joseph T. Glatthaar, who wrote of black Civil War soldiers in *Forged in Battle.*[1]

Works are also available on American soldiers in most other wars. James Kirby Martin and Mark Edward Lender studied the soldiers of the Revolutionary era in *A Respectable Army;* and Charles Royster has contributed *A Revolutionary People at War.* J. C. A. Stagg has written on the American soldier during the War of 1812 in his "Enlisted Men in the United States Army, 1812-1815: A Preliminary Survey." Soldiers of the interwar periods of the nineteenth century are the subject of Edward M. Coffman's *Old Army.* The everyday experiences of the World War II soldier form the basis of Lee Kennett's *G.I.: The American Soldier in World War II* and of Norman Longmate's *The G.I.s: The Americans in Britain, 1942-1945.*[2]

The war with Mexico, however, is a subject that has not garnered the amount of historical interest that most other American conflicts have generated. Graduate students over the years have written M.A. theses and Ph.D. dissertations describing participation in the war by the soldiers of individual states, but there has been little attempt to address the day-to-day activities of all the American soldiers involved. The present study, then, attempts to fill this gap.

No work of this kind may be done without help, and I wish to acknowledge some of those who helped me. Although the staffs of all the libraries I visited were courteous and helpful, certain people seemed to go out of their way to help me. Among these were Michael Musick of the National Archives; Madel Morgan of the Mississippi Department of Archives and History; Gary J. Arnold of the Ohio Historical Society; Randy Roberts of the Joint Collection of the Western Historical Manuscript Collection and the State Historical Society of Missouri Manuscripts at the University of Missouri; and Herbert Hartsook of the South Caroliniana Library at the University of South Carolina. The library staff of the interlibrary loan department of the University of Houston was always helpful in obtaining hard-to-find secondary works for me, and I thank them. I also thank Joseph T. Glatthaar and James Kirby Martin for their critical reading of the manuscript.

Abbreviations in Notes

AH	Atlanta Historical Society
Ala	Alabama Department of Archives and History
Chi	Chicago Historical Society
Dayton	Dayton and Montgomery County Public Library
Duke	Special Collections Department, William R. Perkins Library, Duke University
E Car	East Carolina University Library
Filson	Manuscript Department, Filson Club, Louisville, Kentucky
Ill	Illinois State Historical Library
Ind H	Indiana Historical Society Library
Ind L	Manuscript Collection, Indiana Division, Indiana State Library
LSU	Louisiana and Lower Mississippi Valley Collections, LSU Libraries
MHI	U.S. Army Military History Institute
Minn	Minnesota Historical Society
Miss	Mississippi Department of Archives and History
Mo H	Missouri Historical Society
NH	New Hampshire Historical Society
Ohio	Ohio Historical Society
Rice	Rice University Library
SMU	DeGolyer Library, Southern Methodist University, Dallas

Tenn	Tennessee State Library and Archives
U Mi	Bentley Historical Library at the University of Michigan
U Mo	Western Historical Manuscript Collection-Columbia, University of Missouri
UNC	Southern Historical Collection, Library of the University of North Carolina at Chapel Hill
USC	South Caroliniana Library, University of South Carolina
USMA	Special Collections Division, United States Military Academy Library
UT	University of Texas Archives
UTA	Special Collections Division of the University of Texas at Arlington Libraries
U Va	University of Virginia Library
Va A	Personal Papers Collection, Archives Branch, Virginia State Library and Archives, Richmond, Virginia
Va H	Virginia Historical Society
WM	Swem Library, College of William and Mary
Yale	Beinecke Library at Yale University

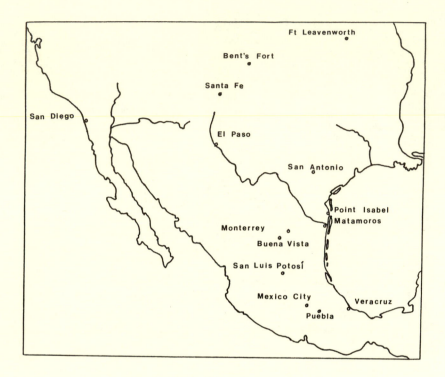

CHAPTER I

"War Exists by the Act of Mexico Herself"*

Seventy years after Thomas Jefferson penned the Declaration of Independence the United States went to war with Mexico—our first foreign war. This war did not begin suddenly; there was no Pearl Harbor. Rather, events from many years previous had sown the seeds for this conflict. Beginning in the early 1820s, Mexico allowed Moses Austin and his son Stephen to bring large numbers of Americans into its northern province of Texas. The new Mexican republic could not get its own citizens to settle in Texas, but it needed to have the area populated as a buffer against both Indian depredations and the already-evident land hunger of the United States. During the first two decades of the nineteenth century, the United States had doubled its geographic area at the expense of its Spanish-speaking neighbors by acquiring the Louisiana Territory and Florida. The Mexican government, therefore, believed that peopling its northernmost territory would make it more difficult for the United States to take this land arbitrarily.

The Americans who followed Austin and other *empresarios* into Texas did so primarily for land. Public land in the United States sold for $1.25 per acre, and buyers had to pay cash. The Mexican government, on the other hand, offered large tracts of land to these colonists for about a tenth of that cost, and even that was not always collected.

*President Polk to Congress

1

In addition, the land grants favored families. Farm families could get 177 acres, and families who intended to ranch got 4,428 acres. The newcomers were required to embrace the Roman Catholic religion and to become Mexican citizens, but they were also exempt from customs duties for seven years and from all other taxes for ten years.

The colonists willingly accepted the conditions that the Mexican government imposed upon them. Since the central government did not provide a priest for these new settlers until about 1830, and even then he was unable to get to all the settlements on any sort of regular basis, the religious requirement posed no great burden. Most of the Anglo settlers became Catholics, but in name only. Mexican citizenship also represented a rather nebulous concept for the Americans. Since dissension and internal turmoil wracked the central government of Mexico, it had very little time to devote to its new citizens in faraway Texas. Coupled with the tax moratorium, this meant that the Anglos were free to continue living very much as they had in the United States. They set up separate communities from the Mexican towns and generally made little effort to mingle with the Tejanos.

By 1830, officials in Mexico City realized that they faced a problem in Texas. The Anglo population far exceeded the number of Mexicans there, and suddenly the buffer against American encroachment had dissolved. To halt this unexpected influx, the government passed a decree on April 6, 1830, which, among other things, forbade further American colonization.

Although this decree had little effect on the everyday lives of most of the colonists, they still resented it. In the fall of 1832 they held a convention and asked the Mexican government to repeal this odious decree and to grant them statehood status within the Mexican nation. A second convention in the spring of 1833 reiterated these demands and took the further step of preparing a state constitution. While Mexican leaders feared that the Texans' real goal was independence, they tried to forestall this by liberalizing certain laws. They allowed a resumption of immigration and a certain amount of religious tolerance, and set up a superior court that allowed jury trials.

In April 1834, Antonio López de Santa Anna took over the Mexican government. Thought to be a friend of reform and of a federalist type of government, much like that of the United States, he quickly turned his back on liberalism. He got the Congress to void the liberal Constitution of 1824 and quickly faced dissension in several quarters. Citizens in the Mexican state of Zacatecas rebelled, only to be brutally crushed. In Coahuila, too, there was a minor revolt and again authorities quashed it; and by late 1835, the Anglo settlers in Texas were also in revolt.

The town of Gonzales, sixty miles southeast of San Antonio, was the site of the opening battle of the Texas Revolution. In early October 1835, a Mexican cavalry detachment rode out of San Antonio to take back a small cannon that the government had provided for Indian protection. The colonists told the officer in charge that if he wanted the cannon he would have to take it by force. The "battle" the next day left one Mexican dead, and the revolution had begun.

Two months later, the Texans defeated a Mexican force at San Antonio and forced the Mexicans—commanded by Santa Anna's brother-in-law—to retreat south across the Rio Grande River. This dual blow to Santa Anna's national pride and family honor would not go unpunished. The dictator himself led an army north to recapture San Antonio and to teach the Anglos a lesson. In the meantime, the plight of the Anglo Texans filled American newspapers and hundreds of volunteers left for Texas to help win its independence.

In late February 1836, Santa Anna's army reached San Antonio and found 150 Americans standing firm in the old mission known as the Alamo. Texas Gen. Sam Houston had ordered Col. William B. Travis and his men to abandon the mission and fall back toward the east where most of the Anglo settlements were, but they had refused. Over the next two weeks, a small group of men managed to pierce the ring of Mexican camps and ride into the Alamo, but large-scale reinforcements were not forthcoming. Just before dawn on March 6, a massive Mexican assault was successful. All the defenders died.

The loss of the Alamo was very disheartening to the Texas rebels, but the worst had yet to happen. While Santa Anna's troops marched toward San Antonio, another Mexican army had moved up the coast toward Goliad, where Col. James Fannin commanded about four hundred men. Like Travis, Fannin had also received orders to abandon his position and fall back. He hesitated, and when he finally decided to move it was too late. The Mexicans caught up with his men on an open prairie a few miles north of Goliad. The Texans were able to keep the enemy at bay throughout the day, but by nightfall it was evident that they could not win. Fannin therefore arranged to surrender his command under the assumption that he and his men would be accorded the traditional treatment of prisoners of war. The Mexicans marched their prisoners back to Goliad, where they imprisoned them in the presidio's chapel. When Santa Anna got word of their capture, he ordered their immediate execution. A week after the surrender, Mexican troops marched the prisoners out of Goliad in three separate detachments. The men thought they were going to the coast to take ship for New Orleans. Instead, after they had marched a half-mile or so from the fort, the Mexican troops stopped the columns and shot the prisoners down.

The loss of these men, murdered, was even more hideous than the loss of the Alamo. A month later, with cries of "Remember the Alamo! Remember Goliad!" Sam Houston led his force against Santa Anna at the decisive Battle of San Jacinto. The Texans brutally avenged both the Alamo and Goliad as they shot Mexicans down even as they tried to surrender. Santa Anna was among the captured, and many of the Texans clamored for his immediate execution. Instead, however, the triumphant Texans forced the Mexican dictator to sign a treaty recognizing the independence of Texas, a treaty that Santa Anna immediately repudiated upon returning to Mexico.

Nevertheless, Texas had won its freedom and existed during the next nine years as an independent republic. They were not years without conflict, however. In the summer of 1841, three hundred Texans—merchants, soldiers, and a few diplomats—set out from Austin for the Mexican town of Santa Fe. They hoped to tap into the lucrative trade existing between that Mexican town and traders from the United States. They also planned to offer the protection of the Republic of Texas to the people living there. Instead of the citizens of Santa Fe welcoming the expedition with open arms, as some Texas visionaries had predicted, Mexican troops disarmed and captured the Texans and marched them to prison in Mexico City. Many died en route.

The year following the Santa Fe Expedition, Mexican soldiers mounted two different retaliatory raids into Texas. Each got as far as

San Antonio before retiring south of the Rio Grande. While these sorties were temporarily disruptive, they did not pose any serious threat to the young republic. After the second such force had returned to Mexico, a party of Texans attempted to capture the Mexican village of Mier, just south of the Rio Grande. After a day-long battle, an overwhelming number of Mexican soldiers forced them to surrender and began marching them to Mexico City. As the prisoners headed deeper and deeper into Mexico, they realized that they might never again return to their loved ones, and they therefore determined to escape at the first opportunity. When the chance presented itself the Texans overpowered their guards and escaped northward in small groups. The rugged Mexican terrain made travel difficult, and most of the escapees soon found themselves back in captivity. Santa Anna was incensed that his prisoners should have tried to escape, and he ordered them to draw lots so that every tenth man might face a firing squad. The Texans drew beans out of a jar to determine their fate. Most of them drew white beans, signifying that they would live, but seventeen drew black beans and faced execution. While the Mier Expedition represented the last instance of open warfare between Mexico and its lost province to the north, things were far from amicable between the two.

Immediately following their successful revolution, Texans actively sought annexation by the United States and, in case that did not occur, diplomatic recognition as an independent nation. Hopes for annexation, however, ran into serious opposition from northern congressmen. They feared that the admission of Texas as a slave state would not only disrupt the balance of power between free and slave states in the U.S. Senate but would also allow the further expansion of slavery into the Southwest. While the debate over annexation continued, President Andrew Jackson, as one of his last official acts, recognized Texas's independence on March 3, 1837. Over the next three years, France, Belgium, England, and the Netherlands followed suit, but annexation always remained on the Texans' agenda. Finally, in the face of Mexican protests that such a measure would represent an act of war, the United States annexed Texas as the twenty-eighth state in 1845. Compounding the situation in Mexican eyes was the fact that the United States recognized Texas's claim to the Rio Grande as its southern boundary when, as a Mexican province, the Texas border had always been the Nueces River, 125 miles to the north.

President James K. Polk placed the American army on alert, and in the summer of 1845, Gen. Zachary Taylor proceeded to Corpus Christi, Texas, on the north bank of the Nueces, with a force of about four thousand men, representing nearly half of the U.S. Army. General Taylor dubbed his force "the Army of Observation" and ordered it to be on the lookout for any Mexican military activity in the area.

As the two nations edged ever closer to war, President Polk still held some hope for a peaceful settlement. He hoped to use the unpaid damage claims of American citizens against the Mexican government as a bargaining tool to negotiate the Texas boundary peacefully. The claims had arisen over a period of years and stemmed from the losses of Americans in Mexico due to various revolutions there. In 1842 an international tribunal had mediated the claims and awarded the U.S. government, on behalf of the actual claimants, slightly more than two million dollars. Mexico agreed to pay the damages over a five-year period but was unable to continue payments beyond the first year.

When Polk learned in the fall of 1845 that the Mexican government was willing to negotiate payment of these claims he sent John Slidell to Mexico City. By this time Polk, as well as many other Americans, had begun to cast covetous glances toward Mexican California. Because of this, Slidell's instructions encompassed not only the settlement of damage claims but also the possible purchase of California and New Mexico. He was to offer the Mexican government a release from their claims debt in exchange for its agreement to recognize the Rio Grande as the border of Texas. This border would also enclose eastern New Mexico. He was then to offer to pay five million dollars for the rest of New Mexico and as much as forty million dollars for California, although Polk privately expressed the belief that the United States could get California and New Mexico for as little as fifteen million dollars. Polk's audacity outraged Mexican officials. They had agreed to discuss only the damage claims. They certainly had no intention of giving up New Mexico and California, and refused to allow Slidell to remain in the Mexican capital.

With the failure of Slidell's mission, and after Texas had formally accepted the terms of annexation, General Taylor moved his force out of Corpus Christi and south of the Nueces in early 1846 to the banks of the Rio Grande opposite the Mexican village of Matamoros. The members of his force—now designated by the more ominous-sounding term "Army of Occupation"—must have known by this time that negotiations must soon give way to war. Young Lt. George G. Meade, who later saw all the action he could have wanted during the Civil War, was very open about his feelings. In a letter to his wife before the actual commencement of hostilities he wrote, "I hope for a war and a speedy battle, and I think one good fight will settle the business; and really, after coming so far and staying so long, it would hardly be the thing to come back without some laurels."[1]

The train of events that led more immediately to open hostilities began in early April 1846, when Mexican Maj. Gen. Pedro Ampudia notified General Taylor that he must immediately retire to the north side of the Nueces River, since Mexico claimed the land south of that river. Taylor, honoring the American claim that extended south all the way to the Rio Grande, refused. Tensions in the area heightened until April 25, when a large force of Mexican cavalry surrounded a small force of American dragoons led by Capt. Seth B. Thornton. The Americans fought gamely, but they faced overwhelming numbers. When the dust had cleared Thornton had lost sixteen men in killed and wounded, and all the rest were prisoners of the Mexicans. These were not the first American lives lost—bandits had occasionally picked off soldiers who had wandered from camp—but it was the first real encounter with Mexican soldiers.

General Taylor immediately dispatched news of this clash to Washington. President Polk received Taylor's message as he was already contemplating asking Congress for a declaration of war. The existence of American casualties erased any doubt in his mind regarding the course to take. On May 11, 1846, President Polk informed Congress that "Mexico has passed the boundary of the United States, has invaded our territory and shed American blood upon the American soil. She has proclaimed that hostilities have commenced, and that the two nations are now at war."[2]

Congress passed a declaration of war on May 13, and now it had to address the business of waging war. The size of the army was not adequate for extensive campaigning and had to be greatly enlarged as soon as possible. Drawing upon a popular perception of the effectiveness of temporary volunteers, the Polk administration called for only a modest increase in the size of the regular army and fifty thousand volunteers.[3]

Unknown to President Polk and other government leaders in Washington was the fact that the level of hostilities along the Rio Grande had already intensified considerably. On April 30, Maj. Gen. Mariano Arista's main force began crossing the Rio Grande a dozen miles below Taylor's position. The American commander hastily strengthened the earthen fort—Fort Texas—across from Matamoros, and started for Point Isabel for supplies with most of his men on May 1. After marching until midnight, the tired American soldiers pushed on early the next morning and finally reached their destination by about noon. They immediately set to work fortifying their position and preparing for a Mexican attack.

Due to delays in crossing the river, General Arista had been unable to intercept the Americans before they reached their supply base, so he changed his plans. While he kept a wary eye on Taylor with the bulk of his force, he detached General Ampudia's brigade and sent it back to help the Matamoros garrison take Fort Texas and the five hundred enemy troops within. The bombardment of the fort began early on the morning of May 3. The American artillery immediately responded. It soon became evident, however, that the Americans would not be driven out of their little fort without some cost. The Mexican cannons were unable to breach the fort's walls, and an infantry attack would result in unacceptable casualties. General Ampudia apparently decided to starve the fort into submission with a classic siege.

Meanwhile, General Taylor had strengthened his supply base and felt it was secure enough to allow him to march to the relief of the beleaguered garrison of Fort Texas. He issued marching orders for the next day, in which he expressed utmost confidence in his small army. He knew that General Arista would very likely engage him in battle, and he reminded his infantrymen that "their main dependence must be in the bayonet." On the afternoon of May 7, he led his force of slightly over twenty-two hundred men, accompanied by two hundred supply wagons, out of Point Isabel. As soon as General Arista learned of Taylor's departure he recalled Ampudia's brigade and hurried to interpose his force across Taylor's line of march.[4]

Near the middle of the next day, the American advanced guard discovered the Mexican troops near a place called Palo Alto. The scouts immediately halted and refilled their canteens as they waited for the rest of the army to catch up with them. The day was very warm. Many of the men had removed their wool jackets, and some had donned straw hats. As the American army moved slowly through the dense chaparral, Mexican artillery opened up at a range of about a half-mile. One American wrote that "the balls were constantly hissing over our heads or mowing their way through the tall grass, and it was astonishing how few struck our ranks." American cannons quickly began a counterbattery fire in reply as General Taylor hastily formed his men into a line of battle.[5]

General Arista's battle plan was to attack and turn the right side of the American line, and then fall upon Taylor's parked supply wagons in the rear. As a force of Mexican cavalry under Gen. Anastasio Torrejón began to head in that direction, two regiments of U.S. infantry moved to block them. One, the Fifth U.S., formed itself into the classic square defensive position while the Third U.S. took up a position nearer the wagons. The American infantrymen in the square steeled themselves to receive the lancers and were surprised when the enemy did not attack and completely envelop them. Instead, the Mexican horsemen pulled up at a distance from the Americans and began firing by squadron, each squadron then retiring to the rear rank to reload. The Americans, despite the casualties they were beginning to take, continued to wait as the enemy slowly advanced in this manner. Then, when the enemy cavalry had closed to within fifty yards, American musketry "emptied upwards of 40 saddles." Rather than risk another attack upon the square, General Torrejón decided to bypass it and head straight for the wagon park. After his men got close enough to see that the Third Regiment was guarding the wagons, and had a pair of cannons to help them, he decided to return to his own lines.[6]

Elsewhere on the field, the muzzle blasts from Lt. James Duncan's cannons ignited the prairie grass. The resulting smoke eventually obscured a good deal of the area between the two armies and the fighting halted for an hour or so until visibility returned. During this respite the men sat and rested, as if from a period of drilling, while General Taylor rode up and down the line visiting with his subordinates. Then, Duncan "went out and blazed away. Every shot was sent home with unerring accuracy."[7]

Once again Torrejón's cavalry advanced on the American right, this time supported by Mexican infantry. And once again the Mexicans met American troops formed into a square, this time an artillery battalion. Infantrymen on both sides traded volleys, but it was the American artillery that made the difference as it cut huge swaths in the enemy ranks. Both armies fought bravely, and it was certainly not an imbalance of valor that determined the outcome.

As darkness began to envelop the field the two sides disengaged themselves and took stock of their respective situations. The Americans had lost five killed, forty-three wounded, and two missing out of a force of over twenty-two hundred men. Mexican losses were much higher. Out of approximately thirty-seven hundred men, General Arista left 102 dead upon the field, with another 129 wounded, and twenty-six missing. Since the Americans retained control of the field, they claimed a tactical victory. Strategically, however, nothing had been settled. The American point of view showed that there was still a large Mexican army on American soil. The Mexicans likewise considered Taylor's force to be a foreign army on their claimed territory.[8]

Taylor's troops awoke the next morning to see the Mexican army slowly withdrawing southward. As one American soldier wrote, "It was a beautiful morning; the winds were singing; the sun was shining bright; and the sweet fragrance of the prairie flowers was wafted along by gentle winds; and yet, surrounded by all this loveliness, were two Christian armies about to meet and kill each other." General Taylor called a council of his top subordinates and asked their opinions on his next course of action. Most of them voted to fortify their present position until reinforcements could arrive. Taylor mulled over the situation for a couple of hours, but he favored an immediate pursuit of the retreating Mexicans and finally ordered his army to advance. First, the able-bodied soldiers erected breastworks and placed cannons to protect the vital supply train from any sudden Mexican thrust, while the wounded began a slow journey back to Point Isabel.[9]

The Americans did not have to go far to overtake the Mexicans. General Arista had suffered defeat at Palo Alto, but this was another day, and he was willing to stand and fight again. The location he chose to defend was strong, one in which American artillery, so decisive at Palo Alto, would not have room to maneuver effectively. Unlike the Palo Alto battlefield, which was fairly open prairie, Arista's position was a heavily wooded, crescent-shaped ravine, or *resaca*, that had once been a channel for the Rio Grande. It was about sixty yards wide and open toward the north. Its four-foot depth made it an ideal defensive position. Arista distributed his infantry, including recently arrived reinforcements from the siege of Fort Texas, along the protective ravine, and placed artillery to command the road that crossed it, and along which the American army had to pass. Then he waited.

By early afternoon the vanguard of the American army approached the Mexican position, and the battle commenced with sporadic skirmish fire. When General Taylor arrived on the scene he ordered one of his field artillery batteries forward along the road and deployed three infantry regiments in the dense chaparral on either side of it. As the fighting intensified, Taylor's foot soldiers slowly worked their way toward the edge of the ravine, the thick underbrush making any cohesive action impossible. As the Americans pushed forward, they became separated from their commands and wound up following the orders of whatever officers were nearest them. One participant, a member of the Fifth U.S. Infantry, matter-of-factly wrote, "There were no tactics used. It was a grand free fight, from right to left." So intense did the battle become that one of Taylor's men was not even aware that a Mexican bullet had hit his cartridge box, exploding it and setting his clothes on fire. He realized what had happened only when his burning sleeve set off the cartridge in his hand as he was tearing it open with his teeth.[10]

Nor were the artillerymen making much progress. Even though they were sometimes firing a load of canister and an explosive shell at the same time, they had been unable to silence the enemy guns and felt a constant threat from Mexican lancers. They had beaten off one attack by these horsemen, but were not sure that they could do so again.[11]

At this point, General Taylor sent forward a squadron of dragoons under the command of Lt. Col. Charles A. May with orders to capture a particularly troublesome enemy battery. May's men hesitated briefly at the American artillery position of Lt. Randolph Ridgely while May inquired about the exact position of the Mexican guns. Ridgely said, "Hold it, Charley, 'till I draw their fire and you will see where they are." He then fired his cannons, and the Mexican gunners immediately replied. As soon as they did, May led his men thundering down the road in a column of fours, hoping to reach the enemy guns before they could get off another shot. So irresistible was their charge that the dragoons swept over the gun position and penetrated deep into the Mexican lines before the men could stop. When they finally halted, Colonel May saw that he only had a half-dozen troopers still in their saddles and could therefore not retain the captured guns. His men did not return entirely empty-handed, however, as among the captured prisoners was Brig. Gen. Rómulo Díaz de la Vega.[12]

Mexican cannoneers quickly recaptured their guns and put them back into action. General Taylor, disappointed in his dragoons, called Lt. Col. William G. Belknap forward with two regiments of infantry. He ordered Belknap to "take those guns and by God, keep them!" It was not an easy task, but finally this Mexican position fell.[13]

Meanwhile, troops on the extreme right of the American line discovered a trail across the ravine about which neither of the army commanders had been aware. This proved to be the turning point in the battle. Even though General Arista rushed troops to this trouble spot, he was not able to stop the American breakthrough. The Mexican army began to fall back again, only this time the retreat turned into a rout as, according to an American witness, "they could not stand the yankee steel and they flew in terror and dismay from the field." Another American recorded a similar impression: "The enemy can scarcely be said to have made a stand after the flight commenced, for a few well directed shots from our batteries drove him from position to position, till he reached the [Rio Grande] river." Indeed, the demoralized *soldados* could not seem to get away fast enough. As one Mexican later wrote, "The most horrible confusion reigned on the field, and everything announced a grievous disaster to our arms." The disaster was magnified by the fact that many of the defeated soldiers drowned in their panic-stricken attempts to cross the Rio Grande to safety.[14]

This time there was no doubt as to the outcome of the battle. The Americans had driven the Mexican army out of the disputed territory. They never returned. Casualties were heavier on both sides than they had been the day before. General Taylor lost thirty-three men killed and eighty-nine wounded of the seventeen hundred men actually engaged. General Arista's losses were, surprisingly, much higher. The attacking force usually suffers greater losses, but in this case even though the Mexicans were fighting a defensive battle, they lost over five hundred in killed, wounded, and missing.[15]

The American soldiers were jubilant. Although the Seminole Wars in Florida had provided combat experience for some of them, the fighting at Palo Alto and Resaca de la Palma was the baptism of fire for most. The twin victories gave a tremendous morale boost after months of inactivity along the Texas coast. One young officer, showing both the elation of a victor and a more sober reflection upon what he had just experienced, wrote his sister that he "would not have missed being in these fights for a great deal but I must say that I do not wish to see another."[16]

The performance of the troops also gave support to the continuing debate over the status of the army, as the men proved their worth to the nation. The mere fact that General Taylor had called for volunteers at all had been offensive to some of his officers. Many of them voiced tremendous elation over the fact that no volunteers, except for a handful of Texans, had arrived in time to take part in the battles. They believed, and rightly so as later events were to prove, that had volunteers taken part in these battles, they would have claimed most of the credit for themselves and "the American people would cheerfully have conceded it to them. Indeed, it would have been said, that the [regular] army was rescued from annihilation; and, unpopular as it was before, it would never again have held up its head. . . . The denunciations of uselessness and imbecility would have been repeated, and West Point graduates [would] have continued to be stigmatized, as merely 'kid glove dandies.' "[17]

The war between the United States and Mexico had by now claimed over a thousand casualties. It was a very real war, and as such demanded very extensive planning. On the evening of May 14, 1846, the day after Congress approved President James K. Polk's war message, the president, Secretary of War William B. Marcy, and Gen. Winfield Scott met to begin this planning. It was obvious to all three men that General Taylor should continue his activities along the Rio Grande and should push on into northern Mexico. They also decided to dispatch a large expedition overland from San Antonio, Texas, to the Mexican town of Chihuahua, and a somewhat smaller force from Missouri to Santa Fe in present New Mexico. The Mexican War had indeed begun.

CHAPTER 2

To the Colors

With the existence of a state of war between the Republic of Mexico and the United States, the most pressing problem became how to raise the strength of the army to a level necessary to ensure victory. Well before the commencement of actual hostilities, authorities in the War Department gave *some* thought to the need for more troops. During the last week of August 1845, the secretary of war requested the cooperation of the governors of the western states in supplying troops to Major General Taylor, should the need arise. Taylor, however, was only to call upon the governors in the event that Mexico declared war on the United States, or if a large number of Mexican troops crossed the Rio Grande. The "incursion" of General Torrejón's cavalry on April 24, 1846, and the next day's skirmish with American dragoons under Captain Thornton fell within these guidelines. General Taylor wasted no time in sending out a call for reinforcements. He asked the governors of Texas and Louisiana, the two nearest states, to forward five thousand men immediately. The actual arrival of troops, however, in the days before rapid transportation, would take time. In fact, had the Mexican force at Matamoros been better organized, it could conceivably have defeated—and perhaps even captured—the small American army under Taylor even before news of the original skirmish had reached Washington.[1]

This initial request for large numbers of volunteers quickly became mired in confusion. At New Orleans, Brig. Gen. Edmund P. Gaines overstepped his actual authority on May 3, 1846, and called upon the governors of Alabama, Mississippi, and Missouri for even more reinforcements than General Taylor had requested. Moreover, Gaines's call was for men to serve for six months, an enlistment period—in light of the time necessary to train troops adequately and to transport them to the seat of war—that was entirely too short to be of practical value. Before the War Department could repudiate his actions, Gaines made a second requisition. Before long more than twelve thousand men were on their way to the Rio Grande in response to Taylor's and Gaines's requests.

At the same time that knowledgeable military men were saying that a six-month enlistment was too short for effective service, someone recalled the wording of a 1795 law that prevented any militia called up for a national emergency to serve for more than *three* months. In order to allay any fears that troops were being readied in violation of this law, Congress, on May 13, 1846, passed an act authorizing the president to call up fifty thousand volunteers—not to be confused with militia—to serve for twelve months or the duration of the war with Mexico, unless sooner discharged.

Not calling upon the militia in this emergency had two effects on the procurement of troops. First, and most obvious, was the fact that the volunteers could legally serve for longer than three months. Thus, if recruiting officers could induce men to volunteer for twelve months —or even twelve years—there was no law that would prevent it.[2]

The second benefit of not relying on the militia was the questionable overall condition of the existing militia units in most states. The concept of a militia brought to mind different images to different people. Some viewed the militia as consisting of all male citizens, who would be called upon in a case of a dire national emergency. This represented the romanticized image of the Minute Men of the American Revolution, ready to leave the plow or shop at a moment's notice and take up their guns in defense of their hearth, home, community, and country. In 1846, however, the Minute Men were long gone, yet there remained two slightly more modern versions of what constituted a state's militia.

A federal law dating back to 1792 required all men between the ages of eighteen and forty-five to enroll in the militia. It also suggested that the optimum-sized militia company would contain two officers, twelve noncommissioned officers, and sixty-five privates. According to this arrangement, then, there were almost two million militiamen in the United States in 1846. In theory, these men were all organized into companies, regiments, brigades, and divisions, each with its corresponding retinue of officers and aides. For instance, when war came each of Mississippi's sixty-eight counties contained a militia regiment. Had these units all existed at full, wartime strength (almost eight hundred men each), Mississippi alone could have furnished almost as many men as eventually served in *all* of the volunteer units raised for the war. Of course, such was not the case. Some of the counties reported fully organized units to the state's adjutant general, while others were only partially filled, and some made no reports at all. Indiana's adjutant general could not order out even a single organized regiment of state militia because none existed. Only one of New York's eighteen militia regiments in 1847 included the recommended ten companies. Four of these regiments contained only one company, while the rest varied between three and eleven.[3]

Thus, with the militias of the various states in such deplorable condition, it was essential that volunteers carry the load. The raising of volunteers quickly got into full stride. The secretary of war called up approximately twenty thousand of the authorized fifty thousand men from Alabama, Arkansas, Georgia, Illinois, Indiana, Kentucky, Mississippi, Missouri, Ohio, Tennessee, and Texas for immediate deployment. He instructed the governors of the other states to enroll another twenty-five thousand men and hold them in readiness.[4]

The bare mechanics of the recruiting process of the nineteenth century were quite simple. After the governor of a state learned his state's quota from the War Department, he would in turn issue a call for volunteers. Sometimes the local militia officers paraded their companies and asked for men to step forward to join a new volunteer company. Prominent citizens unconnected with the militia also advertised that they were raising companies to go to Mexico. Since the volunteers elected their own officers, these citizens usually hoped to be rewarded with a captaincy. When a group of recruits reached company size, their captain reported them to the governor as ready for duty. Then, after the governor accepted them, they traveled to their state's designated place of rendezvous. There they waited to be mustered into federal service.

The general response to the call for volunteers was overwhelming. Fueled by patriotic speeches, bonfires, torchlight parades, and liberal doses of "Canal Water," war fever ran high in most communities. Fearful of the effects of martial passion on his son, a South Carolina history professor who opposed the war sent him to Europe so that he would not get caught up in the war fever and enlist. A young Indiana man who had reservations concerning the morality of the war, calling it "the most unholy war ever waged by a civilized people," nevertheless succumbed to the excitement of the times and joined the "University Guards."[5]

But most of those who enlisted do not seem to have had any qualms about doing so, and very few have left any evidence that they questioned their country's decision to go to war with Mexico. One regular army infantryman, perhaps more perceptive than most, rationalized his actions in a letter to friends: "I do not pretend to say that this war is entirely justifiable, for there is not one war in twenty that is, but I believe and I think I have good reasons for believing that Mexico is more in fault than the United States in bringing on the war." A regular officer, George Meade, entertained similar sentiments, but he was a little more precise as to where he lay the blame for the war, saying that it was "brought on by our injustice to a neighbor, and uncalled-for aggression." However, in the excitement of the moment men of military age, whether they were already in the army or were facing pressure to volunteer, were more than willing to overlook such a thing as who was most at fault in bringing on the war. Their country was at war and Lieutenant Meade and others wished "to see it conducted in a vigorous manner, and brought to a speedy conclusion by its being carried on with energy well directed."[6]

In most sections of the country the response to the call for volunteers was overwhelming. The citizens of Baltimore met their city's quota in thirty-six hours. Thirty thousand Tennesseans rushed to fill the three thousand positions allotted that state. Four times as many Kentuckians volunteered as were required. Ohio met its three-thousand-man quota in two weeks. The War Department sought four regiments from Illinois, but enough men came forward to fill fourteen,

and North Carolina met its quota three times over. Even in Massachusetts, where many citizens objected to the war as merely a ploy to gain
new slave territory, enough men responded to fill its one required
regiment in less than a month. This glut of eager young recruits
created the embarrassing problem of choosing men for service and
sending the rest back home. The governors of Tennessee and North
Carolina drew lots to decide, while Kentucky's governor simply accepted troops on a first-come-first-served basis. Whatever the methods
employed, they left most young men at home.[7]

At Paris, Kentucky, two regiments of state militia gathered to hear
the governor's call for volunteers read to them. In less than an hour,
over a hundred men had come forward. While this was going on,
however, word arrived that Kentucky's quota of infantry had already
been met. Any more volunteers would have to enlist as cavalry and
bring their own horses. This created something of a problem since not
all of the Paris volunteers had extra horses that they could spare for
military service. Nevertheless, the men continued to organize themselves and elect their officers while the citizens collected horses and
donated money to outfit the company as cavalry. By 6 p.m. the
organization was complete, and the newly elected captain and one of
his lieutenants hurried off on the forty-mile trip to the state capital at
Frankfort to report to the governor. Upon reaching Lexington, they
learned that a company had formed there that day and its officers were
even then on *their* way to Frankfort. After getting a fresh horse for
their buggy, the two men from Paris pressed on. They overtook the
Lexington representatives and seemed assured of reaching the capital
before them until one of their wheels splintered. Undaunted, the
captain left the lieutenant to come on foot while he jumped on the
horse and raced on. He reached the governor's mansion about midnight and got the chief executive out of bed only to learn that a local
company had filled the last remaining vacancy just a few hours earlier.[8]

A company of 140 Virginians offered themselves to their governor,
but he would not accept them until their number was pared down to
sixty-four. Likewise, Alabama's "Eutaw Rangers" had to cut back to
sixty-four men before they would be accepted. Many of the men thus
displaced sincerely hated to return to their communities, while others
"pretended to do so who were at heart delighted at it."[9]

Some went to extreme lengths to get into the army. Indianans crossed the Ohio River to join Kentucky regiments. Marylanders enlisted in the Virginia Regiment. And a Memphis newspaper urged Tennesseans not to wait for the governor to call for volunteers, but to go to Louisiana where troops were already organizing. Early in May 1846, a group of Mississippians organized a company at Natchez, even though the War Department had not authorized their state to furnish troops. Indeed, the battles at Palo Alto and Resaca de la Palma had not even occurred. But Louisiana, just across the river, had begun raising troops in response to General Taylor's request in late April. The enterprising Mississippians, therefore, simply crossed the river and enrolled as Company E of the Fourth Regiment of Louisiana Volunteer Infantry. Another Mississippi company took an even more drastic step. Coming from Port Gibson, they were too late for inclusion in their state's regiment. Disappointed but not deterred, they went to New Orleans hoping somehow to join another unit there. With their expectations dashed in the Crescent City they took ship (at their own expense) for Point Isabel on the lower Texas coast. There they finally got their wish when they joined Taylor's army as part of the First Regiment of Texas Volunteer Infantry.[10]

The initial enthusiasm for the war waned somewhat in certain areas, due to the ambiguous wording of the act calling for volunteers. The first section of this act allowed the president to call up fifty thousand volunteers and "the militia, naval and military forces of the United States . . . to serve twelve months, or to the end of the war, unless sooner discharged." The second section, however, stipulated that if the militia were called up, it was to "be compelled to serve for a term not exceeding six months." Thus, many men were willing to serve for six months, but resisted going in for twelve. Entire companies sometimes disbanded, after arriving at their rendezvous points, when their members refused muster into federal service for the longer term. Secretary of War William Marcy further exacerbated the situation in November 1846 by stating that all new enlistments had to be for the duration of the war.[11]

This problem was particularly noticeable in the states farthest from Mexico. In these locations, state authorities were to enlist soldiers and organize companies and regiments. Then they waited until the War

Department notified them before sending their troops to Mexico. Because of this delay, many of the young men who hurried to sign up in the summer of 1846 had lost their earlier zeal by the time the actual call to duty came, usually several months later, and they refused to go. In Fayetteville, North Carolina, some patriotic local women collected money to buy a beautifully engraved silver goblet to commemorate the Fayetteville Riflemen "for their meritorious conduct for volunteering their service for the Mexican War." When North Carolina authorities finally received orders to send their troops to the front, some four months later, over half of the Fayetteville Riflemen decided not to go.[12]

Despite such difficulties, however, the raising of volunteers was generally attended by much patriotic oratory and community involvement. Eager young men electioneered openly for company office and these elections were, according to a Pennsylvania volunteer, just like "all other elections, fighting and knocking one another down was the order of the day." Appeals to patriotism were common, but some held out the promise of plunder. Peter Goff sought the captaincy of Company A, Second Illinois Volunteers. This self-proclaimed murderer of abolitionist newspaper editor Elijah Lovejoy promised that he would show the Mexicans no more mercy than he had shown Lovejoy. Just in case this fiery appeal was not enough, however, he backed it up with a hundred dollars worth of whiskey. He was duly elected. Not all of the officers thus elected were of the same stripe as Captain Goff. Approximately one hundred volunteer officers had attended the U.S. Military Academy, although not all of them had remained long enough to earn commissions. Many had returned to civilian life after leaving the academy and then reentered the army as volunteers. Some of these returnees, Jefferson Davis for one, turned in creditable performances.[13]

As the companies formed, local women would often set to work making uniforms and tents. As much as the volunteers appreciated their efforts, the piece of handiwork held in greatest esteem was the company flag. The usual train of events was that a local woman, or perhaps a group of women, stitched up a flag for the young men to take to war with them. When the flag was complete, there would be a formal ceremony in which one of the young ladies responsible for the flag would present it to the company. Her presentation speech usually enjoined the young men to defend the banner with their lives. She would encourage them to "unfurl its Stars and Stripes upon the Palace of the Montezumas." Of course, to do anything to dishonor the flag was beyond comprehension. It would be better, by far, that the soldiers' "blood dye the plains of Mexico and this flag should be their winding sheet than that they should disgrace themselves or it by dastardly conduct."[14]

One of the officers would then make an acceptance speech, assuring all within earshot that his brave soldiers would not dishonor either the flag or their country. Occasionally, the unthinkable would be mentioned:

But should we not be victorious; if in the Book of Fate it is decreed that we are to be vanquished, and are to fall fighting beneath this Flag, our last prayers shall be, in our last dying moments, that some kind hand may bear it back safely to those who made it, to be preserved by them, as a lasting memento of those gallant youths who poured out their life blood fighting beneath its Stars and Stripes in defence of their country's right and in defence of that liberty, which Valor has won, and Wisdom and Virtue bequeathed unto us.[15]

The holiday mood continued when the soon-to-be-tested soldiers toasted the women whose hands had stitched their flag. A typical salute was, "We honor them for their patriotism, we respect them for their worth and virtue, we admire them for their beauty and love them because we can't help it." A dinner for the volunteers usually accompanied the flag presentation, and the whole event took on the aspect of "a regular Methodist camp meeting."[16]

The formation of the military companies was only the first step in converting eager but usually completely untrained civilians into an army. Each governor appointed one or more rendezvous points in his state to which the volunteer companies came to enter into United States service. This movement often required the expenditure of several days' travel by foot, wagon, canal boat, or railroad—sometimes a combination of all these modes. Even though citizens often donated the use of their wagons to convey the enlistees, meals had to be furnished and other incidental expenses met. In legislation dated June 18, 1846, Congress authorized a payment to each man of fifty cents for every twenty miles traveled to his state's rendezvous to take care of such costs. The men could not collect this money, however, until authorities actually accepted them into federal service. Different states solved this problem in different ways. The governor of Indiana called on his state's banks to loan the necessary money until federal reimbursements were available. In other states, governors asked their legislatures for appropriations. South Carolina put up twenty thousand dollars for its troops. When Florida's lawmakers failed to respond, the governor used his own money. In Massachusetts, the same problem occurred. To meet the emergency Caleb Cushing, the colonel of Massachusetts' lone required regiment, put up five thousand dollars to cover travel expenses and give his troops a one-month advance on their pay.[17]

After the volunteers reached their rendezvous points they still had to form regiments and elect their regimental officers—colonels, lieutenant colonels, and majors. Army officials then assigned regiments to brigades. At this level, however, soldiers no longer elected their leaders. Instead the president appointed brigadier generals to command these units.

The state rendezvous presented the first taste of military life to many of the recruits. Doctors were to examine them there and judge their fitness for the rigors of active campaigning. Before approving enlistees for acceptance in the army, the doctor certified that they had full use of their limbs, did not suffer from rupture or any other disabling infirmities, and would not be the means for introducing any contagious diseases into the army. It was the examining physician's further responsibility "to ascertain, as far as practicable, whether the recruit is an habitual drunkard, or subject to convulsions of any kind, or has received any contusions or wounds in the head which might produce occasional insanity."[18]

Army regulations called for the soldier to remove all his clothing for the medical examination. This provision was generally important for a couple of reasons. In countries such as England and France, where many soldiers entered the army through conscription, this type of examination made it more difficult for these men to make themselves appear unfit. The effects of padded clothing, to simulate deformities, or harnesses, to inhibit mobility artificially, became immediately apparent if the recruit was naked. In the United States, where all soldiers

served voluntarily, this type of examination prevented genuinely unsuitable men, though motivated by the highest patriotism, from entering the army.

Because of the rush to get soldiers to Mexico, the quality of the
physical examinations did not always come up to official requirements.
The men of one volunteer regiment remained fully clothed while
physicians examined them and only forty of the one thousand men
failed to pass. When this regiment got to Mexico, however, many of
its members had to be discharged as physically unable to perform the
duties of soldiers. Had doctors conducted their original physicals in
strict accordance to regulations, however, many of these men would
never have left home in the first place. Subsequently, physicians examined a detachment of replacement troops destined for this same
regiment. This time they more carefully followed regulations and the
doctors rejected 20 percent of these men, most of whom would have
passed had they taken the exam with their clothes on.[19]

Another reason for having enlistees disrobe was to keep undesirable
former soldiers from reenlisting. This class of men appeared normal
when clothed, but stood out when naked because of the brands that
authorities had applied to them. An observer had merely to look for
the letter *D* for deserter, or *HD* for habitual drunkard, tattooed on a
hip or under the arm of a recruit to know that he was not a fit candidate
for enlistment.

The examining physician looked first for obvious abnormalities. He
immediately rejected any men with deformed or missing limbs, or flat
feet. A recruit had to have his front teeth, and they had to be strong
enough to tear open a musket cartridge. He could not be blind in
either eye. A contemporary guide for military surgeons also enjoined
them to have the recruit stand up straight and observe him from all
sides, looking for such things as spinal curvature. They were to check
his sense of balance by having him stand first on one foot, then the
other. He should flex all of his joints to assure that they allowed full
range of motion for his arms and legs. The same book issued a further
caution to army doctors: "Some recruits are so offensive in their breath
. . . as to be intolerable to their comrades; and, for these causes . . .
ought, unquestionably, to be rejected from any army."[20]

Some of the men weeded out by this process probably heaved a secret sigh of relief. They would not have to go to Mexico after all. Others, however, felt a stigma attached to their situation and blamed the physician. A doctor in Mobile, Alabama, wrote to his father that he had rejected nine of the eighty men he had examined, and that "they could not be made to understand that a visitation of providence was not an insult offered by myself to their manliness." Doctors turned an Indiana man away because of a deformed shoulder. With a judicious amount of padding, he made himself appear normal and successfully enlisted into a different company. This again shows that not all of the medical examinations strictly followed army regulations.[21]

In some instances, these nineteenth-century versions of preinduction physicals revealed much more about the soldiers than was usually the case. An Alabama man asked his captain for permission to take his younger brother along. He explained that the young fellow was of a rather frail constitution, but that if he had to leave him in Mobile he would be entirely on his own. The captain, in a moment of compassion, agreed, and the young man came to live among the soldiers. He kept to himself most of the time, declining to participate in any of the rough-and-tumble sports often engaged in by the rest of the men. Eventually rumors began to circulate that cast some doubt upon the true relationship of the brothers. On hearing the stories, the captain asked the battalion's doctor to examine the delicate young civilian, and he quickly discovered the reasons for his apparent frailty. He was not the other soldier's brother at all, but was a young lady of easy virtue. She was immediately forced to leave the camp, still wearing a man's clothing, and her sponsor was the victim of much ridicule from his messmates for some time to come.[22]

A Missouri volunteer in a similar situation faced more than ridicule. Before leaving Fort Leavenworth for Santa Fe this man, a lieutenant, decided that there was no reason to give up all the amenities of civilization. He therefore had a young woman, described as an "abandoned female," enrolled in his company as a man. This arrangement went undetected for some time, as she performed a soldier's duties by day and satisfied the officer's sexual urges by night. She might have continued the charade for some time had she not become pregnant. When the lieutenant learned of her condition he urged her to "desert" and return to Missouri with a supply train that was headed that way.

She was quickly apprehended and the lieutenant found himself facing court-martial charges of defrauding the government. By "tenting, sleeping and co-habiting with the said female," he had deprived the United States "of the service of a good and competent soldier." As a result of the trial, authorities dismissed the lieutenant from the service.[23]

It is possible, although unlikely, that a few women successfully masqueraded as men to enter the army. At least one woman insisted, in a book published after the war, that she had passed herself off as a man and had served in combat. Even after being wounded at Cerro Gordo in the spring of 1847, she claimed that her secret remained undiscovered. A woman was also discovered among Indiana troops. She claimed that she tried to pass herself off as a man because that was the only way she could join her father, who was a soldier in General Taylor's army. Her plight touched sympathetic local citizens, and they subscribed enough money to pay for her passage to the Rio Grande.[24]

Another problem sometimes facing army surgeons was trying to decide the race of the enlistee. The U.S. Army, like many other institutions of American society in the 1840s, was closed to black Americans. While blacks had served well in both the American Revolution and the War of 1812, and would again serve with distinction in the Civil War, no known blacks saw duty as combat soldiers during the Mexican War. The obvious physical differences between the races made it easy for the examining doctor to reject black enlistees. The problem became a bit more difficult, however, in the case of men who were the offspring of mixed parentage. A contemporary manual of instruction for the medical examination of army recruits cautioned doctors to be very careful in this area, as "soldiers would not tolerate the mixed breed as comrades." The manual went on to say that the examining physicians might have to rely on less than fully scientific means to determine whether an applicant might have Negro blood in his veins. In such cases where skin color alone was indeterminate, the doctors should look for the slightly different shape of the skull attributed to blacks. But since this characteristic disappeared after only a few generations of miscegenation, this supposedly left only the texture of the hair as an identifier, and that, too, was often unreliable.[25]

During the first year of the war, a man presented himself for enlistment at Fortress Monroe, Virginia. The doctor who examined him had some misgivings as to his racial stock. Since he was not sure, the doctor called in the commanding officer and both men finally decided that the recruit was a white man and allowed him to enlist. "Some weeks after, a person of respectable standing called on the [commanding] officer, and claimed the man as his slave and his son. Not a doubt could be entertained of the credibility of the gentleman who applied for the youth, who was his son by a bright mulatto woman, his slave."[26]

Army regulations specified that the recruit who successfully passed the physical exam was to receive a thorough, head-to-foot washing and have his "*hair cut close to his head.*" The new soldier then received his uniform and turned in his civilian's clothes. For however long he was in the army, he was not to possess any clothing except that which he received from the government. Of course, in the rush to enlist, army recruiters probably did not demand strict adherence to all of the rules.[27]

The same legislative act that called for volunteers also stipulated that they provide their own uniforms. Whereas this provision certainly alleviated the demand for government-issued clothing, it just as certainly did not contribute to the standardization of dress. The possibilities of variation in cut, color, and trim were limitless. In spite of this, however, most uniforms were reasonable approximations of those worn in the regular army.

The enlisted infantryman of the regular army of the mid-1840s wore a light blue, often referred to as sky blue, wool jacket and trousers. The close-fitting jacket, also called a roundabout, was a single-breasted garment with a single row of white metal (pewter) buttons and a standup collar that fit snugly. Even though army uniform regulations had called for dark blue as the national color for a quarter-century before the Mexican War, the only infantrymen to wear this color were officers. The dyes required to obtain the dark blue color were expensive so the sky blue, which was often a mixed weave of blue and white, became the accepted uniform color. The volunteer uniforms, for the most part, were varying shades of blue or gray, although there were some notable exceptions. One company of Alabama volunteers wore frock coats and trousers of green worsted, while a Mississippian wrote

home that Gen. Zachary Taylor referred to his unit as "the striped
tigers from our uniform being all striped."[28]

Perhaps more important to a soldier's comfort than the color of his
uniform was the number of articles required. Too few meant that he
would be cold in certain climates while too many meant he had to
carry extra weight on long, hot marches. A North Carolina newspaper
published the following list of required clothing for volunteers: one
dress cap, one forage cap, one uniform coat, one woolen jacket, two
pairs of woolen overalls, one cotton jacket, three pairs of cotton overalls, two flannel shirts, two pairs of drawers, four pairs of bootees
(shoes), four pairs of socks, one linen fatigue frock, one neck stock, and
one blanket. This seems to be a close approximation of one year's
regular army clothing allotment as published in contemporary army
regulations, except for an overcoat, or great coat. If, indeed, any
soldier went off to war with this much clothing, it seems certain that
he stored excess articles while actively campaigning.[29]

A discussion of how the government raised and outfitted troops for
service in Mexico is incomplete without some attempt to learn more
about the men who volunteered. It is almost impossible to arrive at
precise quantitative data for the Mexican War soldier. Unlike the case
with the Civil War, there is no central repository for descriptive rolls
of the Mexican War volunteers. It is therefore difficult to gauge such
characteristics as the age, occupation, or nationality of the "average"
volunteer for that war. On the basis of descriptive lists of regular army
recruits and of various published muster rolls of volunteer units, however, one may draw a fairly accurate picture of the American soldier
during the Mexican War.

By way of comparison, a survey of just over one million Union
army soldiers, published shortly after the end of the Civil War, shows
that the average man in that conflict was about twenty-five to twenty-
six years of age upon enlistment. Some were as young as thirteen and
some were octogenarians. An admittedly small and unscientific study
of Mexican War muster rolls shows almost exactly the same results.[30]

One very strong point of similarity is that the soldiers in both wars
were predominantly farmers or laborers. This should come as no
surprise since the general population was overwhelmingly rural.[31]

There were foreigners in the ranks of the regular army in the 1840s, although probably not as many as in the following two decades. One captain, complaining that fully one-half of his company did not understand English, observed that "they never could comprehend the difference between the command to *charge* their muskets, *charge* the enemy, and *charge* the United States for services rendered." Throughout the early nineteenth century aliens had enrolled in relatively high numbers, and by the time of the war with Mexico they comprised about 40 percent of enlisted strength. This figure assumes less significance, however, when one recalls that volunteers outnumbered regulars by a considerable margin during the Mexican War, and the volunteers tended to be overwhelmingly native born. Again, because of the lack of compiled evidence, this is difficult to quantify but the literature appears to bear it out. In the midst of this Anglo-American majority there were a few instances of volunteer units composed almost wholly of other ethnic groups. Some of the companies of Missouri volunteers that accompanied Colonel Doniphan were almost completely German, and Irish predominated in the ranks of the ill-fated Jasper Greens from Georgia.[32]

The armies of the 1860s were likewise predominantly native born but with large leavenings, at least on the Union side, of foreigners. As many as two hundred thousand Germans and 150,000 Irish fought to restore the Union, and there were lesser numbers of men from many other countries, including Mexico. Entire regiments were often made up of men from a particular country. These included the Irish Twenty-third Illinois, Ninth Massachusetts, and Sixty-third New York, the Danish Third Wisconsin, and the German Eleventh Corps. Because immigrants tended to reside in the cities, and because the largest cities were in the North, the number of foreign troops in the Confederate armies was smaller. Nevertheless, there were a few cases—such as some of the New Orleans volunteers—where entire companies were made up of non-English-speaking volunteers.[33]

By and large, the United States Army that went to Mexico was a little less ethnically diverse than were the two American armies that met during the 1860s. Perhaps the most important reason for this is simply that the flood of immigration, spurred by famine in Ireland and

political revolutions in other parts of Europe, was only beginning at
the time of the Mexican War. There were, therefore, relatively fewer
immigrants than in 1861.

All of the foregoing represents an attempt to quantify data that are
readily available (at least for the Civil War soldier), and to use it to
compare the armies in question. The result is that the soldiers in these
armies were remarkably similar.

Delving into the inner man, however, by examining soldiers' letters,
diaries, and reminiscences, indicates other similarities but some differences also. Young men joined the army in 1861 with the same youthful
exuberance that other volunteers had shown in 1846. They seem to
have forgotten the horrors of the earlier conflict, the men who returned
from Mexico with fewer limbs than when they had left, the long lists
of those who had succumbed to killer diseases far from home. These
things were easy to put out of mind because they were so overshadowed by the positive aspects of the Mexican War. The territorial gains
were of immense value, thereby making the sacrifices somehow easier
to accept. And it had been a war in which American arms had not
known battlefield defeat. The very success, therefore, in Mexico simply fanned the flames of desire for martial honors.

The men who flocked to the colors did so for a variety of reasons.
Some went into the army to get away from problems they were having
in civilian life. The lingering effects of the Panic of 1837 still haunted
some men, and they may have hoped to hide in the army from credi-
tors. Some saw the army as a means of livelihood until the nation's
economy improved to the point that they could find other suitable
employment. Many recent immigrants enlisted for this reason throughout
the nineteenth century, and those who came from non-English-speaking countries had a chance to learn the language and American customs
by joining the army. Some—it is difficult to know just how many—
entered the service with the sole purpose of having the government
pay for their transportation to the frontier. Once there, where a man
often had a better chance at a fresh start at making a living, these
recruits deserted. It was not uncommon for a man to enlist, as had
Edgar Allan Poe some years before, under an assumed name. A Texas
newspaper reported the following exchange, perhaps apocryphal, between two volunteers:

"Why have you volunteered" said rather a careworn-looking, newly enrolled volunteer to a fine looking young country soldier. "Why I volunteered because I have no wife, and go in for war," was the unequivocal reply; and now why have you volunteered? he added. "Oh!" said the careworn-countenanced little man—for he was little—with a sigh, "I have volunteered *because I have a wife, and go in for peace.*"

Others joined to escape entangling domestic problems.[34]

A New York City volunteer had one of the more unusual motives for joining the army and he managed to involve his whole family in the decision. He was a German immigrant, and the loss of his entire life's savings to a burglar had left him terribly embittered toward his adopted home. When he heard of a New York regiment being raised for service in California he saw this as his opportunity to start a new life, far from the evils of the big city. This, in itself, was not so different from many other recruits. This man, however, enlisted with his oldest son as privates, while two younger sons were enrolled in the regimental band as drummer and fifer, and his wife and six younger children went along as laundresses, cooks, and scullery moppets.[35]

A study of soldiers' letters, diaries, and reminiscences reveals two major reasons for enlistment. First, there was a desire for personal glory and adventure in a foreign land, sometimes masked in the rhetoric of patriotism. Second, there was a perceived need to avenge the deaths of the men killed during the Texas Revolution and during subsequent difficulties between the Republic of Texas and Mexico.

The same sort of *rage militaire* that swept across the American colonies in 1775 was again evident in 1846. Most young men viewed the war with Mexico as a wonderful opportunity for them to do something memorable. They seemed not to realize the awful price in human suffering that each side pays in any war. An Ohio college student seemed only vaguely aware of the seriousness of war when he notified his father of his intention to interrupt his studies long enough to enlist. "I still want to graduate," he wrote, "and for that reason I should like to know whether you would send me to college after I came back, provided first that I should go & secondly that I got back safe." He and his thousands of comrades in arms expected to march into Mexico and show those people that the mighty United States of

America was not a country to be trifled with. And that would be that![36]

It had been over thirty years since the smoke had cleared over the battlefield at New Orleans, and the memories of America's last major war had faded considerably. The veterans of the War of 1812 were probably not much different than the veterans of all other wars. When they got together to relive their experiences, they likely came to dwell less and less on the bad food, hard marching, and constant threat of death by disease that was their lot. Instead, by the 1840s, they would have tended to play up the "glory" of soldiering. Their war, and in fact every war, was the most dramatic, if not most important, event in the lives of its participants. The war with Mexico was to be, as a Virginia newspaper declared, "the last opportunity that will be presented to this generation" for martial glory.[37]

The apparent ease with which General Taylor's small army had defeated its larger Mexican enemy at the battles of Palo Alto and Resaca de la Palma in May 1846 fueled a feeling of American invincibility in the hearts of young Americans. In fact, many of the volunteers were afraid that Taylor would end the war before they had a chance to participate. A Missourian was on his way to St. Louis to enlist when he heard of Taylor's early victories. So, with no apparent prospect of winning any laurels, he returned home. A volunteer at Fortress Monroe, Virginia, waiting for ships to take his regiment to Mexico, expressed his anxiety in a letter to his father in early 1847: "I am very anxious to get off, fearing that we might not arrive in time for the first great battle, and I believe the last." He apparently did not think too much of Taylor's victories at Palo Alto, Resaca de la Palma, or Monterrey.[38]

Two months later, this same soldier wrote from Mexico, "The expectation that we will be attacked seems to have delighted the men, & I must say that I would be pleased myself, for I can assure you that fighting is the least dangerous & arduous part of a soldier's duty." Although this was a man who had yet to smell powder, he nevertheless expressed a sentiment that most of this war's volunteers shared. It was at once an almost overwhelming desire for battle and a sense of personal invincibility to the dangers of combat. Nor was this attitude restricted to the troops of the Mexican War. During the Civil War soldiers on both sides often exhibited deep anxiety that the war would be over before they could take an active part in it. A World War II G.I. called war a spectacle, "something to see." He went on to write that his contemporaries, too, were afraid that if they could not go into the army they would "miss something worth seeing." A combat veteran of the Vietnam War called war a game, an "escape from the everyday." He went on to declare that "if you come back" from a war, "you bring with you knowledge that you have explored regions of your soul that in most men will always remain uncharted." [39]

Although the volunteers of the 1840s came forward for many of the same reasons that had impelled American men into other wars, there was another spur to enlistment, one that was unique to this conflict. The Texas Revolution had occurred ten years earlier, but it had a tremendous effect on recruiting in 1846. This was, of course, obvious with regard to volunteers from the state of Texas, where a newspaper enjoined its readers to "think of our countrymen martyred at the Alamo, at Goliad, at Mier." People in virtually every part of the United States had reasons for sympathizing with friends and relatives in Texas. It was predominantly American settlers from the older states, after all, who colonized Texas. The makeup of one company of the Texas Army in 1836 illustrates this fact well. Fourteen Pennsylvanians, eight Virginians, four Kentuckians, four from England, three each from Indiana, Tennessee, and Maryland, two each from Maine and Germany, and individual soldiers from Mississippi, Delaware, South Carolina, North Carolina, Missouri, and Scotland comprised it. [40]

The Texas Revolution inspired a certain amount of typical American sympathy for the underdog, and the fact that so many Americans traveled to Texas to join in the struggle guaranteed a considerable amount of personal interest in its outcome. Had things happened differently during the revolution a large part of the anti-Mexican feelings would probably have subsided by 1846. But the massacre of over 180 men at the Alamo and the execution of nearly four hundred of Col. James Fannin's men at Goliad after they had surrendered kept passions high. Men from almost every state in the country had died at the Alamo, and the casualty list from Goliad showed some fifty-four Kentuckians, three Pennsylvanians, five companies of Georgians, and

141 Alabamians. This geographic dispersion kept alive a widespread
thirst for revenge. It was this strong desire to avenge the perfidious
deaths of friends and relatives that drove many of the volunteers of
1846.[41]

The memory of these events loomed large. One company of Georgia volunteers even called itself the Fannin Avengers. Survivors of the
two most recent Texan expeditions joined the American army in 1846,
and a Tennessean was undoubtedly correct when he assured his brother
and sister that these men "did not enter the service altogether through
motives of pure patriotism, but for the sake of the spoils, and to glut
their vengeance." Many other soldiers remarked upon incidents of the
Texas Revolution when passing near the site of one of them. They saw
where members of Fannin's ill-fated command had scratched their
names into the walls of the chapel at Goliad before their execution.
They were anxious to fight the Mexicans under Gen. Jose Urrea "as
he is the same individual who, ten years ago, ordered the massacre at
Goliad. . . . If we find him . . . we will pay him up for old scores."
They saw the names of other Texans, captured at Mier, on the walls
of their prison cells in Perote. They viewed the ruins of the Alamo in
San Antonio "where Col. Crockett & his little band of heroes 'fell their
rights defending.' "[42]

And so it was that in the summer of 1846 thousands of young men
from across United States rushed to enlist in the new volunteer regiments bound for Mexico and glory. They determined not to miss out
on this, their generation's war. Just like soldiers before and since, they
would strive for personal laurels, putting their manhood to the ulti-
mate test. Unlike volunteers in other wars, however, these young men
went forth with another—unique—purpose. They intended to avenge
in blood the treacherous fates of those who had died to win Texas
independence. But it would be a while before any of these patriotic
volunteers met the enemy. They must first be trained, equipped, and
transported to the seat of war.

CHAPTER 3

Off to War

The enthusiasm with which young Americans hurried to join the army made it easy for the government to attain its manpower quotas. But before these thousands of eager recruits could actually face the enemy the army had to make sure that it trained its soldiers and provided them with the proper types and amounts of equipment, such as weapons, ammunition, food, medical supplies, tents, and blankets. This had not been a difficult task before the outbreak of war with Mexico. The army was small, less than seventy-four hundred officers and men, but suddenly the secretary of war was calling for twenty thousand volunteers immediately, with the possibility of thirty thousand more to be available in the near future. In fact, before the wartime emergency subsided, over 112,000 men had joined the army.[1]

The least critical item, in terms of what was already available, was weapons. The two national arsenals, at Springfield, Massachusetts, and Harpers Ferry, Virginia, constantly turned out muskets, and there were thousands of them stockpiled at various armories around the country. There were plenty of guns on hand in the summer of 1846. By the middle of June, there were already enough muskets and rifles at a depot in Galveston, Texas, to arm all of the expected Texas volunteers many times over. The Allegheny Arsenal dispatched weapons to Alton, Illinois, and Louisville, Kentucky, and the arsenal at Baton Rouge sent guns to Fulton and Fort Smith, Arkansas, Mobile, and Memphis for distribution to the volunteers gathered there. Many

35

other troops stopped at Baton Rouge on their way down the Mississippi River to pick up their muskets.[2]

These thousands of muskets were of no practical use, however,
unless the recruits knew how to use them effectively. The commanding general of the army, Maj. Gen. Winfield Scott, recognized the
need for training and advised that the newly enrolled volunteers remain in the United States for several months while they received the
necessary education. Some of the new troops, because of previous
militia duty, were familiar with basic military instruction. For others,
though, including some of the company officers, this was their first
exposure to such things. The martial ardor of some men rapidly waned
when they reached their rendezvous points and discovered that army
life was not to be one big frolic. In order to become effective soldiers,
they had to learn to drill. And learning the drill took hours and hours
of repetition.

Still, the men found time for less military pursuits. Many of them
were away from home for the first time in their lives and wanted to
kick up their heels a bit. Kentucky volunteers quickly wore out their
welcome among the civilian population of Louisville. In fact, their
antics so disturbed a local newspaper editor that he wrote, "An order
for the speedy embarkation of the volunteers would be hailed with the
liveliest satisfaction by the citizens of Louisville." Sometimes the antics
of the soldiers were more serious than mere drunken carousing. A
handful of Alabama volunteers came upon a Creole family in the
vicinity of their camp near Mobile, and mistook them for mulattoes.
After several visits the head of the family, himself a slaveowner,
discovered their mistake and tried to convince them of their error. The
soldiers were not easily dissuaded, however, and had already resolved
to return at night and satisfy their lustful cravings with the old man's
dark-complected daughters. That night the men, fortified with whiskey, returned and demanded admittance. The Creole, of course, refused, and told them to leave before someone got hurt. Not about to
be put off by one man, the Alabamians proceeded to break down his
door, whereupon he fired and killed one of them. In the ensuing
confusion, the family fled to the city and sought the protection of the
local sheriff until the regiment left for Mexico.[3]

The root cause of many of these problems was alcohol. Hundreds of young men with a lot of free time on their hands made an inviting prospect for all the whiskey peddlers in the neighborhoods of the camps. Some camp commanders went to great lengths to cut down on the drinking, but enterprising groups of soldiers just as often found ways of circumventing such measures. At Camp Toulmin, for instance, sentinels patrolled the camp's perimeter with orders to arrest any man attempting to enter the camp with whiskey. Soldiers soon found a small country store nearby and arranged with the proprietor a way to satisfy their thirsts. They would visit the store during the day and pay for a jug of whiskey. Then, after dark, the merchant would pass along the road bordering the camp with a long cord attached to the jug. Finding a spot between two guards, he would throw the cord into the edge of the camp. The waiting soldiers then carefully hauled in their prize.[4]

With organization complete, the men still had to be armed, trained, fed, clothed, and transported to Mexico. The law that called the volunteers to service also specified that the federal government furnish them with weapons. This provision lessened the supply problems that would have occurred if the men had brought along their own guns. Trying to supply ammunition to a campaigning army whose soldiers were carrying everything from the government issue .69 caliber smoothbore flintlock muskets to .36 caliber rifled percussion squirrel guns would have resulted in chaos. And even though the individual state militias periodically drew weapons from government arsenals, the War Department could not depend on the numbers or conditions of those weapons still on hand in state armories. Among the arms drawn by the state of Ohio since 1816, for instance, were over fifteen thousand muskets, seven thousand rifles, and eleven thousand pistols. Yet on the eve of the Mexican War, that state's adjutant general could not account for almost six thousand muskets, nearly twenty-four hundred rifles, or some sixty-nine hundred pistols. He further reported that the accoutrements that normally accompanied these arms, such as bayonets and cartridge boxes, were almost entirely lost. Indiana's adjutant general reported that a large part of his state's allotment of weapons were "scattered throughout different parts of the State, in some places

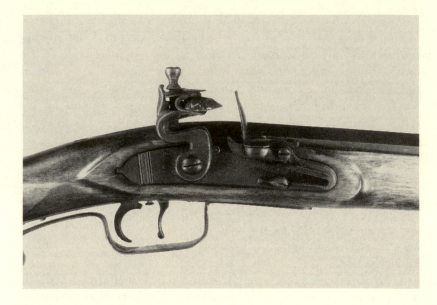

Flintlock rifle ready to fire.

stacked up in a house, . . . lying in shops, broken and rusted, . . . and
distributed among the citizens [and] used for hunting, and claimed by
those who hold them as private property."[5]

The Mexican War occurred at a time when many of the world's
armies were phasing out their flintlock muskets in favor of more advanced percussion weapons. Flintlock muskets had been around for a
long, long time. Their operation relied upon the simple principle that
sparks result when a sharp piece of flint strikes steel. On a flintlock
musket the jaws of the cocking piece, or cock, gripped the flint securely. With the pull of the trigger, the flint struck a hardened steel
frizzen. The frizzen then pivoted forward, allowing the sparks to fall
into a small pan of gunpowder. This powder burned and transmitted
a spark through a small hole in the gun barrel and into the main
powder charge, thus firing the weapon.

Loading and firing a flintlock musket was not a rapid process.
Holding the weapon horizontally, the soldier pulled the cock back to
half-cock and tipped the frizzen forward to expose the pan. He then

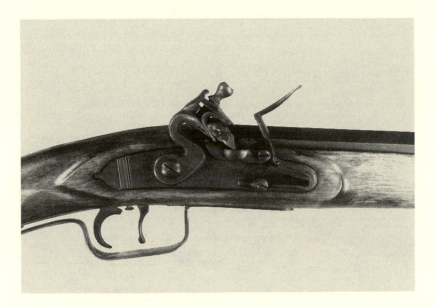

Flintlock rifle after firing.

reached into his leather cartridge box, suspended by a shoulder strap and worn on his right hip, and drew out a cartridge. Cartridges were paper and contained a measured amount of gunpowder, a round lead ball slightly smaller than the inside diameter of the gun barrel and weighing just over an ounce, and, just above that, three smaller lead balls, or buckshot. (This type of cartridge was therefore known as "buck and ball.") It was all held together by glue or string, or a combination of the two. Next, the shooter tore the end of the cartridge open with his teeth and poured a small amount of powder into the pan and closed the frizzen over it. He then placed the butt of the musket on the ground and poured the rest of the powder down the barrel. Next, he placed the projectiles, complete with the remaining cartridge paper, into the barrel and seated them firmly on the powder with his ramrod. He then cocked the weapon, and he was ready to fire.

A percussion musket was somewhat simpler to load. The soldier poured *all* of the cartridge powder into the barrel, and then rammed home the lead balls. Then he pulled the cocking piece, or hammer, to

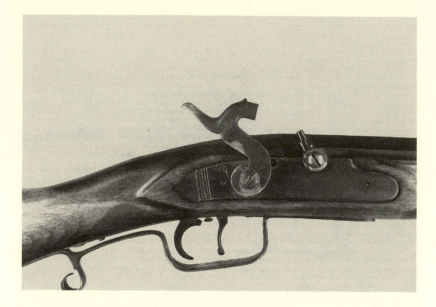

Percussion rifle ready to fire.

half-cock. He placed a small copper or brass cup-shaped percussion cap on the gun's cone, or nipple, and loading was complete. To fire, he merely cocked the hammer and pulled the trigger. The hammer fell onto the nipple, exploding a small charge of fulminate of mercury in the percussion cap, and sending a spark through the cone and into the main charge.

The percussion system had been in use on sporting weapons for over twenty years, but the military was slow to adopt this new technology. By 1840, England and other European countries had commenced manufacturing the new arms, and they were also altering their flintlock guns to percussion. American ordnance officers also recognized the superiority of percussion guns and advocated their adoption. In 1844, the government arsenal at Springfield, Massachusetts, started manufacturing percussion muskets, and the following year the arsenal at Harpers Ferry, Virginia, also began to turn them out. By 1846, these two factories had built over seventeen thousand percussion muskets. The war with Mexico inspired increased production, and during

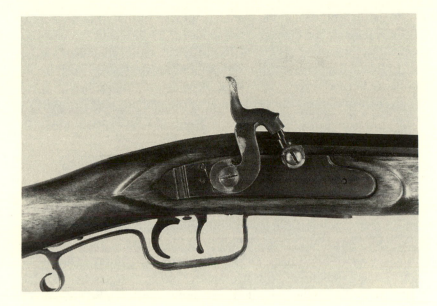

Percussion rifle after firing.

the war years, the national arsenals produced over seventy-eight thousand more of them.[6]

In spite of the recognized superiority of the new arms, very few of the troops who went to Mexico carried them. This has puzzled some people, but the answer is simple. Ordnance officials did not want the soldiers to fight a war with unfamiliar weapons. They feared that there was not enough time to train troops with the new muskets before their deployment to Mexico, particularly since virtually none of the drill manuals then in print addressed percussion arms. In fact, Jefferson Davis, who commanded one of the few regiments that did use these newer rifles, felt constrained to write his own manual for his unit. Lack of training time was not the only factor, however, that concerned the ordnance officers. They also worried about maintaining an adequate supply of percussion caps. A soldier who lost the flint out of his weapon could often make do with a piece of flint that he might find lying on the ground, but there was no such easy substitution available to the soldier who used up or lost all of his percussion caps.[7]

Regardless of the ignition system employed, the effect of the musket
balls and buckshot delivered from massed ranks could devastate an
equally compact body of enemy troops when within a hundred yards.

Individually, however, the smoothbore muskets were woefully in-
accurate beyond a very short range. A soldier of average height, firing
with the barrel of his musket parallel to the ground, might reasonably
expect his bullet to hit the earth a scant 120 yards from where he
stood.

In 1860, long after the end of the Mexican War and on the eve of
the Civil War, army ordnance officers tested several types of rifles and
muskets then in service, and among these were the .69 caliber muskets
of Mexican War vintage. The test firings took place at various distances
and under conditions somewhat approximating those facing troops in
the field. For example, ten soldiers fired by volley, or all at once, five
times at a two-foot-square target a hundred yards away. Out of the
fifty bullets thus fired, only five hit the target. Targets beyond that
distance remained untouched. Even under ideal conditions, with a
shooter firing five times from a bench rest, the results were dismal. At
a distance of one hundred yards it took a forty-two-inch diameter
circle to enclose these shots. It was this level of performance that
prompted Ulysses S. Grant to observe, "At the distance of a few
hundred yards a man might fire at you all day without your finding it
out."[8]

Many of the soldiers, particularly those from rural areas, already
knew how to use firearms, having spent considerable time in the woods
hunting game. The aspects of training that were new to almost all the
men were marching and the manual of arms. Gen. Winfield Scott had
written a tactics manual back in 1830 that attempted to unlock the
mysteries of the various movements involved. His book was probably
the most well known, but there were also others in print from which
the volunteer officers could choose. Some of the volunteer units were
fortunate enough to have members with West Point training, and these
men, usually elected officers because of their military background,
were able to lend some experience when the troops began learning the
drill. There were also some very conscientious officers without prior
training who strove mightily to educate themselves. One such man
provided himself with a copy of *Army Regulations* and two drill manuals

—Scott's and one written by Samuel Cooper—and drilled his regiment relentlessly.[9]

Of course, these circumstances did not occur in every volunteer unit, and even when they did the results were not always good. For example, the top two officers in the regiment of Alabama volunteers did not have prior military training, but some of the officers beneath them did. Unfortunately, these junior officers became very frustrated when trying to instill in the men a proper amount of precision in drill. The major, a West Point graduate, thought it a hopeless task to ever prepare the regiment for actual warfare. One of the company commanders, another West Pointer, found it difficult at times to control his mirth at some of his less military fellow officers as they tried to bring order out of chaos.[10]

Sometimes even the seemingly simple task of teaching men to march met with less than satisfying results. Nor was it always the fault of inexperienced volunteer officers or inept recruits. When the army decided to form a company of engineer troops, it appointed three regular army officers to lead it. The captain was a well-versed military engineer who had either never learned infantry drill or had forgotten it. Since the men in his company would sometimes serve as infantry, his two West Point-trained lieutenants taught him the infantry drill, and he in turn taught them the latest advances in military engineering. Finally, after a certain amount of this private tutoring, the captain felt confident enough to begin drilling his men in infantry tactics.

One of the first things a drill instructor teaches his men is how to march in step with the rest of the unit. And right away the captain got into trouble. During the 1840s, there were three rates of speed for marching soldiers. In "common time," the men covered ground at the rate of ninety steps per minute, each of which was twenty-eight inches long. "Quick time" raised the rate to 110 steps per minute, and "double quick time" was a run, or 165 steps per minute, each of which was now thirty-three inches long. This all seems simple enough, but it confused the captain. While marching his company at common time, he continually complained that the pace was too slow. He kept urging the men to greater speed until they were nearly running. He was still not satisfied, but eventually ended the drill for the day.

As the exhausted soldiers returned to their quarters, the two lieutenants approached the captain and diplomatically suggested that he order the men to march at quick time, or double quick time, if he wanted them to march faster. He replied that all he wanted was common time, ninety steps per minute, and that by timing the men with his watch he determined that the best they were doing was eighty-five steps per minute. The lieutenants continued to mull it over that night. It had certainly seemed to them that the men were marching much faster than common time. Finally, they figured out what had gone wrong. When the captain had been counting steps, he counted every time the left foot came down as one step, thereby undercounting by half. While he complained of this eighty-five-step-per-minute pace as being five short of common time, the company was actually covering ground at a rate of 170 steps per minute, or five greater than double quick time. The trainees were undoubtedly grateful that the lieutenants discovered the error before the captain tried to make them march at his idea of double quick time![11]

In spite of the obvious need for intensive training of the volunteers, President Polk, definitely not a military man, thought that time thus spent was a needless delay, and he urged that volunteers be sent to Mexico as quickly as possible. Consequently, many units soon began leaving their state rendezvous points for Mexico with little or no military training. As a general rule, the soldiers from the western states (today's Midwest) descended the Ohio and Mississippi Rivers in steamboats to New Orleans, and from there they boarded oceangoing ships bound for the mouth of the Rio Grande. After March 1847, men from the Southeast and Northeast sailed from Mobile, Charleston, New York, and other Atlantic ports directly to Mexico.

For many of the inland volunteers, the trip down the river to New Orleans was merely a continuation of the festive living they had enjoyed ever since signing up. They still had no clear idea of what lay ahead for them in Mexico. They railed against authority and complained when their officers imposed such basic restrictions as requiring them to stay on board the riverboats when they docked along the way, unless they first gave an assigned password to go ashore. The recruits were able to circumvent such rules easily in the crowded river ports. The boats often docked so closely together that the men simply jumped onto the deck of a neighboring vessel and walked ashore via its gangplank. At other times, young enlistees bent on sampling the sights and sounds of a river city waited in the vicinity of the gangplank until one of their comrades went ashore legitimately. Then, after overhearing the password, off they went![12]

There was some sickness on the riverboats—a portent of things to come—and a few accidental drownings. An Indiana volunteer, reportedly suffering with delirium tremens, jumped overboard several times, but he was always rescued. A Georgian had a problem with sleepwalking as his company was descending the Alabama River toward Mobile. One night he awoke to find himself in the river. After crew members hauled him back aboard the steamer, he apologized profusely to the vessel's captain "for having delayed his boat on its important mission." On this same river (it may even have been the same trip), the pilot sounded his whistle as the boat moved past Selma, Alabama. A company of rural recruits on board had never heard this sound before, and they had no idea what it was. Some thought that the ship's steam boiler had exploded, a very real source of river traffic danger, and jumped overboard to escape. Sadly, some of them drowned.[13]

Not all of the losses that the volunteer companies suffered before reaching Mexico were so tragic. Many men decided that perhaps they had allowed themselves to be unduly swayed by the excitement surrounding the call for volunteers, or they may have realized that a person going off to fight in a war faced a not insignificant risk of never coming home again. For whatever reason, some men deserted their comrades before ever leaving the United States. One New York City company of seventy-seven recruits lost fifty-five of them before even leaving the city, including thirty in a single day. It seems that the longer the volunteers waited before leaving for Mexico, the more time there was for some of them to decide that they were, after all, too young or too old or too frail for military life. A South Carolinian made it known that he did not want to continue, so the other members of the Palmetto Regiment shaved his head and marched him out of the camp to the tune of the "Rogue's March." Col. Stephen Ormsby, commander of one of the Kentucky regiments, told his recruits after they reached New Orleans that if any of them were too cowardly to go on, they should identify themselves and he would allow them to go home. Four men stepped forward, whereupon the colonel ordered

them to strip off their uniforms and leave. They did as they were told
and donned civilian clothes. Their recent comrades-in-arms, however,
looked upon this as an opportunity for "fine sport." They hoisted the
poor unfortunates onto fence rails and paraded them through the camp
so all could witness their disgrace. Tiring of this, the soldiers uncere-
moniously dumped their unwilling passengers into a nearby pond. At
least one of the four was expected to return to Louisville. If he did,
warned one of the volunteers in a letter home, "I want you to run him
away from there as he is a very trifling fellow."[14]

Something that virtually all the volunteers shared was a sea voyage
of varying length. (The few mounted units, the Missourians who went
to Santa Fe, and the Texas volunteers were about the only troops who
missed this experience.) An overwhelming percentage of soldiers who
commented upon this phase of their journey did so with extreme
distaste. The most often-mentioned causes of their displeasure were
the poor food served on the ships, the overcrowded conditions, and
the almost universal seasickness.

The recruits were crammed into the holds of the ships like so many
cattle going to market. Some ships provided rough pine bunks, four
men to a bunk. Rank, however, had its privileges, and the officers
shared small cabins away from the holds. The officers enforced this
social gap on some ships to the point of segregating themselves from
the enlisted men when they were off duty and not allowing them any
social contact with their superiors at all. An Illinois soldier complained
of this segregation, referring to the officers' staterooms as "their sanctuary." He went on to observe that the officers had posted sentries to
ensure their privacy, and that the guards did their duty as if they were
protecting "the portals to paradise." The necessity of transporting
horses and mules made the close quarters aboard ship even worse.[15]

The food that the soldiers ate while in transit to Mexico was, at
best, monotonous. Bacon, biscuits, and coffee were the staples. One
soldier sadly related his failure to vary his diet: "I could neither steal
any thing or buy it." Some fared better than this man, however, if
they were able to catch some fish. And in one case, a ship's captain
bought his passengers a 250–pound turtle from an islander at Little
Caymans.[16]

On the longer voyages from the Atlantic coast ports, the lack of fresh water also caused problems. Before leaving port, large casks were filled with drinking water. But with the uncertainty of wind and weather, the ship's passengers and crew sometimes exhausted this supply well before reaching their destinations. Even when the quantity of water was sufficient for the entire trip, the quality sometimes left something to be desired. A Virginia officer found the drinking water on his ship so foul that the only way that he could bring himself to drink it at all was to mix it first with a little molasses or claret.[17]

Had the finest chefs in the world prepared fresh, sumptuous meals daily aboard the ships, though, a lot of the men would not have cared. For when one's insides are knotted up with seasickness, food of any kind is not high on a list of immediate priorities. In fact, rare indeed was the soldier who did not suffer from this malady. A few fortunate ones had mild cases. "I was sick only a few minutes, vomited only once," admitted one volunteer. Most, however, were not that lucky. According to one man,

I had all along anticipated a severe attack of that most uncomfortable malady [seasickness], and I can assure you that my expectations were a great deal more than realized. For a week or more I scarcely left the cabin, ate scarcely anything, and in fact did nothing but drink a little water or suck a piece of ice and throw up bile. The quantity of the latter that I discharged would astonish a landsman.

Seasickness was not limited to those making the long trip from the eastern seaboard. On the relatively short journey from New Orleans to Brazos Santiago, near the mouth of the Rio Grande, an Indiana volunteer related that half of the men on his ship were seasick. They would not, or more probably could not, always make it to the rail before vomiting: "Sometimes you would find yourself eating and someone close by would let slip right on your dinner and your clothes; and then you will imagine how pleasant our trip was."[18]

Occasional storms only made a bad situation worse. A victim of seasickness did not welcome the roll of the ship in heavy seas, and some of these unhappy travelers even tied themselves to their bunks for safety. More serious than that, however, was the very real possibility of the ship going down with the loss of all aboard. A fifty-eight-year-old South Carolina quartermaster sergeant thought that his experience crossing the Gulf, buffeted by storms, was almost beyond comparison to anything else in life: "after 16 days of the most perilous voige [voyage] ever experienced we encountered three Northern Storms, one lasted 48 hours it caused me to suffer beyond description we suffered every thing that mortals could suffer except a ship reck." A Mississippian described a Gulf of Mexico storm that his ship encountered:

It was a dreadful sight, the mules & horses got loose & ran into the cabin. at the same time chairs tables & trunks were dashed to pieces—the mules & horses [moaning] & falling about the blood spouting the well [men] rushing out of the cabin & the sick crawling a little & retreating to their berths. This was a dreadful sight.

While this volunteer did not relate the fate of the horses and mules, a regular army artilleryman described a similar occurrence. "During the voyage the horses would break loose, the watch would be standing by, sledge in hand, knock the horse in the head, hoist him up and throw him overboard. This was the only remedy we had to save the vessel." [19]

Obviously, the soldiers bound from the East Coast for California had the greatest chance for unpleasant experiences at sea. In fact, the six-month voyage of Col. Jonathan D. Stevenson's New York Volunteer Regiment was probably as full of excitement for those troops as the time they eventually spent in California. For example, as one of the three ships carrying the regiment neared the equator, the regimental surgeon suggested that baths would enhance the comfort of the men. Since they had been at sea for two months by that time, baths were surely overdue. The ship's crew provided a large tub on the deck, and each company of men was to take its proper turn of bathing. Some of the volunteers, those who were far down the list of bathers, protested that they did not want to sit in a tub in which so many other filthy bodies had already been washed.

One of the officers, West Point trained and willing to brook no insubordination, ordered the troops from another company to enforce his order, and when they refused he had them all confined in the ship's guardhouse. The reluctant bathers and their comrades packed into the small, poorly ventilated enclosure, and before long some of them fainted from the oppressive heat and overcrowding. That night, sympathetic comrades, perhaps as many as a hundred of them, tied a rope to the grated door of the cell and pulled down the entire wall. A guard sounded the alarm, but by the time the officers arrived, the mutinous volunteers had thrown the demolished guardhouse wall overboard. The officers, badly outnumbered by the surly soldiers, wisely decided to let the matter end, and they rescinded the order for baths. After reaching Rio de Janeiro three weeks later, the ship's crew obtained enough lumber to rebuild the guardhouse, but on the first night out of port it met the same fate as its predecessor.[20]

The New Yorkers spent a week in Rio de Janeiro, a week in which their rowdy behavior caused so much trouble with the local populace that the Brazilian government temporarily broke off diplomatic relations with the United States. Colonel Stevenson seemed almost to welcome the rupture, and he told his men to prepare for immediate combat. Luckily for the outnumbered Americans the Brazilians averted a clash of arms by accepting the recall of the American ambassador.[21]

After a week in Rio de Janeiro, a week in which many of the New Yorkers spent time in local jails for drunkenness and disorderly conduct, the three ships continued their journey. Because of the problems in Rio, the colonel of the regiment ordered the ship on which he was sailing to go on to California without stopping at the next major port, Valparaiso, Chile. The other two ships had to stop for supplies, but their officers refused to allow the men to go ashore. As these two ships prepared to leave port, the troops on one of them forcibly prevented the sailors from raising anchor. The mutineers demanded shore leave. The lieutenant colonel defused the dangerous situation by allowing the men to go ashore for one day. Some of them got in trouble again, just as they had at Rio, and twenty-nine deserted, but the ships were soon on the way again and reached San Francisco without further incident.[22]

For some soldiers, their trip on the open seas was not only the worst event of their lives, but the final event as well. The bodies of those who died at sea were disposed of in time-honored naval fashion. A blanket or a piece of sail cloth served as a shroud. A member of the ship's crew would sew this up around the body after placing a couple of heavy cannonballs near the feet. Several men then lifted the wrapped body onto a plank and balanced it upon the rail of the ship. An officer, the ship's captain, or perhaps one of the volunteer officers on board read a short prayer or made some other appropriate remarks. After this brief eulogy ended, the plank was tipped up, and the body, weighted down by the cannonballs, plunged into the sea.

When the volunteers finally splashed ashore at Brazos Santiago or, by the middle of 1847, Veracruz, they found themselves in an environment that was alien to anything with which they were familiar. The heat was oppressive, especially to those clad in dark-colored, wool uniforms, and the insects and other vermin were also quite troublesome.

The men occasionally felt the stings of tarantulas and scorpions, and six-foot rattlesnakes with well over a dozen rattles were not uncommon. A snake of this size bit a soldier in the Fourth U.S. Infantry Regiment, and also an army mule. A surgeon treated the man's wound by excising it, allowing it to bleed a bit, and then treating it with aqua ammonia. The afflicted area swelled up, turned black, and caused the man a considerable amount of pain, but he eventually recovered. The mule was less fortunate. While it is unclear what treatment, if any, the mule received, it died.[23]

Snakes were not the only dangerous creatures to bother the volunteers. Even though only a minute fraction of the soldiers incurred the bites of poisonous snakes or insects, they all suffered the torments of the immense clouds of flies, mosquitoes, and fleas, as well as wood ticks, ants, and chiggers. An Alabama officer complained that the flies were "ten thousand times more numerous than I ever saw them before," and an Illinois sergeant lamented that there was "nothing in the shape of a Swallow or Bat to lessen their numbers." A Tennessean reported that mosquitoes were sometimes so troublesome as to prevent him from sleeping. He had never been particularly bothered by mosquitoes at home, "but these on the Rio Grande seem to me to be larger and can bite harder & make more noise while they are at it than any I ever heard or saw before." Others felt that they could easily endure all the flies and mosquitoes if there were just some way to get rid of the fleas. A couple of Indiana soldiers went on a flea hunt one evening and killed 250 of them in a short space of time. An officer from the same state was convinced, based upon his experiences, that "if all the flees in the world could be collected together, at least one half of them would claim residence in Matamoros." Another volunteer complained to his sister that "if [we] dont soon get a ship load of blood brought over we [will] be in a bad fix for the flees and gnats have sucked all the blood out of us and eat our hides up." Wood ticks and chiggers also proved bothersome. An Ohioan described the latter as "a most trifling little bug which bores a hole in your hide and deposites an egg there, to torment you out of your life with as little ceremony as a gad-fly would serve a two year old in the same manner in Ohio."[24]

By the time they reached Mexico, the eager recruits believed they were ready to meet the enemy. Most of them had survived the ordeals of seasickness in the Gulf of Mexico and even though the oppressive heat and the hordes of insects they now encountered were bothersome, they were anxious to test their manhoods on the field of battle. Many, however, would never get the chance to test their courage because far more deadly "bugs" were at work. The germs that would cause thousands of men to sicken and die were too small to see but left many graves in their wakes.

CHAPTER 4

"Nearly All Who Take Sick Die"*

Sickness began thinning the ranks of the soldiers even before they left their home states and continued as they made their way to Mexico. But after reaching their destination, their health declined precipitously. Diarrhea, malaria, and dysentery were the most pervasive diseases, but other killers such as smallpox, cholera, and yellow fever also appeared in the camps. Even such illnesses as mumps and measles proved fatal to many. Disease, which killed almost eleven thousand American soldiers and led to the discharge from service of several thousand more, was Mexico's greatest ally in this war. In fact, the death rate of the men serving in Mexico was ten times what it was among the general population of the United States at that time.[1]

Sickness was so prevalent at times that camps resembled hospitals more than military installations. The disease rate, according to an Illinois soldier, was truly alarming: "Measles, mumps, diarrhea and fever of an intermitting type were all at work upon the troops." Nor was this an isolated complaint. An Alabamian "never saw anything like the extent to which the diarrhee prevails in camp," and an Ohioan, commenting on the debilitated state of comrades from Illinois, noted, "They are the most sickly, enfeebled set of men I ever saw. They

*James L. McCloughlin to James McCloughlin, Sr.

ought all to be sent home for their health." Another soldier maintained that the military musicians spent so much time playing the funeral march that the mockingbirds in the area added it to their repertoires.[2]

Indeed, isolated cases of sickness seemed rare. Instead a disease tended to roar through a camp like a prairie fire. An outbreak of measles among Tennessee volunteers spread so quickly that two-thirds of the regiment was soon laid low. With huge numbers at sick call, ordinary camp routines ground to a halt. "We Dont pretend to Drill now," an Illinois soldier wrote, "for thare ant hardly anough well ones to take Care of the Sick."[3]

Losses to sickness approached 60 percent in one of the Tennessee regiments, and illness depleted several other units by as much as 40 percent. In the American army as a whole sickness caused fully seven times as many deaths as did Mexican musket balls. As dreadful as this statistic may be, it is not so very different from those of other wars of the eighteenth and nineteenth centuries. Precise figures are not available for American losses to illness in the Revolutionary War, but from the Seven Years' War through the Napoleonic Wars the ratio of deaths by disease to those by hostile causes in the British army was about eight to one. The proportion evened out somewhat during the Civil War, where sickness only claimed two lives for every one lost to enemy fire. This seemingly rapid improvement in health probably was due less to any dramatic increases in medical knowledge than to the nature of the war itself. The Civil War saw American armies of unprecedented size engage one another in battles of uncommon ferocity in which Union and Confederate troops killed each other so fast that the balance between combat deaths and noncombat deaths began to even out. The 1862 Battle of Antietam, where *each* side lost as many men in one day as the American army lost during the entire war with Mexico, amply illustrates this theory. Disease-related fatalities again overwhelmingly predominated after the Civil War, and it was not until World War II—and after great medical advances—that the trend reversed itself.[4]

The high incidence of death by disease during the Mexican War is easily attributable to the state of medical knowledge at the time. The medical profession in general did not yet understand disease transmission, or the need for sanitation in dealing with the sick or wounded. But a greater contributor to the ever-lengthening lists of dead was the status of the medical profession in the United States.

American medical schools in the early nineteenth century generally required their students to attend two terms of lectures, each covering the same material, and each lasting only three or four months. Students attending schools that offered more than one term per calendar year could satisfy this requirement rather quickly. Others began their studies well after the beginning of classes, or left before the close of a term, and still earned credit for having attended the full slate of lectures. In addition to this rather meager education, students worked closely, in apprenticeship fashion, with practicing physicians. Finally, they took an examination, although the degree of difficulty of these final exams varied from one institution to another. One prominent American doctor, speaking in 1846, characterized these tests as being extremely easy to pass. "Hence, the rejection of candidates is . . . a matter of exceedingly rare occurrence, and almost all who have complied with the most essential requisite of paying their teachers are sure to be honored with the title to which they aspire."[5]

Most American medical students obtained their knowledge by apprenticing themselves to a practicing member of the profession for three or four years, paying the teacher for the privilege of studying under his guidance. The apprenticeship consisted of two parts. First, the student studied such topics as anatomy, chemistry, botany, physiology, drugs and their actions, pharmacy, and clinical medicine. During this phase the apprentice also assisted the doctor in compounding prescriptions, bloodletting, wound dressing, and other minor tasks. Sometimes he got the chance to do some dissecting on animal or human cadavers. During the second phase, he went with the doctor to call on patients and sometimes helped out in surgery. At the end of the training program, the doctor certified his student's ability to practice medicine.

One eminent physician of the period thought that many of his fellow doctors had gone into the field of medicine for the wrong reasons. Some, he claimed, were physically unfit for hard farm labor, or perhaps too lazy for such a calling. Sometimes parents pushed a son into the study of medicine so they could have a "gentleman" in the family. This doctor also thought that too often a man studied medicine because he was "too stupid for the Bar or too immoral for the Pulpit."[6]

Given this rather dismal picture of the state of the medical profession, it is small wonder that so many soldiers died. Most Americans in the middle of the nineteenth century believed that men who joined the army as enlistees only did so because they were too lazy or inept to make a living in any other way. If, in addition, the doctors who signed on for army service were of a similar lowly caste, then the quality of medicine available to the troops was surely abominable. But this was not the case. Surgeons appointed to army units had to pass a special examination. The fact that these tests had an unusually high failure rate indicates that the applicants who passed were at least decent doctors. In fact, when the newly founded American Medical Association in 1847 looked into the state of medical education in the United States as one of its first orders of business, it paid particular attention to the requirements of the Army and Navy Boards of Medical Examiners.[7]

The surgeon general was the head of the Army Medical Department and from his office in Washington, D.C., he oversaw general health in the army. At the beginning of the Mexican War his department consisted of only twenty surgeons and fifty assistant surgeons. Regulations provided one surgeon and one assistant for each of the army's fifteen regiments, but these positions often became vacant and remained that way for long periods of time. The act calling for volunteers also specified that the regiments thus formed should contain the same proportion of doctors as the regular army units. Legislation providing for ten new regular army regiments in early 1847 also authorized a slight increase in the size of the medical department. In addition to an extra assistant surgeon for each of the new regiments, two more surgeons and a dozen more assistant surgeons joined the department.[8]

Whenever vacancies occurred among the numbers of authorized medical personnel, the Army Board of Medical Examiners compiled a list of doctors whom they invited to take the examination. In July 1846, this board met in New York City. Only forty-three of the sixty-three invited applicants arrived to take the exam, and fifteen of them decided not to take it after all. The board found three others physically unfit, and administered the exam to the remaining twenty-five doctors.

Seventeen of them failed! The results of another examination, in the spring of 1847, were similarly discouraging. This time the board invited 103 physicians. Again, only about half of them responded. Of the forty-five doctors who took this test, only eleven passed.[9]

Those who failed were defective in a wide range of topics within their chosen profession. Some lacked a sound knowledge of human anatomy because their training had not included the dissecting of cadavers. In fact, as one examining board discovered, it was "not very uncommon to find that no dissection at all has been done, because forsooth, the cost was a few dollars for subjects, or it may be, that dainty fingers might not be soiled." The same board found several applicants who, even though they were highly recommended graduates of medical schools, lacked any experience in even minor surgery, and in some cases they had not even had instruction in the subject. Navy medical boards encountered the same sort of lack of training among the doctors who appeared before them. One man identified castor oil as the oil of an animal called a castor. Another stated that the solar plexus was in the sole of the foot. When this board asked one young man to give the respective temperatures at which water boiled and froze, he was unable to do so, and further contended that such knowledge was of no practical use to a physician.[10]

Such appalling performances before the various military examining boards for surgeons had far-reaching effects. Perhaps most obvious was the fact that these screening processes helped to keep inept physicians from practicing medicine in the army or navy. Unfortunately, however, there was nothing connected with their test results that would prevent them from inflicting themselves upon the American public at large.

Compounding the problems of health care for the soldiers was the fact that since most doctors stayed with their regiments, any hospitals set up at intermediate points along the line of march were chronically short of competent medical personnel. This shortage was particularly acute in Veracruz during the late spring and summer of 1847. The army hired civilian doctors, many of them from New Orleans, but this appears to have been a stopgap measure at best. One army doctor characterized these newcomers as utterly worthless adventurers "who had come to Veracruz to see what they could pick up," while another called them an embarrassment to their profession.[11]

Even if one could assume, through some stretch of the imagination, that all military surgeons and assistant surgeons were highly capable men, there still remained a desperate need for nurses, orderlies, cooks, and hospital matrons. The situation at Veracruz was probably typical. When the bulk of the army moved inland to begin the advance on Mexico City, General Scott ordered that each regiment that left hospital patients behind also had to leave men to care for them. The doctors of the hospitals would determine how many such attendants each unit should leave. The exigencies of the campaign, however, required as many able-bodied men as possible in the ranks, so those left behind were usually either convalescents themselves or misfits that commanders were trying to get rid of.[12]

When a soldier felt himself falling ill, he knew that there were three things that could happen to him. The doctor might be able to give him some medicine that would cure his ailment in fairly short order. But if a cure was not immediately forthcoming, the sick man might find himself discharged from the service due to his inability to perform his duties. He would then try to recover at his home in the United States. The third possibility, and the one that befell eleven thousand unfortunates, was death far from home.[13]

The sick soldier presented himself to his regiment's physician early in the morning. If the doctor decided that the man was truly ill, he prescribed some medication and sent him to the hospital. The military hospitals of that time, particularly the field hospitals, were by no means rest havens. Sometimes they consisted of only a few leaky tents where a patient's recovery seemed to depend as much upon luck as upon the ministrations of medical personnel.

Along with the genuinely sick, some of the less enthusiastic soldiers responded to sick call because they had grown tired of playing the part of soldiers and wanted to go home. If they could convince the doctors that they were sick enough, they would gain disability discharges and be on their way. In a letter home to Indiana, one soldier named a dozen members of his regiment who had received such discharges and were en route to their homes. He believed them to be malingerers and enjoined his correspondent to report their names to the local newspaper for publication. He thought that "many of them are babies and are so badly home sick that they would die if they staid away from home any longer." Others were quite honest about their intentions with regard to visiting the doctor. A physician with a Mississippi regiment noticed a man at sick call one morning who had not come forward and stated his complaint like the others had. When the doctor asked him what was wrong, he replied, "Nothing, Sir; I just came to learn from the others *what to say when I wanted to get sick.*" [14]

Much of the sickness was due to the quality of the drinking water available to the soldiers. Many times on the march the troops had to cover great distances through parched and arid deserts with only the water in their canteens to quench their thirst. When they did find water it was often extremely contaminated, yet they drank it anyway. An Ohio officer saw his thirsty soldiers "drink with avidity the green, dirty, standing water of the quarry holes by the road side and declare it *excellent.*" Illinois troops came to a spring in which some cattle had defecated. This represented only a minor inconvenience, however, because, as one of them wrote, "we were too thirsty to be bluffed off in that way so we diped [dipped] round and quenched our thirst." [15]

The soldiers had to contend with impure water in their permanent camps as well as on the march. Camps were routinely situated on rivers or streams, but the soldiers' unsanitary practices quickly polluted these watercourses. The San Juan River at Camargo was particularly bad. A North Carolinian called it "the nastiest river in the world," and later wrote that he would "as soon drink the water out of Father's tan vats [used for tanning animal hides into leather] after it had been run in there 3 weeks." Another volunteer, whose writing skills left a little to be desired, nevertheless made his feelings known quite clearly when he wrote that the water at his new campsite was "gud water in comparison to the water we had bin useing for we had to use pond water all the wa threw and sum of it thick with mud and perfumed with ded mules." [16]

The greatest continuing threat to health was malaria, an ailment that was a traditional scourge of military camps. A soldier suffering from this disease would experience a high fever accompanied by aches and pains in the joints and a general feeling of exhaustion, which sometimes proved fatal. These symptoms did not manifest themselves in the same way in every patient. Some victims would recover from the fever temporarily only to have it return again and again. Doctors often diagnosed this—because of its nature—as intermittent fever. Others experienced a similar cycle of fever, but their body temperatures never quite returned to normal. Nineteenth-century doctors called this remittent fever, although it actually may have been typhoid fever or what is now known as *Falciparum malaria.* An accurate diagnosis was also difficult because so many other ailments exhibited similar symptoms. For instance, if a person also complained of nausea, stomach pain, and vomiting, the physician might judge that he had cholera. To further obscure the issue, doctors not only referred to the disease as intermittent or remittent fever, but might also call it ague, marsh fever, or miasmatic fever.[17]

It did not really matter under what name doctors treated malaria because according to contemporary medical thought, all fevers had the same basic causes and responded to the same types of treatments. The most popularly ascribed reason for most diseases was the gases, or miasma, that rose from rotting animal or vegetable matter. This explains why some diseases went by the name marsh fever. Medical treatment was equally nonspecific. Medical men believed that anything that lessened a patient's symptoms must be acting upon the disease itself and was therefore good. In the event of fever, any measure that lowered the sufferer's temperature was deemed effective.[18]

One popular form of treatment was venesection, or bloodletting. Doctors of the early nineteenth century used this technique to treat a wide range of ailments, and they thought it to be particularly effective with all kinds of fevers. So firmly entrenched was bleeding as a form of treatment that many medical men considered it almost a panacea. One wrote that bleeding a patient would "ameliorate all the symptoms, afford a refreshing sleep, cause the skin to perspire, and the bowels to relax, increase the appetite, and give a feeling of relief and ease which no other remedy or any mode of diet is able to supply." Bleeding was even a common practice in conjunction with surgical amputations. The theory doctors employed was that they should remove the estimated amount of blood that would have circulated in the severed limb.[19]

Bleeding as a therapy was imprecise at best. Doctors disagreed on the amount of bleeding a person should undergo in order to effect a cure. One doctor claimed that in the course of his career, he had probably bled patients enough to fill a hundred barrels with blood. The predominant belief was that the patient should bleed until unconsciousness resulted. A doctor in Pennsylvania reportedly bled a feverish patient every day for a week and a half, taking an average of fourteen ounces per day! Almost miraculously, the man survived. Others were not so fortunate. Another doctor, treating a case of malaria, "bled the patient till he was too weak to shake, and then the disease and the patient went off together."[20]

Luckily for the soldiers, it appears that army doctors employed other methods of combatting disease much more often than they used bleeding. Liberal doses, or "heroic draughts" in nineteenth-century parlance, of quinine sulfate was the preferred treatment for malaria. Adequate supplies of this drug, however, did not always keep up with its demand. Long, tenuous supply lines, often subject to guerrilla raids, caused army doctors to turn at times to other measures. Doctors in Monterrey substituted sulfate of zinc and myrrh, sometimes accompanied by opium. When the sulfate of zinc also ran short, Dr. John B. Porter reluctantly treated his patients with arsenic. Soon thereafter the army was able to secure the supply lines to Camargo and Matamoros, which once again brought the much-needed quinine.[21]

After malaria, the most frequent health complaints were due to dysentery and diarrhea. Dysentery showed up as a fever, accompanied by inflamed intestines, abdominal cramps, and bloody diarrhea. Because of this latter characteristic, it was often referred to as the bloody flux. Some men had diarrhea for so long that it became a way of life for them. Those diagnosed as merely being afflicted with diarrhea usually did not have the fever or severe cramps. In fact, however, some of these latter cases may also have been dysentery, but of a less virulent strain.

Common treatments for dysentery and diarrhea often resembled those for other maladies. Dr. Nathaniel Chapman, a prominent civilian doctor and the first president of the American Medical Association, favored bleeding the patient every two or three days. He cited certain cases where he had bled a patient a dozen times, each time drawing up to eight ounces of blood. He recommended the use of gentle emetics every few hours composed of torrified rhubarb, ipecacuanha, and opium. Other doctors favored the substitution of cerated glass of antimony for the rhubarb and ipecacuanha. Another staple in the treatment of these ailments was calomel, which Chapman regarded as indispensable.[22]

Contaminated food, polluted drinking water, poor camp sanitation, and a general lack of concern for personal hygiene were the main causes of these diseases. By modern standards, the level of cleanliness that army regulations required does not seem very stringent. "Bathing is promotive of both comfort and health," regulations stated, and soldiers were to make every effort to bathe at least once a week. They were also to wash their hands and faces daily, and their feet twice a week. These rules went on to say that, "it is essential to cleanliness and health that the soldiers should change their linen [underwear] at least three times a week in mid-summer, and twice a week during the remainder of the year." In spite of these admonitions, many men became very sick because they refused to keep themselves clean. This appears to have been particularly true of the volunteers. An army doctor in Puebla wrote that many of his patients were men "who probably have not washed their persons for months, and who for weeks have not changed their underclothes, and who are not only filthy but covered with vermin. . . . Now, it is impossible for men to be healthy under such circumstances."[23]

The fact that the volunteers suffered more from ill health than their regular army comrades seems perplexing at first glance. And yet examination of data from both the American Revolution and the Civil War shows a similar pattern. Since the United States was a predominantly rural nation until the twentieth century, most volunteer soldiers arrived in camps from farms or small villages where disease seldom reached epidemic proportions and the people had little resistance to them. When an illness then struck an encampment, this lack of immunity meant great suffering among the troops. Gradually, those who survived the early onslaughts began to build up their resistance against recurrences. This process of "seasoning" usually took about a year. Monthly strength reports from Gen. George Washington's army verify this by showing large numbers of troops on sick report early in the

Revolution, but, with only an occasional exception, a relatively low level for the final five years of the war. During the Civil War, too, sickness proved most debilitating to a unit's strength early in its existence. Since the war with Mexico was so much shorter than either of these other conflicts, and since the maximum term of service for most volunteers was only one year, it is impossible to validate the effect of "seasoning" on these men. The regulars, on the other hand, generally came from large cities where they had probably already survived several periods of illness. This early exposure, coupled with the fact that many of them had already served in the army long enough to have survived various camp fevers, inured them against subsequent attacks.[24]

Of all the illnesses that plagued American troops in Mexico, yellow fever, which scourged low-lying coastal areas, was perhaps the most feared. One army doctor was certain that the Mexicans counted on yellow fever and other tropical diseases as weapons against the invaders. They hoped, he contended, "that the lethal heats of the *tierras calientes* would be as fatal to our troops as the cold of Russia was to the troops of Napoleon." An Illinois soldier's letter home reveals a great deal about the fear of this disease among the general public. He told his brother of the recent yellow fever deaths of three of his comrades at Matamoros, but he cautioned him not to disclose the cause of these deaths to others unless it had already become generally known that the fever had broken out. He did not want to panic the folks at home unnecessarily. A young regular army lieutenant named Ulysses S. Grant probably expressed the feelings of most American soldiers in Mexico when he wrote to his fiancée, "We will all have to get out of this part of Mexico soon or we will be caught by the yellow fever which I am ten to one more affraid of than the Mexicans."[25]

The specter of yellow fever loomed so prominently in the thoughts of all that military leaders planned an entire campaign around it. When they began to look at the possibility of capturing Veracruz or some other Mexican port city, they had to consider the fever. Gen. Winfield Scott wanted to be sure that his men could capture the city and push on into the interior of Mexico before the onset of the fever season in late March or April. Consequently, Scott's command landed near Veracruz on March 9, 1847. To avoid a protracted siege that might have extended into the summer, American troops immediately began to bombard the city. Within a month the city had capitulated, and the bulk of the American force had moved away from the coast. In spite of this careful planning, however, soldiers who remained to garrison the city did contract the disease, and some died.

Since yellow fever shared symptoms with other diseases, it was sometimes difficult to diagnose accurately until it had gone into its advanced stages. Generally, a person struck with this disease suffered excruciating headaches, high fever, pains in the limbs and back, constipation, and vomiting. As the sickness progressed, the sufferer's skin took on a yellowish cast due to a reduced excretion of bile. Internal hemorrhage darkened the vomit with blood, giving rise to the disease's Mexican nickname of *vómito negro* (black vomit) or simply *vómito*.[26]

Virtually no one in the medical profession, civilian or military, had begun to blame mosquitoes for the spread of the disease, and it was to be another half-century before army doctors, during another tropical war with another Spanish-speaking enemy, isolated the *aedes aegypti* mosquito as the culprit. The generally accepted causes of yellow fever, like most other fevers, were heat, moisture, and decaying animal and vegetable matter. Doctors in Veracruz, therefore, issued guidelines to the troops for avoiding infection. They urged the men, first and foremost, to be temperate in what they ate and drank. They should limit their consumption of alcohol, as well as rich foods and green fruit. They should avoid exposure to the sun between the hours of 7 A.M. and 2 p.m. if possible, and should stay out of the damp night air. Finally, they stood a better chance of staying healthy if they dressed a little too warmly for the season. Some soldiers undoubtedly looked upon these suggestions as merely a ploy for getting them to lessen their drinking. Others were convinced that the doctors were right. One young man confidently wrote his father, "I have no fears of loosing my health here as long as I refrain from the use of intoxicating liquors but the intemperate use of liquor in this country will kill any person in time I care not how vigorous a constitution they may possess."[27]

In spite of the fact that army doctors did not understand how yellow fever spread, certain measures that they took did help control the disease. The men could not do anything to alleviate the heat or humidity, but they could certainly tackle the problem of rotting garbage and dead animals in the streets of Veracruz. Gen. William J. Worth, the temporary military governor, hired some two hundred Mexicans to rid the city of the offensive matter, which eliminated many potential mosquito-breeding sites.[28]

Medical personnel in Veracruz urged the soldiers to report to them as soon as they noticed the slightest symptoms of yellow fever. Doctors believed that they had a much better chance of effecting a cure when they began treatment early.

Dr. John B. Porter was the doctor in charge of the large hospital in Veracruz, and he left a detailed account of how he and his medical staff dealt with yellow fever in the summer of 1847. As soon as a patient reported to the hospital he received a warm mustard bath. Then, if he suffered from chills or gastric irritation, hospital personnel applied mustard plasters to various parts of his body. Dr. Porter then prescribed generous doses of quinine and calomel every three to four hours. Later advances in medicine have shown that quinine has no effect on yellow fever, but in the 1840s quinine was universally believed to be essential. The calomel, or mercury chloride, was intended to ease constipation. Many doctors regarded it, too, as a sort of panacea. Dr. Porter began to be aware of calomel's deleterious side effects, such as excessive salivation and sore gums and teeth, but still thought that its benefits outweighed its liabilities. It was an effective laxative only because it broke down into poisonous components that irritated and purged the intestines. The patient also underwent salt-water enemas every hour or two to further cleanse the bowels. Doctors believed that the calomel and enemas served the dual purpose of relieving the constipation that was so often one of the patient's symptoms, and of preventing nausea and vomiting. Dr. Porter also resorted to venesection, or bloodletting, when the patient complained of hot skin and a bounding pulse, but he did not repeat the process after its first use. Finally, at the end of the first day's treatment, the sick soldier received a small dose of morphine with his calomel and quinine. In spite of these efforts, over one-fourth of all the yellow fever patients died.[29]

Precise medical statistics for the Mexican War are not available, so it is impossible to determine the fatality rates of individual diseases. This unfortunate lack of information appears due simply to the hustle and bustle of active campaigning. Regulations required all medical

officers in the field to submit monthly reports to the medical director
in Mexico, who then sent a consolidated report to the surgeon general
in Washington. After the war, the Army Medical Department attempted to collate all these reports and compile abstracts, but the task
proved to be fraught with insurmountable obstacles. Sometimes the
monthly reports from surgeons in the field did not reach the medical
director. At times, it was because these doctors were just too busy, or
too lazy, to write their reports. At other times these reports were
included in mail shipments that Mexican guerrillas intercepted. Record
duplication was also a source of error. There were cases of soldiers
being reported on their respective regiments' sick lists, and then the
same men might be reported again by one or more general hospitals to
which they had been transferred. So while there is a general sense of
the numbers of men who died of sickness, there is no way to determine
mortality rates for specific diseases. Suffice it to say that while the
death rate was extremely high by modern standards, it was still not as
bad as what a young Tennessean morosely wrote to his father: "nearly
all who take sick die."[30]

In addition to all of the diseases of the body to which the American
soldiers were subjected when they reached Mexico, there was another
malady that they brought with them. It was more a way of thinking
than a physical illness. It was the Americans' overwhelming feeling of
superiority over all other men, particularly those—such as the Mexicans—who had darker skins.

CHAPTER 5

"Reptiles in the Path of Progressive Democracy"*

In the summer of 1845, John L. O'Sullivan, editor of the *Democratic Review*, coined a term with which the Mexican War would forever be linked. He wrote that it was America's "manifest destiny to overspread the continent allotted by Providence for the free development of our yearly multiplying millions." Although the phrase "manifest destiny" was new, the idea behind it was not. As early as 1801, Thomas Jefferson had envisioned a time when citizens of the United States would spread over all of North and South America. A few years later, John Quincy Adams expressed the same sentiment, but in language more closely resembling O'Sullivan's, when he wrote, "The whole continent of North America appears to be *destined by Divine Providence* to be peopled by one *nation*, speaking one language, professing one general system of religious and political principles, and accustomed to one general tenor of social usages and customs." By the 1840s, the most obvious exhibition of this philosophy was the displacement of the American Indians as the line of white settlement crept inexorably westward. The war with Mexico focused American attention on the sparsely settled northern reaches of Mexico, which seemed to bar further expansion toward the Pacific Ocean.[1]

As U.S. troops penetrated northern Mexico they encountered an

* *Illinois State Register*

alien terrain, people, religion, language, and culture. No earlier American army had experienced anything quite like this. The soldiers' responses to what they encountered, as exhibited in letters, diaries, and contemporary newspapers, clearly reflect the temper of the times throughout the United States.

Much of what the soldiers saw of Mexican territory in the early stages of the war was desolate and forbidding. Indeed, one man left a colorful description of the landscape of New Mexico: "The bible says that it tuck [took] God almighty six days to make the world, and that on the seventh day he rested. Now *I* never believed a d——d word of this before, but now I do:—and all this region . . . was made late Saturday evening—when he was d——d tired *and in a bad humor at that!*"[2]

Other areas of enemy territory, however, particularly along rivers, were rich and fertile. This did not go unnoticed by the largely agrarian Americans. Many of them commented upon its value, and they also remarked what a shame it was that the land's current owners did not realize its full productive potential. They saw rich areas apparently unattended, and even when under cultivation, the farming methods and implements that the Mexicans used were fifty to one hundred years behind the latest agricultural technology. This backwardness did not have to be permanent, however, because "whenever the direction of American enterprise shall tend to this country," it could be made as productive in sugar and cotton as the richest plantations in Louisiana. All it would take was American "energy and *go-a-head-a-tiveness.*" Another soldier echoed this sentiment when he observed that "were Mexico peopled with Americans and blessed with American laws and institutions it would soon become the richest country in the world."[3]

These sentiments reflect the apparent change in what historians have called America's sense of mission. The founding fathers viewed their work as an example for other nations to follow. They believed that the American form of government would serve as a key to world prosperity, and it was up to Americans to bring this message of republicanism to those peoples less fortunate than themselves. By the middle of the nineteenth century this view had lost some of its currency, but was not universally discarded. Some Americans began to abandon their roles as missionaries of democracy. They now assumed that some races were innately inferior and would never be able to enjoy the benefits of a free society. (The thriving institution of black slavery was an obvious aspect of this belief, as was the treatment of American Indians.) One soldier believed that the American forces were merely "carrying out the designs of Providence. Mexico is a large and beautiful country now in the possession of a population unworthy to enjoy it." He went on to say that whatever the outcome of the war, the result would be "not only beneficial to our own country, but a material change for the better" in Mexico as well. An Indiana officer thought that the Americans were doing a favor by bringing to Mexico "a settled form of free government."[4]

The idea that the war with Mexico was also a crusade of sorts was the sentiment most soldiers expressed. In fact, the Indiana officer went on to write of the Mexican people that "it requires no gift of prophecy to foretell their doom, and they are destined soon to fall before the all grasping & all conquering genius of genuine Americanism." A South Carolinian did not believe that he even had to view the Mexican countryside or meet the Mexican people to hold a similar view. Writing before the war even began, he said that the American people, with "a gigantic effort . . . could sweep the continent from Panama to the Pole and from ocean to ocean *in a year*." Another soldier matter-of-factly relegated the Mexicans to extinction when he wrote, "As to the miserable inhabitants the same fate will await them that happen to the Indian tribes of our own frontier. [t]hey will naturally vanish before civilization."[5]

Americans easily rationalized the concept of manifest destiny by equating the Mexican people with what they considered a lesser form of human. Sam Houston, with a longer history of anti-Mexican feeling than many Americans, declared that Mexicans were no better than Indians, and he could "see no reason why we should not go in . . . and take their lands." An Alabama volunteer reiterated, probably unknowingly, the policy of early settlers of the eastern seaboard toward Indians when he confided to his diary, "It is an outrage, for the Mexicans to own such a country. They are too lazy to till the soil; they make no improvements whatever in the implements or mode of culture and make but few improvements in the useful or mechanic arts or in civilization." In other words, if a people did not measure up to the

American concept of culture, government, or progress, they should prepare to step aside. The *Illinois State Register* for July 17, 1846, carried an article that put it quite succinctly. It said that the Mexicans "are reptiles in the path of progressive democracy . . . and they must either crawl or be crushed."[6]

The whole concept of manifest destiny rested on a foundation of racism, or, more politely, ethnocentrism. White Americans quite frankly thought of themselves as a chosen people and looked down upon all those with darker skins than their own. And the population of Mexico appeared to encompass the entire spectrum from European white to African black. Many American soldiers commented upon the various skin tones they saw. Very few of them failed to distinguish the fair-skinned Mexicans, whom they invariably labeled Castilians, from the darker-skinned natives.

These feelings of racial superiority had not sprung up suddenly. As early as the sixteenth century when English King Henry VIII broke with the Pope, he and his successors found it very convenient to shift part of the animosity thus engendered onto Catholic Spain. Later, reports of near genocide carried out by Spanish *conquistadores* among the natives of the New World contributed to further ill feelings. (This last may have been tempered by jealousy over the fact that Spain was drawing such rich mineral wealth from its American colonies.) The intolerance for all things Spanish was passed along to English colonists in North America, from whence it diffused among all white Americans.[7]

Americans also found it convenient to stereotype the Mexicans as lazy, immoral, and corrupt in order to conceal the expression of any such traits in their own characters. In psychological terminology, the Americans used the Mexicans as their collective alter ego and projected onto them their own unacceptable inner strivings. Historians have made use of this concept in dealing not only with American-Mexican relations but also with Americans' perception of the black African slaves and the American Indians.[8]

Ethnic differences were not the only things that the soldiers in Mexico found worthy of comment. They made note of everything from architecture, people, and food to laziness and religion. A soldier's view of a Mexican village elicited comments upon its size, often comparing it to towns in the United States. Sometimes these initial views were positive, sometimes negative, but many times they were neutral. The one- and two-story houses in cities such as Matamoros or Monterrey were different from any these men had seen before, but not necessarily better or worse. During the early part of the war, the Mexican villages along the Rio Grande served as the American soldiers' first view of Mexico. For many, those border towns projected a most unflattering image indeed. The crude huts in which the poorer residents lived had walls of vertical logs daubed with mud, and roofs of thatch or palmetto leaves. The more affluent citizens lived in flat-roofed stone or adobe houses of very solid construction. These homes, with iron bars on the windows and heavy wooden doors, presented a stern visage to passersby.

The Scottish-born wife of a Spanish diplomat, traveling in Mexico a few years before the war, remarked that it "certainly does require some time for the eye to become accustomed to the style of building" there. American soldiers felt no need to be so tactful in their descriptions. Some found the larger cities such as Matamoros to be pleasant surprises, with large, roomy buildings and well-laid-out streets. Others thought Matamoros was "mean and miserable to the last degree." A deck hand on a Rio Grande steamboat painted all of the river towns with the same broad brush. He convinced himself that Matamoros, Reynosa, and Burita would, in the United States, "rank no higher than a villiage of Hog-pens." When a Missourian, after enduring a long, dusty overland trek to New Mexico, glimpsed Santa Fe for the first time, it presented to him the appearance of an "immense brick yard with some of the kilns whitewashed. The streets (if they be so called) are narrow, and dirty, in the extreme."[9]

In the spring of 1847, American troops under Gen. Winfield Scott landed at Veracruz and began to push inland toward the capital city. The fortified coastal city of Veracruz gave rise to the same variety of comments as had Matamoros. While one regular army officer thought it to be "the most filthy & stinking place" he was ever in, an Alabama enlisted man compared it favorably to New Orleans. Mexico City, at the opposite end of the line of march, possessed all the virtues and vices of comparably sized cities in other parts of the world. The extreme poverty evident in certain sectors of the city disturbed an

Ohio officer, who described the place as "the most *stinking city* I ever smelt." Another soldier likened Mexico's largest city to Sodom and Gomorrah, and found it to be "full of more dissipation and sin than I had ever seen or imagined."[10]

The aspects of Mexican towns that almost all soldiers were compelled to describe to their correspondents were the Roman Catholic churches. These buildings occupied central positions, both geographically and spiritually, for the residents. Comments upon these churches by American soldiers, most of whom were Protestant, were usually less than complimentary and were often degrading. The first thing many mentioned was that these churches had no pews or other furniture, and that the worshippers stood or knelt on the bare floor. In contrast to this were the rich furnishings—"pictures, statues, gold, silver, jewels and tapestry in the greatest abundance"—that the soldiers considered so out of place in the midst of the congregations of paupers.[11]

A Virginian found the interior decor of a Puebla church particularly offensive: "It is there that one finds Mary, the Mother of Jesus, the simple virgin, the pure and holy parent of God, decked out in gold and purple and tinsel and brass with cheeks of wax bedaubed with rouge and eyes of glass." A fellow soldier described a statue of the Virgin Mary, perhaps the same one, as wearing a dress adorned with diamonds and a diamond-studded gold crown. Another man noted the ornate carvings in a cathedral in Monterrey. There were "images of the apostles and every body else they could think of." Still a fourth soldier sarcastically told how some Mexican churches had "pieces of the *true* Cross, by the cord, bones of Saints by the bushel, gorgeous altars resplendent with barbaric gold."[12]

These descriptions of church riches must have seemed incredulous to those who read them back in the United States. Could the cathedral at Puebla really have an altar worth seven million dollars or a chandelier that cost forty thousand dollars just to clean? A German volunteer from Ohio declared that the altar in the Mexico City cathedral was of pure silver, and that "most churches are entirely gold-plated on the inside."[13]

Even though only a small percentage of American soldiers were Catholics, many of them attended religious services in the Catholic churches of Mexico. For some it was a chance to learn more about the Mexican people and their culture. For others it represented an opportunity to go to church—any church—on Sunday. Some few undoubtedly attended merely out of boredom and for something to write home about. Among the tolerant few who kept open minds about these religious services was a North Carolinian who wrote his mother that when he went to Mass he was filled with "feelings of religious awe & reverence for the *Wise Being* whom they worship, although we may not approve the doctrines & religious tenets which they entertain." Another volunteer told of going to Mass in Matamoros. He, too, felt a sense of "reverential awe and devotion," even though he found parts of the service meaningless. Still, he "could not censure a form because it did not concur with our preconceived opinions of religion." Finally, an Alabamian observed, after attending Mass, that "there is something of solemnity in their worship notwithstanding the ridiculousness, to us, of some of their forms and ceremonies." [14]

Such tolerant attitudes among the American soldiers were exceptional. In fact, the prevailing feeling was one of hostility and ridicule. Americans regarded the mere existence of the Catholic faith as one of the basic flaws in Mexican society and advocated that it be "rooted from the soil." They labeled the Catholic liturgy, which they did not understand, as "senseless flummery." They did not see how any rituals so different from their own could possibly be acceptable to God. A regular army officer seemed almost condescending when he wrote that "the mummery of the service would have been laughable had it not been so melancholy to reflect that 'twas an attempt at the worship of God." [15]

The soldiers often mocked, and sometimes mimicked, Catholic church services. In the spring of 1848, some Ohio volunteers in Puebla observed a priest performing the traditional application of ashes—from whence Ash Wednesday derived its name. He used the ash residue from the burning of the dried palm leaves left over from the previous year's Palm Sunday celebration. Then, with his thumb, he inscribed a small cross on the forehead of each of the members of the congregation. To the Catholic faithful this was a symbol of penance and marked the beginning of the Lenten season. The soldiers knew nothing of the ceremony's significance. They only knew that it resembled nothing they had ever seen. Not content with verbal ridicule, the soldiers took a piece of cork and used it to apply similar marks all over their faces until the Mexicans, offended and embarrassed, wiped their own foreheads clean.[16]

Many men found particularly offensive the lifestyles of Mexican priests, whose dissipation the soldiers often commented upon. One of the rare regular army officers who was himself a Roman Catholic found the Mexican clergy to be very different from the priests in the United States. While in Santa Fe he quickly lost all respect for the local priests. "It is notorious," he wrote, "that they are the greatest debauchers, gamblers and drunkards of the community. A priest at a fandango, a few evenings ago, became so much intoxicated as to fall from his seat." Later, this same officer had similar comments about the priests in California: "Their immoral behavior is not so public as with the priesthood in New Mexico. Yet they are proverbially ignorant and exercise by no means a moral influence over the people."[17]

One reason why American soldiers had so much contact with the Mexican people was because the army's long-term camps were always in, or very near to, Mexican towns and villages. The soldiers soon got first-hand exposure to the people and their way of life. Due to the fact that the army contracted locally for food and various other supplies, there was a considerable amount of interaction with local businessmen. And since the camps were usually not particularly restricted, local peddlers and food vendors plied their wares to the men. It was at this level that many of the Americans met the Mexican people. The relationship seldom approached anything resembling friendship, as the soldiers seemed to regard the Mexicans with whom they dealt as "treacherous devils." An Illinois soldier applied a broad brush when he painted the entire population of the Mexican city of Monclova as obtaining "a precarious living by murder and robbery." Not to deny women a place in his estimation, he characterized them as "all of the most common character and the men, regular assassins."[18]

While some American officers became acquainted with Mexicans of the upper social stratum, most soldiers formed their opinions of the Mexican people on the basis of their dealings with various merchants and citizens of the lower classes. Not surprisingly, the commercial dealings often resulted in one party feeling as though the other had tried to take unfair advantage of him. Consequently, while there was a great deal of trade, the Americans always appeared to be wary of those with whom they did business. Some had the feeling, expressed by one volunteer, that the Mexicans "seem to be anxious for the continuance of the war for the purpose of making money off of the Americans." Another was just as sure that these same smiling traders would, in the event of American military reverses, "be the first to cut our throats." [19]

On a general level the American soldiers regarded the Mexican people as being of a lower racial order. One thing that particularly bothered them was the amount of miscegenation in Mexican society. They came from a country where interracial marriages were, with rare exception, strictly taboo. Early Spanish settlers in Mexico had had few qualms about taking darker-skinned mates, usually Indians, so that by the 1840s every hue and color from white to brown to black comprised the Mexican population. This, in turn, led to the American character-ization of the Mexican people as a "mongrel race." One young regular army officer called them "a mixture of Indian, negro, and Spanish blood—apparently a great deal below and more ignorant than either race." The lower classes came in for most of the negative comment. The editor of an American newspaper, published in Mexico City after most of the fighting was over, gave a recipe for a Mexican:

Blacken a man in the sun; let his hair grow long and tangled, or become filled with vermin, let him plod about the streets in all kinds of dirt for years; and never know the use of a brush, or towel, or water even, except in storms; let him put on a pair of leather breeches at twenty and wear them until forty without change or ablation; and overall place a torn and blackened hat, and a tattered blanket begrimed with abominations; let him have wild eyes and shining teeth and features pinched by famine into sharpness; . . . combine all these in your imagination and you have a recipe for a Mexican lepero. [20]

The conditions of abject poverty in which many Mexicans lived reinforced their lowly image in American eyes. In rural areas, the people often incurred debts to large landowners and were then unable to repay them except by working off the loans. Many American ob-servers compared this system of debt peonage to the slavery of the southern United States. One volunteer officer from Illinois declared that the living quarters of these workers were worse than those he had seen slaves occupying along the Mississippi River. Another volunteer, this time from the slave state of South Carolina, considered this Mexican form of enforced servitude to be "infinitely worse than ours."[21]

Soldiers also drew comparisons between the urban poor and American slaves. The entire village of Burita, near the mouth of the Rio Grande, came in for a blanket condemnation when a soldier wrote that "the meanest negro huts in Tennessee are far better than the houses here." Another man found that the poorer citizens of Monterrey were less well clothed than American slaves, and several commented upon their ignorance: "As regards their intellectual powers little can be said in their favor. As a general rule I believe our negroes are their superiors in mental abilities, comparing them, as they both are, without education." Another soldier was even more convinced. He wrote his daughter that the Mexicans "are ignorant in mind imbicile in body . . . not equal as a man to our slaves."[22]

Not all American soldiers harbored such resentful feelings toward the Mexican people, although scarcely any regarded them as equals. A Tennessean wrote his mother that the local population "invariably treated us with great respect and kindness." He repeated this sentiment four months later and seemed to be willing to live and let live. Another soldier, in a letter to his niece in Vermont, said that even though he believed them to be treacherous and untrustworthy, he felt no hostility toward the people. One volunteer officer, probably more perceptive of human feelings than most of his comrades, described his visit to a Mexican church in Monclova. Because of previous orders, this officer carried his sword while in the town. He described his reception by the churchgoers: "They looked at me with any thing but a pleasant expression . . . & in fact I did not blame them much for it did not look right to me to walk armed into the sanctuary, & no doubt they thought it the greatest desacration. In fact I don't feel half as mad at the Mexicans as I did when I left home."[23]

As is the case in most wars, the soldiers of the opposing armies in the Mexican War spoke different languages. This fact presents obvious military difficulties, particularly for the invading army. It was also a problem for the soldiers on a more personal level. Between active campaigns, many men had daily access to towns or villages. It was necessary, therefore, when engaging in any commercial transactions, that some form of communication exist. It seems likely that local businessmen would have attempted to learn the language of their sudden new clientele. Likewise, many soldiers began at least a rudimentary study of Spanish.

Different reasons motivated different soldiers in their desire to learn the new language. Some, like the colonel of the Massachusetts volunteers, recognized the obvious military importance of such knowledge. Knowing that he faced a long sea voyage to Mexico with plenty of idle time, he took along not only some books on tactics but also some Spanish grammars. Others waited until they arrived in Mexico before buying books and beginning to study. A typical book of this sort contained Spanish and English equivalents for the alphabet, a vocabulary, some poetry and passages from the Bible, and various useful phrases. Unfortunately, many of the soldier-students found that the language as it was written in the books differed significantly from the language as it was spoken around them.[24]

While some men studied Spanish because they believed it to be "well worth acquiring for its literature," they were probably outnumbered by those with less cultured pursuits in mind. Most shared the motives of a young man who wrote to his brother about his frustration when attending local Mexican dances—or fandangos: "I enjoyed myself very well with the . . . young ladies. I could enjoy myself as well with them as with the Americans if I understood their language better. I am at a loss what to say to them which causes some uneasiness with the ladies and myself."[25]

Regardless of their reasons for studying Spanish, the soldiers delighted in describing to the folks at home their real or imagined progress. Some openly stated that they were learning, or had already become fluent in, the language. Others simply dropped occasional Spanish words or phrases into their letters, followed by English translations for their less learned correspondents. Within this latter class of "students" there was quite a range of mastery. One man, writing from his hospital bed in Saltillo, described an attractive Mexican woman to his friend back in Kentucky as being "*mucha bonita* that is rather handsome." Another man, perhaps less literate, used the phonetic approach. He wrote that something was "(much awayner) [mucho bueno] that means very good."[26]

Conversations between American soldiers and Mexicans, which began with high hopes by both parties, sometimes degenerated into bits and pieces of both languages, with liberal doses of sign language thrown in for emphasis. An Illinois volunteer officer tried desperately to converse with a local boarding house proprietor and her daughters:

When at fault for a word I take an English one & give it a Spanish ending & pronunciation & make a salaam or two. . . . If that don't go, I throw in a word or two of Latin & French, & occasionally a little German, & conclude with "Senora" or "Senorita." Thus I generally succeed in calling up a smile, & a gentle "Si, Senor" . . . then they let loose a torrent of Castillian on me, & I stand & look knowing, & say "Si Senorita" when I've no more idea of what they are saying than if Moses was talking to me in his native tongue.[27]

Not all of the invaders went to such lengths to make themselves understood, and some were more easily disconcerted by the language barrier than others because of their mispronunciation of the few Spanish words they had learned. This was the case when one of Taylor's men encountered a Mexican while looking for a lost horse. "Look here, my man," the American began, "have you seen anything of a d——d *caballo* a *barnosing* about here, with a *cabrista* on his neck?" The Mexican, who spoke no English, quite understandably had no idea what this man was saying. The American then, in a pique of Anglo-Saxon exasperation, exploded, "Don't understand! Why the d——d fool *don't know his own language!*"[28]

Even General Taylor picked up a smattering of the language, although he sometimes became flustered when trying to recall the proper words for a particular situation. Early in 1847, an irate Mexican citizen came to Taylor's quarters to complain that some of the volunteers under his command had stolen wood from him. The volunteers often caused problems for the general, and he was just not in the mood to hear about another such incident. The fact that the man rattled off his complaint in Spanish further upset the general. Not wishing to deal with the matter, Taylor fumbled around for the right Spanish word with which to dismiss the man. "Huevos! Huevos! Huevos!" (Eggs! Eggs! Eggs!) he thundered at the surprised civilian. "This was the nearest thing to Vamos that he could think of."[29]

When it came to dealing with Mexican women, the American soldiers generally invoked a double standard. While they constantly belittled the character, or lack of character, of the civilians around them, they were willing to put aside these feelings where the women were concerned. They had been away from home, and American women, for a long time, and the chances for their early return were slim. The longer they were in Mexico, the more likely they were to appreciate the beauty of Mexican women. One historian put it quite succinctly when he wrote that the soldiers "allowed their hormones to overcome their ethnocentrism." [30]

Not all, however, felt that way. One soldier thought the Mexican women no more attractive "than the majority of the negro wenches about Cincinnati." An officer of the Seventh U.S. Infantry was less charitable when he stated that he had "never seen any old Negro half so hideous and disgusting in appearance as very many of the wretched hags of this ill-famed race." He also declared them to be without exception the "most revolting, forbidding, disgusting creatures in the world." Of course, both of these men were writing to their wives, so they might have been trying to reassure them of their own continued fidelity while far from home. Another man, without so obvious a reason to modify his description for the benefit of his correspondent, held a similar view. He laid to rest any rumors about the dark-eyed beauties south of the Rio Grande: "I have seen but few women that are worthy of the name. they are not good looking either in form or feature and the rest of them are rather disgusting in their manners otherwise." One man wrote to his wife that he did not even like those women with the fairest complexion—and therefore closer to his own —because he thought that even they possessed a "sort of dirty mottled appearance that looks like a mixture of negro, or Indian." Another man, an army doctor, tried hard to maintain decorum when describing in his journal the women he had seen. Although he did not like their dark complexions, he was certain that they had the most attractive ankles he had ever seen. He went on to write that Mexican women "walk with a natural grace but then that can't be otherwise with that inimitable ankle." Finally, a young volunteer seemed not to know exactly how to describe the women to his mother. First, he told her they were very beautiful, but then hastened to add that they would hardly bear comparison to the girls back home. Had he stopped there, his mother could have rested easy, knowing that her son would not give in to temptation. His continued indictment, however, probably did not do much for her piece of mind. He condescendingly declared that the Mexican women's "greatest attraction is their grace in the dance, Their sylphlike figures, & beautiful faces; They are also excellent musicians."[31]

Those who saw beauty in Mexican womanhood were not always shy about expressing their admiration. One volunteer declared that the women in Mexico were so beautiful that he could not keep himself from falling in love with them. Another maintained that some of them were "*very,* yes *extremely* handsome," while a North Carolinian confidently let his cousin know that the beauty of Mexican women far surpassed any he had ever seen.[32]

Taken as a group, the American soldiers of the late 1840s were the embodiment of the concept of manifest destiny. They were unwilling to allow anything to stand in the way of their nation's course to greatness. They regarded all human beings with darker skins as being on a lower level of human evolution than themselves. Many gave evidence of this in their frequent comparisons of the Mexican peasants with Indians of the American West and black slaves of the American South. This debasement of the Mexicans served a military purpose in that the troops had less difficulty in taking the lives of enemy soldiers if they considered them to be subhuman. This pattern of violence was not always restricted to the battlefields, as soldiers with too much free time between campaigns often alleviated the boredom of camp life by committing crimes of varying magnitude against the civilian population. Fortunately there were also other ways to relieve the tedium of military routine.

CHAPTER 6

"All the Varieties of a Soldier's Life"*

One of the major adjustments facing the volunteers as they got to Mexico was the humdrum of everyday military life. Even considering the living standards of the 1840s, most of these men left more comfortable surroundings than they were likely to find in the tent camps and garrisons in Mexico. A few took to army life with enthusiasm. A Georgian wrote his wife, "As I become acquainted with Camp duty I become more fond of the Army—it is a pleasant life—this will not be pleasant news for you." A New Yorker agreed when he wrote of how he and a friend "boath like solegern verry well."[1]

Most soldiers, however, were bored with the dull routine of camp life. In one extreme case, an officer who was making his rounds inspecting sentries overheard one of them talking to himself: " 'Well this is the G——d damnedest shot of work I ever saw yet. I voted for old Polk G——d d——n him and here I am in wind & rain & misery. I came out here to fight and instead of fighting I have to tread this [illegible] for four hours. What a d——d fool I was. I ought to be in Hell for a d——d fool.' " At this time the officer approached the sentry and playfully answered his challenge of "Who comes there" by responding, " 'James K. Polk.' " The officer's humor was apparently lost on the soldier who, raising his gun and taking aim, ordered,

*J. R. McClanahan to Mrs. James R. Taylor

" 'Stand, James K. Polk for I'll be d——d if I don't shoot you if you give me the least chance.' "[2]

Living accommodations in the camps varied. When the troops were stationed in cities, they occupied permanent buildings, such as former government offices, schools, or convents. When such quarters were not available they lived in tents. The enlisted men generally slept on the ground in these tents, but the officers often had cots or camp beds on which to sleep. If the army stayed in a given spot for any reasonable length of time, the soldiers attempted to make their tents more home-like. One man, undoubtedly an officer, wrote to a friend and proudly described his surroundings: "I wish you could take a peep at our camp, particularly into *my tent* & see for yourself how comfortably fixed I am. I have a large wall tent with a brick floor & fireplace." Others had less pretentious furnishings. One man simply drove four sticks into the ground and placed a board across them for a table, while the side of a candle box, similarly balanced, served as his washstand.[3]

It is safe to assume, given the available evidence, that most soldiers found the general routine of camp life to be boring and uninteresting. They seldom mentioned any aspects of this life that were agreeable or unoffending to them. Negative features, however, often came in for extensive commentary. The weather is an example. Although soldiers were unlikely to comment upon the times when the weather was mild and dry, they were quick to complain about such things as leaky tents and blowing sand. One officer even wrote to his wife about how leaky his tent was in *dry* weather: "A vertical sun comes through the sleazy canvas . . . with force enough to bake one's brains, however thick the skull may be." In addition to the heat that most of the Americans found so unusual was a weather phenomenon known as a norther. A norther results from a very rapid reduction of temperature, often accompanied by icy winds. One man, writing from Brazos Santiago, near the mouth of the Rio Grande, told his father that the thermometer fell from eighty-six degrees to below zero and that "ice of considerable thickness was formed." While such a change in weather as this would have been extremely rare, even more moderate drops would still have drawn comments from those unused to them.[4]

The hot, dry climate that the soldiers encountered in Mexico also produced great amounts of dust, which, along with sand in certain parts of the country, caused a great deal of discomfort. The soldiers sometimes seemed to feel that their entire world had become nothing but dust. A North Carolina volunteer told his sister the dust was so pervasive that "we cook in dust, eat in dust, sleep in dust, and live in dust. Some of the boys are swearing like Turks in consequence of the dust that is blowing into their victuals." Equally troublesome was the sand, more gritty than the dust, which seemed to prevail in some areas. One man noted that he and his comrades could "neither eat, sleep, nor drink without having our eyes and mouths full of wet sand." Another related the story of a volunteer who believed that he had swallowed so much sand as to endanger his health. This poor unfortunate approached the doctor and asked him if he had anything that would remove a sandbar. When told that he did not, the afflicted soldier replied, "Well, then, I am a *gone sucker*. I've got a sand-bar in my innards, upon which every thing grounds, and I can't get any thing up nor down." [5]

Even when the weather was pleasant such routine camp chores as drill and guard duty rapidly became nothing more than bothersome drudgery. While army leaders undoubtedly wanted their men to spend a good deal of time on the drill field, the actual practice varied from camp to camp and from time to time. Many of the volunteers drilled for long hours, several times a day. After a while, however, the newness and excitement of military life wore off. Even a seasoned regular army officer expressed the prevailing sentiment when he wrote his wife that an army camp "where there is no active service is a dull and stupid place, nothing but drill and parades, and your ears filled all day with drumming and fifeing. All this is very pretty for such as have never seen it, but fifteen years of such business takes off the edge of novelty." The fact that some of the volunteer officers were totally unfamiliar with the drill also drew wry comments from the men. An Illinois volunteer noted in his diary that his company seldom drilled, and the main reason was that his captain did not know the drill: "He makes the biggest blunders; any private knows more of regimental drill than he does." [6]

The prospect of nearly endless drill was even less appealing when the chances for actual engagement with the enemy continued to be so slim. One soldier combined his distaste for drilling with an ethnocentrist bias, quite common at the time, when he observed that "as for drilling we dont think worth while taking the trouble to drill. It is very little use in fighting the Mexicans for they will not stand long enough to show us a chance."[7]

Sometimes the periods of drill were occasions of some excitement in the camps. An Ohio volunteer accidentally shot his best friend while drilling. This sort of accident should never have happened, since the foolhardiness of drilling with loaded muskets appears to be so obvious. In fact, some officers ordered their troops to replace their flints with pieces of wood while drilling and the new edition of *Army Regulations* (that was published during the war) required the soldiers to use a piece of bone in place of the flint when drilling. Each of these measures would protect the frizzens from being scratched by the steel jaws of the cock, and at the same time would prevent the accidental striking of sparks by a flint hitting the frizzen.[8]

Such injudicious behavior on the drill field was not strictly reserved for the enlisted men, either. Early in the war a Louisiana volunteer colonel was drilling his regiment and had formed them into a hollow square, as if to repulse a cavalry assault. Then, perhaps intending to test their resolve, he mounted his horse, drew his saber, and charged upon the square. These volunteers undoubtedly knew that they were to stand firm in such a situation, but this was their own colonel riding down upon them and they gave way, allowing him to ride into the center of the square. Had they followed their training exactly they quite possibly would have caused a serious injury to the colonel or his horse. But the colonel was trying to instill the utmost discipline in his command and ordered them to try it again. This time the square did not give way and the colonel's horse received a rather serious bayonet wound in the process. The worried enlisted man who had wounded the horse soon had his fears of retaliation laid to rest when the colonel proclaimed proudly, "Well, the horse did his duty—the rider did his —and the soldier did his—in fact, all did well."[9]

The environment of an army camp offered many other opportunities for life-threatening accidents besides those on the drill field. These often occurred at night and involved nervous sentries who, far from home and in a strange land, often fired at the slightest movement, thinking the entire Mexican army was at hand. One such occurrence took place early in the war along the Texas coast, and it had rather far-reaching effects. A small hunting party was returning to a volunteer camp about dusk. Not far from camp they spied a small herd of cattle that, in the deepening gloom of night, they mistook for enemy cavalry. As soon as they fired on these supposed Mexicans, their comrades in camp rushed to grab up their muskets, thinking they were about to be set upon by the enemy. They spent the next several hours nervously fingering their triggers and peering into the darkness. The occasional sounds of distant bugles only deepened their anxieties, although they later discovered that they were only hearing music from one of the American ships anchored in the harbor. The nervous volunteers finally returned to their slumbers, but their story did not end there. The next morning, as a safety precaution, they all fired their muskets into the air to unload them. Americans at another camp several miles away heard the gunfire and thought it represented a Mexican attack on the first camp, and they in turn spent some time on full alert.[10]

Sometimes the actual targets of the nervous sentinels were other American soldiers. A guard mistook Robert E. Lee and Pierre G. T. Beauregard for enemy cavalry as they returned from a nighttime scouting mission and fired. In this case neither officer was injured, although the ball passed between Lee's left arm and his chest. At other times sentinels shot at nothing more than bushes or small trees. Occasionally, they wound up shooting themselves or each other. At the Mexican town of China, a guard discharged a load of buck and ball at a Mexican and each of the four projectiles took effect. The Mexican was severely wounded, as was one of his mules, and his dog and his other mule were both killed. A Pennsylvanian related how "a poor Jackass, not being able to give the countersign, received eleven balls."[11]

Some of these accidental shootings took place not only in spite of precautions, but because of precautions. Army regulations, for instance, warned of the danger of having loaded weapons about the camp and strictly prohibited this practice unless the men were expecting an immediate attack by the enemy. A Tennessee volunteer faced five days of hard labor when he violated this rule. His musket accidentally went off and wounded a lieutenant standing nearby. But accidents also occurred involving legitimately loaded weapons, as when the troops in camp loaded their muskets in anticipation of an enemy attack that never developed. There were also times when soldiers returned from scouting missions with loaded muskets. In either case, the guns needed to be unloaded for safety's sake. There were a couple of ways to unload a muzzle-loading musket. The fastest and easiest was simply to point the weapon in a safe direction and fire it. The men had to exercise some care in choosing where to point before they fired, but this was also the safest way to unload. Another method was to draw the load from the weapon. This entailed using the ramrod with a fixture on the end of it resembling a wood screw. The soldier would put the rammer down the barrel and turn the screw into the soft lead of the bullet. Then, when a firm grip on the ball was assured, he would pull it out. Common sense would seem to dictate that anyone using this method would make sure that there was no powder in the pan, and that the flint was in no danger of coming in contact with the frizzen and causing sparks.[12]

But not every soldier possessed the requisite amount of common sense, and accidents did occur. A volunteer described one such case when two of his comrades were trying to draw the load from a musket after they had returned to camp. Apparently one of them held onto the stock of the musket while the other tried to extract the load with the ramrod. For some reason the gun fired. Perhaps the pan still held powder, and perhaps the soldier holding the gun had assumed a grip whereby his finger automatically came to rest on the trigger. At any rate, when the weapon fired, the rammer tore through the grip of his companion and skewered a passerby in the neck. The load that the men had been trying to extract then lodged in the chest of the soldier who had held the rammer, killing him instantly.[13]

Indeed, the number of soldiers killed accidentally—whether through true accidents, suicides, or homicides—was quite high. The records of the surgeon general's office list 361 such accidental fatalities, compared to 1,429 who were killed or mortally wounded in battle. Chroniclers of later wars might label these men victims of "friendly fire," but, as in the later wars, they were just as dead as if they had fallen in battle.[14]

Such events as these only emphasized how far away from home and family the troops really were. And like soldiers of all wars, these eagerly awaited the arrival of mail from home to break the monotony of camp life and make their lives a little more bearable. Letters were "like angels visits," according to one man, and were read and reread. Another homesick volunteer informed his cousin that a recent letter from him "gave me more pleasure than to receive 30 dollars wages." Hometown newspapers were also extremely popular items in the camps, often being read cover to cover "a dozen times over, advertisements and all" and then passed on to other eager readers.[15]

It is difficult to ascertain the frequency with which the soldiers received mail from home because these letters do not seem to have held up to the rigors of active campaigning. But the frequency with which the men mentioned the receipt of mail, or the absence of mail, in their letters home indicates that most soldiers did not receive nearly the number of letters that they hoped for. Young Lt. Ulysses S. Grant gently chided his fiancée for having sent him only eleven letters over the preceding twenty months. A soldier from Yorkville, South Carolina, was more impassioned:

i never intend to show my face in carolina again. if i was Discharged now i would not come back to carolina. i am shure i have wrote some *thirty* letters to york District and I never received answers yet. tell them that . . . i am much obliged to them for their kindness to me. i Don't keer A dam whether i ever heare from them again or not. i can think as little of them as they can think of me.[16]

The soldiers were so starved for mail that when one of them *did* receive mail, he often passed it around among his friends so they could share in the feeling of being connected with home again. Sometimes this vicarious behavior was even more pronounced. An Alabama officer found a pile of letters in a back room of the hotel in which he was quartered in Matamoros. The hotel had previously served as the Mexican customs house, and the letters he found had been aboard a Texasbound ship captured by the Mexicans nine years earlier! He gleefully shared them with his friends, but later confessed that "it was not fully acting up to the golden rule of 'doing unto others as we would that they should do unto us.' "[17]

Again, it is difficult to determine what sort of news the soldiers received in their mail, but the plethora of extant letters *from* them gives a good indication of the types of things that were on their minds. One such topic was women. Married men constantly expressed their desires to return home to their wives and families. Unwed soldiers were just as anxious to return home to marry the women they had left behind. Sometimes they were so anxious to return home and marry that the actual choice of a bride did not seem to matter very much. One soldier commented from Santa Fe that "matrimony will be perpetrated to an unusual extent—as every man seems now determined to court the first American woman he sees." Another asked that the unmarried women at home be given plenty of warning because he was "coming home to marry and he wishes it determined by the time he arrives which of them is to take him." A Pennsylvanian was similarly inclined and was even less particular. He just knew that the people at home would surely shower returning veterans with affection, and he would "feel 'tarnal bad' to see all the hugging and kissing and fussing without getting a share. Don't care much, though, for I'll kiss something or somebody, even if it should be one of Mrs. Moore's little red, white-spotted cows!"[18]

Among the things that do not seem to have changed over time is the fact that not all the women at home were content to await the return of their warriors. "Nearly every mail we get brings the distressing news about the boys' sweethearts getting married," commented a Missourian. Of course, as soon as one such incident became known in camp, others began to worry about *their* girls at home. "John Kelly has gone wild since he heard of Minerva Norton's marriage. I think he will take to the mountains soon. Joseph is in better spirits since he got your letter stating Miss Hartin was still single. Horance Johnson is . . . afraid Miss Waters will marry before he gets back, and if she does he is a goner." Some lovesick soldiers even went so far as to threaten suicide if their sweethearts married anyone else, and there were at least a few cases of these threats being carried out.[19]

Although the men sometimes worried about the girls they had left at home, they still had plenty of time to form opinions of their leaders and they did so with little encouragement. Gen. Zachary Taylor came in for a large amount of comment in soldiers' letters and diaries. His troops generally held him in high esteem. Taylor was a regular, through and through, but his unaffected manner and his habit of wearing casual comfortable civilian clothes rather than his uniform endeared him to the hearts of the volunteers. One man described Taylor's dress as "a pair of coarse linen pants, a common frock coat—with side pockets, & a chip hat. I believe he rarely if ever puts on a uniform." A civilian deck hand on a Rio Grande steamboat assured a friend of his that Taylor looked "much more like an old yankey Farmer than the General in command of the American Army." A German immigrant, serving in an Illinois regiment, was a little less subtle in his description of the general: "Taylor is short and very heavy, with pronounced face lines and gray hair, wears an old oil cloth cap, a dusty green coat, a frightful pair of trousers and on horseback looks like a toad."[20]

Such characterizations of General Taylor as "one of the boys" were not universal. Taylor himself certainly did not regard himself as being on the same level as the volunteers with whom he felt himself saddled. A Tennessee volunteer held Taylor personally responsible for keeping his regiment out of the battle for Monterrey, and thus out of a chance for glory, while a regular army infantryman believed that Taylor had unnecessarily impugned the honor of the regulars as a group by calling for volunteers in the first place. Opinions of officers were also subject to change depending upon circumstances. A couple of weeks after the Battle of Monterrey, a soldier wrote of how little confidence he felt in General Taylor's ability to lead the army, but following the Battle of Buena Vista he had changed his tune. Now Taylor was the greatest hero. Generally, however, the men seemed to hold a favorable opinion of the future president.[21]

Other high-ranking officers received mixed reviews. Gen. Gideon J. Pillow is a case in point. As a former law partner of President Polk, Pillow was one of a group of influential civilians appointed to general officer status. Some of these appointments were made for purely political or personal reasons, with no regard for any actual qualifications for the job. At about the same time that one Tennessean was assuring his brother and sister at home that General Pillow was esteemed by both officers and men, a captain from the same state wrote in his diary that Pillow had "a slight touch of the Big head." Yet another soldier, far less taken with any good qualities the general might possess, told his sister that he was "about as consumate an ass as any army modern or ancient has ever been inflicted with."[22]

The same pattern seems to hold with regard to another political general, Caleb Cushing of Massachusetts. A fellow officer, in this case a doctor in the Second Mississippi Volunteers, was very pleased with General Cushing, but then medical officers often do not see the same side of a commanding general as the foot soldiers who serve under him. A soldier of the latter class assured his brother that General Cushing was no general in his opinion, and, in a none-too-kind reference to Cushing's prewar status, stated that "his appearance on horseback is the most perfect Caracature of a mounted militia officer I ever saw." Cushing's penchant for strict military discipline earned him few accolades among the enlisted men, and one summed up what appears to have been the general opinion of the general: "Cushing is about as much fit for a General in an active campaign, as one of the 'flathead' Indians is for a United States Senator."[23]

In many cases the soldiers may have written their opinions of these high-ranking officers to impress their correspondents, perhaps to make them believe that they were personally acquainted with the likes of General Taylor and others. Then again, they may have based their estimations of these men totally upon hearsay and were merely repeating the rumors to the folks at home. Whether either of these scenarios prevailed and if so, to what extent, does not change the fact that the soldiers of the Mexican War were not bashful about criticizing their officers. They formed opinions about not only the upper echelons of the army but also the lower-ranking officers and noncommissioned officers with whom they came in contact on a daily basis.

While soldiers often did not deem it worth mentioning when one of their officers was acceptable to them, they were quick to point out any shortcomings they observed. These complaints were sometimes sweeping generalizations of the entire officer corps, and at other times were aimed at particular individuals, usually known to the soldier's correspondents. An Illinois volunteer, for instance, told his brother about the man who had become a sergeant in his company. This person apparently had "the ill will of every man in company. he is so oficious and thinks he noes it all. . . . he is as dum as an ox and will never make a soldier."[24]

On more than one occasion, conscientious soldiers blamed their field grade officers for the fact that their regiments did not get to participate in battle. A lower-ranking Alabama officer found it mortifying to have to serve under his regimental officers, whom he characterized as "contemptible wretches." He believed that the poor reputation of his superiors had rubbed off upon the entire regiment, and that, therefore, "When there is fighting to be done or any chance for gaining glory & honor we will not be allowed to participate in it." An Indiana surgeon echoed like sentiments after the Battle of Monterrey, during which time his regiment was still encamped along the Rio Grande: "As long as we have jackasses at the head of the Regiment we will remain on this sand bank."[25]

Some soldiers had sterner warnings about their officers. An Illinois soldier expressed some concern when he learned that one of his lieutenants was going back to Illinois to recruit more men for their company: "Had we a *Captain* worth a dime I should advise some of the young men of Schuyler [County] to come out, but as it is I wish them to exercise their own judgement about the matter." Another Illinoisan, probably a member of the same company, counseled a brother back home *not* to join his company if the opportunity presented itself, but instead to "join a company that has a man for a Captain."[26]

Many times the soldiers had only themselves to blame for having elected unsuitable volunteer officers in the first place. Most volunteers chose their own company grade officers, and some even elected their regimental officers. Since most of the volunteers, both soldiers and officers, had no prior military training, it was easy to make poor choices. A member of the Second Mississippi Regiment lamented his regiment's selection in a letter to a friend in September 1847: "We selected inefficient officers. Our Col. has shown himself eminently so. Our Lt. Col. has not been with us since May, and has now resigned. Our Maj., a good officer and clever man, has been sick for five months."[27]

The offenses of these officers ranged all the way from general worthlessness to fraud and cowardice. An Ohio man used several long paragraphs in a letter home to berate his company commander. His list of complaints included the fact that the captain appeared to have gone into the army only in order to obtain high rank and that he had misappropriated funds that were earmarked to buy uniforms for the men. "The next thing which did not seem very praiseworthy, was, the appointment of his own son as drummer, who knows no more how to drum than a horse knows how to fiddle, with the object of relieving him from duty, that he might cook for his father and save the expense of a servant."[28]

The soldiers could put up with a lot of shortcomings in their officers, but cowardice was not one of them. The mid-nineteenth century was a time when military leaders *led*, and led by example. Any hint of timidity on their part could rapidly communicate itself to their troops with disastrous results. Since officers occupied a higher plane than the enlisted men, it probably also gave some soldiers a perverse sense of accomplishment to discover that their leaders sometimes gave in to their fears. An Alabamian commented to his diary that when a fellow officer shot himself in the foot, no one believed that it had been an accident. "What added to the firm conviction of every one as to the act being designedly done," he wrote, "he was said to have cut off a finger once in Florida to have an excuse to return home" from the Seminole Wars.[29]

But the enlisted men did not confine their complaints to their letters and diaries. They sometimes physically threatened unpopular officers. On one occasion a curious Arkansan stopped to look around the inside of General Wool's tent. The general could ill afford such casual interruptions, so he told his orderly to escort the intruder out. As the orderly leveled his musket, the nosy volunteer pointed his weapon at the general and said, "Old horse, damn your soul, if you give such orders I will shoot you for certain." The general then prudently allowed the man to retire at his own pace.[30]

On another occasion, the Arkansas troops were making too much noise to suit the old regular army Wool, and he sent his orderly to request that they quiet down. The men irreverently responded to this request by informing Wool's messenger that he should "tell Johnny Wool to kiss our————."[31]

Actual cases of soldiers murdering their officers, now called "fragging," are obviously difficult to verify, but there are enough hints in soldiers' correspondence to suggest that it did happen. The same Illinois soldier who commented upon General Wool's relationship with the Arkansas volunteers was certain that if these volunteers felt sufficiently provoked by Wool they would "blow out his life" at the first opportunity. A Pennsylvania soldier, serving in one of the new regular army regiments, believed his own captain to be a fair person but that most officers he met were brutal and tyrannical, and often drunk. He followed this observation with the seemingly innocuous statement, "The men seem to form an opinion that some of the officers will soon depart from this world."[32]

Finally, there is at least some evidence of American soldiers trying to kill some of their own unpopular officers. Capt. Braxton Bragg had engendered the ill will of many of the troops under his command by his strict adherence to military regulations. At least two attempts were made on his life. In one instance, a disgruntled soldier from Ohio secretly placed an eight-inch shell under Bragg's bed, with a powder train running outside of the tent. Then, after the captain had retired, the would-be assassin lit the powder. The shell blew up with a roar and, though chunks of metal went completely through Bragg's bed, he was somehow untouched.[33]

Not quite as well documented, but interesting nonetheless, is the theory proposed by an Illinoisan about the death of Col. J. J. Hardin at the Battle of Buena Vista. This soldier claimed that buckshot was discovered in the colonel's thigh after the battle, the kind of buckshot that lay over a musket ball in the buck and ball cartridges issued to American troops, hinting that Hardin may have been intentionally killed by his own men. "This was considered accidental," he said, "but believed otherwise, as battles often decide private grievances, as well as those of nations."[34]

The soldiers did not spend all their idle time complaining about their officers or the weather—they also complained about their food. During the Mexican War, as indeed during every war, the efficiency of the troops depended to a great extent upon the amount and quality of food they received. Army regulations specified a basic ration, but varying circumstances prevented this from being strictly adhered to at all times and at all locations. The soldiers of the 1840s faced a simple and unimaginative diet for their breakfast and dinner fares (many Americans had not yet begun to eat a third meal per day). It consisted essentially of meat, bread, and beans. The daily meat ration was to consist of twelve ounces of pork or bacon, or twenty ounces of beef. The bread was either in the form of eighteen ounces of soft bread or flour, twelve ounces of hard bread, or twenty ounces of cornmeal. The supply of the third staple was to be eight quarts of peas or beans per every one hundred men, or, in lieu of peas or beans, ten pounds of rice. The troops were also able to wash down their food with government-supplied coffee.[35]

Of course, this represented the "ideal" ration. Quite often soldiers on the march fared differently. Sometimes, as in the case of the regular army troops stationed in Texas before the outbreak of actual hostilities, they were able to supplement their rations with fish and wild game. The islands along the coast contained deer that were so tame that even the least experienced hunters had no difficulty. One young officer killed three in an hour's time. Another officer described what he claimed was a typical meal in August 1845. It contained "the smoking haunch of a Buck or doe, flanked with huge roast, fried, and boiled red-fish; and with Turtle pies and steaks."[36]

The troops who marched overland from Missouri to Santa Fe also added to what the government supplied them. The great shaggy buffaloes, which roamed the southern plains in the millions at this time, provided a new taste for these men. Some soldiers took to buffalo meat enthusiastically, exclaiming that they had never consumed better meat in their lives. Others found it less tasty. A Missourian described how he and his companions prepared it over a buffalo chip fire, which gave off an "ammoniacal odor":

Our buffalo meat, which we simply roasted on the live embers, of course partook largely of this flavor, supplying the want of pepper. . . . The part most esteemed by hunters is the small entrails, about a foot in length, and called by the delectable term, "marrow guts." These, although highly relished by the old hunters, never looked very inviting to me! To tell the truth, I was much disappointed in the flavor of buffalo-meat, and would rather have a piece of good beef.[37]

The detachment that continued from Santa Fe to California, however, often faced severe food shortages. It moved through country that was virtually uninhabited by either man or game, and the troops had little opportunity to replenish supplies as they went. Since they had to carry all of their food with them, some were surviving on nothing but meat and water when they reached California.[38]

Whatever the source of the soldiers' food happened to be, they had to prepare it themselves. This meant that several soldiers who were compatible with one another would form into "messes" for the purpose of cooking and eating their meals together. Some of these messes might consist of only three or four comrades, while others had twice that many. The advantage of a large mess was that each individual's turn to cook, haul water, or chop firewood did not come up as often as in the smaller groups. (Officers sometimes avoided such menial duties altogether by hiring a servant.)

For some of the volunteers the idea of cooking their own meals seems to have been a new experience, and they viewed it from different perspectives. A Kentuckian seemed quite pleased with his new-found skill. As he informed his brother-in-law, "it would pleas you to se how manny ways we invent to make ourselvs comfortable and the different ways we have to cook." He then went on to describe how he and his messmates prepared something they called butter cakes. They mixed a little salt with some flour, and then thinned this mixture with water and fried it in grease. On the other hand, an Alabama volunteer decided that such routine camp chores as cooking were "not very pleasant to one that has been in the habit of having such things done for them." [39]

Garrison troops usually had plenty to eat, but the variety was often limited to just what regulations provided. While some found little fault with this menu, others were unhappy. An Illinois soldier was particularly bitter when describing the food he and his messmates were eating:

Starvation is the cry here. Our fare is truly bad enough. We have very fat, rusty side meat, a kind of hard, square bread sent us in barrels . . . together with coffee. Sugar & Butter, eggs, milk, vegitables or indeed anything but fat meat & coffee are out of the question. I can hardly manage to get enough down to preserve me and am some what lean just for want of something good to eat.

A North Carolinian was a bit more succinct: "We eat such Victuals her[e], that no man or woman w[o]uld look at in N.C." A Missourian gave voice to a sentiment that was undoubtedly widespread when he wrote his wife that if he "could only get a glass of Butter Milk & a corn cake I would get a long well enough." [40]

Some soldiers waxed philosophical about the poor quality of their food. One soldier, for example, observed a friend peering intently into his frying pan and asked him what could possibly be so interesting about its contents:

Oh, said he, "I thought I would wake them up." I looked into the pan, where he had placed a cracker, in the grease fried out of his pickled pork, and was amused at seeing a respectable squad of bugs playing on the cracker, and seemingly greatly annoyed by the unceremonious manner in which their winter quarters had been immersed in the hot grease. Sometime the bread is literally eat up by the bugs and worms, but we lose nothing by the operation, as I know of no good reason why well-fed bugs should not make as good fresh meat as well-fed hogs.[41]

The troops soon learned that there were several ways to add to their boring fare. If they were camped away from civilian contact, they could always buy edibles from the army sutlers. When they were located in Mexican towns, they could patronize the local merchants, who usually had a wide variety of food for sale, ranging from fresh fruits, vegetables, and breads to cooked horse meat. In some locations soldiers who were short of ready cash used their uniform buttons, at a rate of twelve and a half cents each, to buy food. Sometimes soap was a means of legal tender.[42]

Sutlers were civilian merchants who operated under license from the army within army camps. They sold all manner of merchandise to their soldier clientele. In addition to food items, which were probably the most sought after of their wares, the sutlers also stocked such items as clothing, tobacco, writing paper, lanterns, camp stools, and hair combs.

At each camp that boasted a sutler, a council of officers was supposed to establish a table of maximum prices to keep this merchant from overcharging the soldiers. In spite of this protective provision, exorbitant prices were a constant source of complaint. One soldier seemed amazed to find the sutler charging five times as much for a plug of tobacco as what it cost back in Ohio. An Indiana newspaper printed a letter from Mexico in which the soldier stated, "It would amuse you to see the prices they ask here. . . . Ice water, 12 1/2 cents per glass; ice, 30 cents per pound; . . . other articles in proportion." (One should keep in mind that these were prices being asked of soldiers who were only being paid seven or eight dollars per month.) The Indiana volunteer ended his report by saying how lucky it was that most of the members of his company had no money, because they had therefore "not suffered from them [the sutlers' high prices] as they would have done were they in a more healthy condition in their finances."[43]

With high prices and low wages, the only way that many soldiers could buy from sutlers was on credit, and the sutlers were more than willing to provide such a service. They knew that on payday, which was every other month, they would post themselves at the pay table, along with their records of amounts owed. Then, before any soldier drew his wages, the paymaster subtracted the amount due the sutler and paid him first. Although regulations specified that sutlers were not to extend more than half of a soldier's salary on credit, many men walked away from the pay table with nothing.[44]

Sometimes the combination of low wages and high prices led to unpleasant confrontations. The soldiers complained constantly of the prices charged by the sutlers, comparing them to prices they were accustomed to paying at home for the same articles. They do not seem to have accounted for the extra cost of transporting these goods to Mexico. Indeed, a sutler attached to the Second Kentucky Volunteers lost his entire stock—twelve thousand dollars worth—when the ship on which he was traveling grounded on a sandbar and his goods were jettisoned to lighten the load. Other sutlers suffered losses at the hands of their erstwhile customers, as the soldiers did not always wait until they had reached Mexico to carry out depredations. At New Albany, Indiana, volunteers who were disgruntled at the high prices and fortified with alcohol demolished the establishments of several sutlers and "helped themselves to such as suited their tastes." Alabamians carried out a similar raid on a sutler's store in Camargo. An observer stated that on the morning following this outrage, "it was not necessary to be close up to hear him [the sutler] 'cuss.' His epithets were long & loud."[45]

Soldiers lucky enough to have any money in their pockets and unwilling to patronize the army sutlers or the village markets for their food sometimes sampled prepared Mexican meals. As one might expect, the use of large amounts of red pepper in some Mexican dishes was disagreeable to those used to milder food, while others took to the local cookery with gusto. A Mexican gentleman in Santa Fe convinced a regular army officer to sample some turtle soup that his cook had prepared and of which he was particularly proud. The American, however, found it so disagreeable that he "had to supplement it with a small lump of opium." An Illinois volunteer officer, on the other hand, left a glowing description of his encounters with Mexican food:

Mexican dinners are quite the rage now among the officers, & I have tormented myself, to be in fashion, by eating several. The peculiarity of the cookery consists in putting a great deal of pepper & garlic in all their dishes. The first course is generally a young kid or lamb, stuffed with rice & raisins & highly seasoned with pepper & garlic. Then a dish of beef alamode with ditto. Then fried eggs & peppers again, & then a dish of real red peppers, stuffed with raisins and pecan nuts & dipped in batter & fried.

It is little wonder, then, that after this meal the young officer felt as if his "throat was the crater of a volcano."[46]

It was not always the food itself that caused comment among the Americans, but the manner in which it was prepared. A North Carolinian told of buying a cupful of goat's milk from a Mexican, but he had to strain it through his handkerchief to remove the dirt and stray hairs before he could drink it. Of course the Mexicans would not drink it either if it was dirty, and "if the old mexicans sees a fly or peace of litter of any kind in it they will souse their fingers in up to their wrist but what they will have it out." Alabama soldiers were avid purchasers of honey and turkey eggs for a time, but honey sales declined abruptly when the men learned that the Mexicans transported it in a raw cowhide bag with the hair to the inside. The popularity of the turkey eggs likewise quickly diminished when "it was found out that another name ought to have been added to the fowl that laid them; they were really turkey-buzzard eggs. . . . After this, it was dangerous for a Mexican to offer turkey eggs for sale in that camp."[47]

The Mexicans also made butter from goat's milk, but it did not appear to measure up to what most of the American soldiers were used to. They found it "too dirty to suit our taste." One man described how the Mexicans made the butter, and then commented that "it is hard to tell which has the predominancy in it—grease or dirt. And its taste is just about as insipid as a piece of an old wool hat, there not being a particle of salt in it. As a matter of course we did not *luxuriate* much in the butter line."[48]

Rounding out the list of dairy products that goats provided for the Mexicans was cheese. Its preparation also caused some Americans to have second thoughts about consuming any. A Mormon volunteer related that the pail used to collect the milk for goat cheese "caught frequent droppings of nanny-berries, which were carefully skimmed out with the fingers. Possibly," he continued, "this may, in some degree account for the extreme richness of the goat's milk cheese."[49]

The combination of wild rumors and the difference in language provided some interesting exchanges between Americans and Mexicans on the subject of food. One American officer had heard a rumor making the rounds among the civilian population that U.S. soldiers ate small children. Deciding to see what kind of fun he could have with this, he approached a Mexican man and asked if he knew where the officer could get a nice juicy boy for his dinner. The man may not have understood clearly what it was that the American was asking for, so the American asked him again, this time for a young girl to eat. Still not getting a positive response, the officer asked if the civilian could direct him to a market where he might purchase a full-grown man. By this time, there was no mistaking what the American was looking for, and the Mexican ran from the scene as fast as he could.[50]

Soldiers also turned to the age-old tradition of foraging for their food. Officers issued numerous orders that the troops were to pay for any such food commandeered from the population at fair prices. Unfortunately, not all soldiers abided by these instructions, and instead they helped themselves to the cattle, pigs, and chickens they encountered. They occasionally employed euphemisms when describing these activities to others as a means of justifying their pilfering. Mexican cattle became "slow deer" or "short-horned elk." One man described how he and his messmates lived "on fat pigs, Chickens, wine, Brandy, and other good things such as we could Draw after knight."[51]

Nor were the enlisted men the only ones who carried out these midnight requisitions. Officers, both volunteer and regular, occasionally participated. Some Alabama volunteers, along with their lieutenant, came upon some Mexicans on their way to market with wagons full of fresh oranges. While the officer distracted the civilians in conversation, the men filled their haversacks with the fruit. And young George McClellan, who had no love for the volunteers or their lack of discipline, casually admitted stopping to kill a "slow deer" while he was out reconnoitering.[52]

Sometimes the Americans committed these misdeeds while drinking. Many soldiers chose liquor as the weapon of choice when it came to fighting the boredom of camp life. The fact that they liked to drink did not mark them as very different from American civilians of the time. In fact, during the early nineteenth century, the United States was one of the heaviest-drinking nations in the world. By the time of the Mexican War, the effects of the various antidrinking crusades had successfully reduced the per capita consumption of alcohol among the civilian population. But in spite of the existence of temperance societies in some of the army camps in Mexico, several factors appear to have worked to lessen their effect among the soldiers.[53]

First of all, most of the regular army enlisted men still came from the lower echelons of society, where drinking was a popular pastime. Many of these men were in the army because they were unable to make a living in any other way. Thus, with a pattern of failure behind them, they were less likely to respond to the protestations of any temperance advocates. Young Lt. Ulysses S. Grant, who himself had a drinking problem in later years, observed that "soldiers are a class of people who will drink and gamble let them be where they may."[54]

Most of the soldiers in Mexico, however, were volunteers, and most of the volunteers came from higher socioeconomic levels than the regulars. These men were representative of a society in which the consumption of liquor had been steadily declining for several years, yet they were often among the worst offenders when it came to public intoxication. This may be attributed to the fact that they were away from home, and all of its restrictions, for the first time. And, just as modern-day college students often rebel against various forms of authority when they are away from parental control, the young recruits in Mexico also tested the limits of authority. An Illinois soldier explained in his diary how he turned to drink: "it alway was agains my princable to Drink when I was at home though I have altered my notion now for it is a great help to a mans helth and allso to Dround trouble for when a man is about half Drunk thare is nothing on his mind only good things . . . he imagines Ever button on his Coat is gold."[55]

Not all of the offenders were enlisted men. A young volunteer officer described how he and his companions celebrated Christmas of 1846 with an eggnog concocted of two dozen eggs and four gallons of spirits. "Some got pretty mellow and I was made very sick by what I drank." A regular army officer told of a similar celebration a week later, on New Year's Eve. "I have some indistinct ideas of my last *sensible* moments being spent in kneeling on my bed, and making an extra eggnog on the old mess chest. I dont recollect whether I drank it or not, but as the pitcher was empty the next morning, I rather fancy that I must have done so."[56]

The newcomers to Mexico obtained their liquor in much the same way they got their food—with the obvious exception of government issue. They could buy whiskey from the sutlers, who often charged as much as one month's salary for a gallon. Others patronized the local economy and drank concoctions known as mescal and pulque, made from the maguey plant, or sometimes a raw brandy called *aguardiente.*

The Americans found that these beverages—just like the local cuisine—called for an acquired taste. And some, after a good sampling, decided not to drink enough to cultivate a liking for the harsh Mexican liquor. A Missouri volunteer, for instance, drank some mescal that others assured him was of particularly good quality. "It appeared," he later wrote, "to draw my tongue half way down my throat, and took my breath away for an instant. It was the first and last glass of mescal I ever drank."[57]

A Scottish woman, traveling in Mexico with her husband shortly before the Mexican War, described pulque: "Here also I first tasted *pulque;* and on a first impression it appears to me, that as nectar was the drink in Olympus, we may fairly conjecture that Pluto cultivated the maguey in his dominions. . . . It is said, that when one gets over the first shock, it is very agreeable. The difficulty must consist in getting over it."[58]

One of Capt. John C. Fremont's topographical engineers has left an equally graphic description of *aguardiente.* "Like the small pox," he said, "a little goes a long ways. I think that it is the meanest liquor in the world for a man to drink. As he gets ornery and mean. I have heard it said that when a man drinks a little of it he wants to steal something, and I have heard it said that when he can't find anything else to steal he will steal his own knife from one pocket and hide it in another, just so as to steal something."[59]

Sometimes even disciplinary actions were not enough to stifle the thirst for alcohol. An Illinois soldier told of being on duty at the guardhouse on a night when twenty of his comrades were locked up for drunkenness: "All night long there was a frightful racket in the guard house; we had three soldiers at each door to guard against the prisoners escaping, nevertheless two of them got out by way of the chimney and later returned by the same route with two bottles of whiskey whereupon the whole crowd got drunk again."[60]

Some drinkers went to even greater lengths than this to quench their thirsts. An Indiana captain, of perhaps a more inquisitive nature than most, spent some of his time in Mexico collecting local specimens of snakes, lizards, scorpions, and horned frogs that he preserved in jars of alcohol. One night two of his subordinate officers found themselves harboring powerful thirsts but without the wherewithal to satisfy them. Desperate, they decided to drink the alcohol from the captain's specimen jars and greedily gulped it down. The next morning the captain noticed his loss and soon ascertained who the guilty ones were. Confronting one of the culprits he said, "I don't care a d———n about the liquor, but I do protest against your eating my scorpions."[61]

The consequences of drinking too much were sometimes more severe than the simple hangovers that many of the soldiers experienced. A heavy drinker might experience the effects of delirium tremens after a particularly serious bout of drinking, or when unable to obtain his usual amounts of alcohol. The sufferer became irritable and his muscles often twitched uncontrollably. In addition to these "shakes," he began to hallucinate, often complaining of being chased by either very large or very small people or animals. Deep sleep would follow, after which complete recovery was possible—but so was death.[62]

Sometimes, before reaching the deep sleep stage of this affliction, these men would behave irrationally and do harm to themselves or others. In the midst of a bout of rowdy behavior while suffering from delirium tremens, a man was finally subdued and taken to the guardhouse to sleep it off. Instead, he borrowed a short, single-bladed pocket knife from a fellow inmate and "completely excised the whole of the genital apparatus, close to the body. Flinging them violently into one corner of the room, he very heroically remarked—'Any d——d fool can cut his throat, but it takes a soldier to cut his privates off.' " A doctor arrived within ten minutes of the self-inflicted castration, but was unable to do much except try to stop the bleeding, which was severe. One of the attending physicians commented that "eight or ten minutes after the bleeding commenced, complete consciousness was restored, nor did he exhibit a symptom of *delirium tremens*, afterwards."[63]

While there do not appear to be many soldiers who left personal accounts of their battles with delirium tremens, several men mentioned companions who had thus suffered. A Missouri volunteer commented, without any apparent rancor, that a member of his command was discharged for disability because he "was laboring under delirium tremens." The apparent acceptance of such behavior is reinforced by the fact that those who experienced fatal bouts of this drink-related malady were "buried with the honors of war."[64]

Drinking was not the only way the soldiers occupied their free time in Mexico. The soldiers often found that they could spend their money on drinking and gambling under the same roof. Numerous observers wrote that the popularity of gambling seemed to transcend all distinctions of class among the Mexicans, "from the priest down." While bull fights and cock fights were appealing in some quarters, the most popular form of gambling was cards, specifically a game called monte. This game was a novelty to the American soldiers. Indeed, the very cards themselves were different, having such suits as clubs, swords, suns, and cups. And although the Mexicans were apparently very adept at this game, a soldier summed up how it must have seemed to many of his comrades when he wrote, "The mysteries of the game can only be learnt by losing at it."[65]

Female companionship was another much-sought-after diversion. Being in a foreign land presented certain difficulties along these lines, however, because the number of women at hand—American women, that is—was very small. Each company of soldiers was allowed to hire four laundresses, but these women were often the wives of men in the company. A few of the less virtuous undoubtedly did more for the men than wash their clothes. At the end of the war, for instance, as one of the regular dragoon regiments was preparing to march to California, some single women made application to go along as washer-women. The officer in charge, fearful of the effect these women might have upon his command, denied their requests by saying that only married women might accompany them—whereupon they speedily arranged "marriages" with some of the men and were accepted for the journey. One of the women was already married to at least two soldiers in different regiments, but she offered herself again. One soldier stepped forward and declared, "I have no objections to making you my wife, if there is a clergyman here to tie the knot." Not being one to stand on ceremony, the "bride" responded, "Bring your blanket to my tent tonight and I will learn you to tie a knot that will satisfy you, I reckon!"[66]

In spite of feelings of racial prejudice, the desire for female compan-ionship led a great number of American soldiers to seek the company of Mexican women. Some were able to meet local women at church or in the marketplace, but the major meeting place was at the fandangos, or dances, that seemed to be held almost every night in some Mexican towns. So popular was this form of entertainment among the civilians that women in very advanced states of pregnancy still attended. In fact, one of these women even gave birth at a fandango in Santa Fe.[67]

One volunteer officer expressed a sentiment shared by some of the Americans who were not very impressed by viewing the locals dancing at these functions: "There is much less of grace and man[n]er in their movements than even I expected to see. They are not either well formed or do they dress well." He went on to describe the dances being performed as resembling more "a Maryland negro dance than any thing I can compare it to." Such low opinions of these social gatherings were definitely in the minority. Most soldiers were willing to overlook any shortcomings in style of dance or grace of movement and instead looked upon these events as opportunities to escape the boredom of military routine. A Texan described a fandango where the step "of every negro dance that was known was called into requisition and admirably executed." This did not bother him, however, as he and his companions danced the double shuffle, the back balance lick, the Arkansas hoedown, the Kentucky heel tap, and the Virginia break-down "with unbounded applause and irresistible effect."[68]

Others found great entertainment at the fandangos. The Mexican women readily danced with the soldiers, and the only problem many of the men faced was how to communicate with their dance partners. As one soldier wrote, "I am at a loss what to say to them which causes some uneasiness with the ladies and myself. They are great galls for kissing. they do love it admirably and so do I."[69]

Records indicate that a fairly large number of the soldiers and their "galls" did not stop at kissing. A volunteer surgeon from Missouri made frequent entries into his journal describing the high incidence of venereal disease among the men. He described one such victim: "His disposition being decidedly amorous led our reverend friend . . . into an illicit intercourse with some Mexican damsel, who being not by any means the purest of maidens left our good friend with unequivocal marks of his amours (viz. the gonorrhea)." In a later entry, the same surgeon injected ethnic prejudice: "Venereal disease [is] prevalent to an extent that could not be imagined in our land of steady habits where this gross licentiousness is restrained by a wholesome condition of public opinion."[70]

Army doctors treated venereal disease according to the medical knowledge of the times. They cauterized whatever "was found upon the organs after a suspicious connection, whether pustule, excoriation, or inflammation." Common practice also included treatment with mercury-based compounds, variations of which continued until the discovery of penicillin a century later. Doctors recognized that the mercury produced undesirable side effects in some cases, and one army doctor feared that "a patient must be mercurialized to death in the first stage of syphilis, for fear that secondary symptoms may appear." This same doctor treated a young artillery officer in Saltillo who had allowed himself to go untreated until faced with "the immediate loss of the organ." Deciding that normal treatment would not suffice in this case, the doctor applied pure nitric acid, which apparently effected the cure.[71]

Since many of the American soldiers in Mexico never witnessed combat, the camp or garrison experience was the one they most commonly shared. Not all soldiers behaved in the same manner when encountering a given set of circumstances, but the conditions they faced were fairly constant. There seems to have been plenty of opportunity to drink, yet there were also soldiers who started temperance societies in the camps. Female companionship, although probably not as easily obtainable as alcohol, was certainly not a rarity, yet some men refrained from debauching themselves. Although the American army's official policy called for full compensation to Mexican civilians for all goods appropriated, the temptation to plunder the defenseless citizens of the enemy nation was great. And even though acts of robbery and assault were not rare, the American army, as a whole, was a far cry from being a band of lawless brigands. Perhaps one reason for this was the sometimes severe methods of discipline that the army invoked to control its men.

CHAPTER 7

"Keeping Down Unruly Spirits"*

Sometimes the ways by which American soldiers in Mexico sought to relieve the boredom of camp life resulted in infractions of military regulations. Even though most of the soldiers were not bad men, some had been misfits in civilian society and continued to be troublemakers and lawbreakers in the army. These individuals faced the army's elaborate justice system and risked a wide range of penalties. Military courts handed down sentences that varied from mere reprimands to death.

Between these two extremes was an assortment of punishments. A soldier's punishment might be to march for several hours at a time while carrying a heavy weight. Particularly recalcitrant prisoners found themselves put into dark holes in the ground for several days at a time with a minimum of nourishment. Gen. Caleb Cushing had stocks built for offenders in his command. Commenting upon this, a soldier wrote that one culprit "was sentenced to eight hours per day for two months in the stocks but the first day nearly finished him and the Doctor put a stop to it." Another method of punishing soldiers was called "bucking." An offender who received this sentence would sit on the ground with his knees drawn up close to his chest. Next, his hands would be tied together in front of his shins. Then, to make movement almost impossible, a pole was passed under his knees but above his elbows. Bucking was sometimes further refined by placing a gag in the mouth

*DeWitt Clinton Loudon diary

of the sufferer, in which case he was said to be bucked and gagged. An extended period of time in such a position was extremely painful. An Ohioan, having observed a fellow soldier being thus punished, decided that bucking "does not seem to me very military, yet is a very good way of keeping down unruly spirits."[1]

By the time of the Mexican War, the American army had abandoned flogging as a means of punishment except in cases of desertion, which crime also carried the possible penalty of death. The soldier facing a flogging knew that it would be a very painful experience. Law limited the number of lashes to fifty, but that was often more than a man could stand. An officer had the offender tied securely for the whipping, sometimes to the wheel of a cannon or sometimes to a tripod of muskets. As the drum major or trumpet major called out the number of the blow, a drummer or trumpeter would lay it onto the bare back of the offender. The whip used was a cat-o'-nine-tails having a drumstick, or similarly sized piece of wood, for the handle. Each of the cat's nine tails was a sixteen-inch length of whipcord tied to the handle, and each of these had three knots tied into it. A surgeon was to stand by to make sure that the lashing did not prove fatal, but this punishment left life-long scars on the backs of those who endured it. One soldier viewed such a whipping in which five men were so punished. While he accepted this type of punishment for them on an intellectual plane, he still found that "it chills one's blood to see free born Americans tied up and whipped like dogs, in a market yard in a foreign land."[2]

No soldier was supposed to receive such punishments without due process of law, although this process differed somewhat from that followed in civilian life. The army dealt with all manner of offenses through a formal three-tiered arrangement. At the lowest level, for instance, a soldier accused of some wrongdoing could ask his commanding officer to appoint a court of inquiry to look into the charges. The court, consisting of one to three officers, acted in much the same way that a grand jury operates in civil life. It could hear testimony but could not pass judgment. At most, it decided whether or not the charges were sufficient to warrant a court-martial.

There were two levels of courts-martial. A regimental or garrison court-martial would convene to judge lesser, noncapital offenses. Usually a captain and two subalterns made up this court, with the duty rotating among the various officers at the post. These officers were rarely lawyers. Though not trained in the legal intricacies, they did their best to adhere to the spirit of the laws as they saw it. As a safeguard for the rights of the accused, the commanding officer of the post or regiment had to approve all sentences issued by this court. A soldier displeased with the outcome of his case in one of these courts could always appeal to have his case reviewed by a general court-martial.

A general court-martial was the highest of military tribunals. Only the president of the United States, a general commanding an army, or a colonel in charge of a separate department could appoint such a court. Between five and thirteen officers made up this type of court, with the higher number always preferred. In addition, a general court-martial had the assistance of a judge advocate for counsel on legal details. But the judge advocate had more than just an advisory function. He presented the government's case as prosecutor *and* assisted the accused as a defense counsel! Theoretically, he was to act in the latter capacity only when the defendant did not have his own attorney, but in reality this was most of the time since soldiers could seldom afford the expense of a lawyer.

The trial began with a formal reading of the charges and the defendant's plea. If he refused to enter a plea, or in some other way attempted to disrupt the proceedings at this point, the court went ahead on the assumption of a plea of "not guilty." As the trial continued, a defendant could very well feel quite lost and alone. Even if he had benefit of outside counsel, he had to present his own defense. A contemporary army court-martial manual makes note of the fact that

Courts Martial are particularly guarded in adhering to the custom which obtains, of resisting every attempt on the part of counsel to address them; a lawyer is not recognised by a Court Martial, though his presence is tolerated, as a friend of the prisoner, to assist him by advice in preparing questions for witnesses, in taking notes and shaping his defense.[3]

After the members of the court had heard the evidence, they retired to decide the guilt or innocence of the man on trial. Military law specified that a prisoner was guilty if a majority of the court so ruled. However, in the event of a tie vote, the defendant was set free.

If the court deemed a defendant guilty, it then had to decide his punishment. Regulations allowed the courts great leeway in determining how a guilty man should pay for his indiscretion. Very few types of crimes carried automatic sentences, and only one *required* the death penalty. This crime, called forcing a safeguard, occurred when a soldier disregarded a duly assigned guard over civilian property in a foreign land. In addition, the Articles of War mentioned over a dozen other crimes in which the punishment was to be "death, or such other punishment as shall be ordered by the sentence of a General Court Martial." These included such obvious transgressions as deserting in time of war, participating in a mutiny, or aiding the enemy by supplying him with food, money, ammunition, or information. A soldier might also forfeit his life, however, if a court-martial found him guilty of sleeping on sentry duty, striking or threatening to strike a superior officer, disobeying an officer's lawful command, or harming anyone bringing food supplies into a military camp or garrison.

And so strong was the belief in capital punishment as a deterrent that whenever an execution was scheduled at any particular place, all the soldiers at that place were required to witness it. They would form their ranks so as to make up three sides of a hollow square while the condemned man stood alone on the fourth side, next to his own open grave. After an officer read the charges against him, he offered the prisoner a blindfold. The firing party, meanwhile, would have received their loaded muskets and be standing by. Often, in recognition of the emotional strain of being ordered to shoot a fellow soldier, one or two of the muskets would be loaded with blanks. That way, each member of the firing squad might convince himself that he had not actually fired a fatal shot but had had one of the muskets without a bullet in it. For some this was not enough reassurance, and they intentionally aimed to miss when given the order to fire. This sometimes meant that the victim was only wounded and would either have to wait for the firing squad to reload and try again or be dispatched by an officer's pistol shot to the head from point-blank range. Such was the case of an Illinois volunteer sentenced to die for threatening the life of his captain. (He had caught his Mexican mistress in bed with the officer.) Perhaps this soldier had witnessed botched executions before because he enjoined his executioners to "take good aim." Unfortunately they did not do so and instead of dying outright he was only wounded. The officer in charge had two more muskets loaded and fired directly into the victim's head, "blowing it to atoms." Observers thought this punishment rather too severe for the crime, and one man labeled it "military butchery."[4]

With the Articles of War allowing the courts considerable leeway in sentencing, however, it is not surprising that soldiers convicted of the same crime at different places and at different times often received vastly different sentences. This resulted, as a prewar inspector general reported, in "a greater variety of punishments for the same offense than there are definable offenses." It was not unusual, then, for one rule breaker to receive a much more severe punishment for a particular crime than another offender who had committed an identical offense. When this happened, morale problems resulted. As a contemporary authority on military law recorded, "This is not justice, and destroys the confidence of the soldiery in courts martial."[5]

Perhaps the most serious crime a soldier could commit in time of war was desertion. Army regulations recognized the gravity of this crime by mandating that convicted deserters receive the death penalty. In practice not all deserters paid with their lives. An Illinois volunteer who deserted received the death sentence, but had it commuted. Instead of death he had his head shaved and the letter *D* tattooed on his buttock, and was given fifty lashes with a whip before being drummed out of camp.[6]

Desertion was a serious concern for a couple of reasons. First, and most obvious, it weakened the army by lessening the amount of available manpower with which to conduct the war. More importantly, desertion was often symptomatic of more serious problems, such as insufficient pay, poor food, or tyrannical officers.

While the numbers are not entirely reliable, it seems that of the 112,000 American soldiers on duty during the Mexican War, over sixty-seven hundred, most of them from regular army units, deserted. The fact that almost as many men deserted as would have filled seven regiments seems ominous. Statistically, however, deserters represented less than 7 percent of total strength and this is considerably better than at other times in American history. George Washington, for instance, lost as many as one-fourth of his army through desertion,

and during the Civil War losses were correspondingly high. In fact, by
the end of that war there were more Confederates absent from their
commands than there were soldiers in the field.[7]

There are several factors among these wars that make a straight
comparison of numbers subject to interpretation. First is the relative
lengths of the wars. The number of deserters during the Mexican War
would probably have been much higher if that war had lasted as long
as either of the other two. Many of the Revolutionary War and Civil
War deserters were conscripts—men forced into the army against their
wills—but the war with Mexico did not last long enough for the
government to resort to a military draft. This meant that virtually all
of the soldiers in this war had voluntarily entered the army and were
not as predisposed to leave before the termination of their enlistments.

A second reason for the lower desertion rate during the Mexican
War—and one that applies to regulars as well as volunteers—might
well be the unbroken string of victories on the battlefields. In spite of
all the elements contributing to the soldiers' disillusionment—bad
food, low pay, tyrannical officers—this unparalleled success in combat
provided periodic lifts to their spirits. Since so many American soldiers expressed such a great desire for martial glory upon entering
military service, it became more and more difficult for them to leave
an army that was constantly winning more laurels. It seemed somehow
less onerous to abandon an army that was forlornly struggling in a
losing, or marginal, cause. Evidence of this occurred in the large
numbers of Mexican soldiers who fled their army and in the high
desertion rate among Confederate troops late in the Civil War.

Third, since this was a foreign war, soldiers who did leave the ranks
found it much more difficult to make their way back home. During
both the Revolution and the Civil War deserters were at least in the
midst of a generally friendly population after they left the army. In
Mexico, particularly in General Scott's army, malcontents found
themselves among a society that was at least ethnically different from
their own. At worst it was a hostile people more than willing to waylay
the lone American as he tried to escape to his own country.

Finally, the very existence of the war may have *slowed* the rate of
desertion in the regular army. The annual rate at which regulars
departed the service without permission was, at slightly over 6.5 per-

cent, not significantly higher than for volunteers. This was considerably less than the 20–21 percent of regular army enlisted personnel who deserted every year during peacetime. The regulars, too, found that the excitement of active campaigning far overshadowed the boredom of garrison life, and this undoubtedly caused many of them to remain in the army at least until the end of the war.[8]

Soldiers began to leave Gen. Zachary Taylor's small army almost as soon as it reached the Rio Grande in March 1846. The proximity to a national border was apparently too much of a temptation for some of the troops, who were perhaps just waiting for a chance to desert anyway. One regular army officer faithfully recorded these events in his diary with such notations as, "Two men swam the river and deserted" and, three days later, "Several of the men have deserted." In just one night in early April fourteen men deserted, but two of them were shot dead by guards as they tried to swim to freedom. Another officer noted that he knew of a deserter who safely made it to the Mexican side of the Rio Grande, only to be killed by an American sentry firing across the river. "It was a capital shot for a musket," he reported.[9]

Soldiers were not the only ones who escaped into Mexico. Army regulations allowed officers to have servants, and many of them brought slaves with them for that purpose. As with many disgruntled soldiers, the nearness of Mexico was an overpowering lure for some of these slaves. A Matamoros newspaper of April 11, 1846, claimed that six slaves had thus gained their freedom already. One slave, who inexplicably returned, declared that his Mexican hosts had treated him with the utmost consideration.[10]

Not all of the American runaways received such consideration at this time. One returning deserter related that his comrades were being forced to work in the mines or to join the Mexican army. He also mentioned that Mexican authorities had accused one of the deserters of being a spy, since he was fluent in the Spanish language, and they had imprisoned him. A short time later he was hanged in retaliation for the death of a Mexican sentinel killed in a brief exchange of gunfire. Commenting upon his fate, an American officer wrote that since he was a deserter, "of course we do not care what they do with him."[11]

Soon, however, Mexican officers realized the debilitating effect on

American morale that large numbers of deserters would have and actively sought to increase those numbers. They had leaflets printed in as many as six different languages to appeal to the polyglot of nationalities within the American army. These notices offered tangible rewards to those soldiers who would desert and join their army. Such deserters would receive comparable rank and large grants of land in Mexico. The pamphleteers also employed another gambit. They sought to appeal to the large numbers of American enlisted men who were Roman Catholics. Portraying the war as a persecution of Catholic Mexico by the Protestant United States, they hoped to convince some of them to come over to their side.[12]

Loyal American soldiers found such practices to be thoroughly repugnant. When army authorities caught a Catholic priest trying to entice American soldiers into the Mexican army, another American soldier wrote that if "he gets his deserts, he should be hung, [in] spite of his sanctity. The recruiting officer's duty is hardly in keeping with that of the priest." This same observer also confidently noted that such attempts illustrated Mexican ignorance of the character of the American soldier. He avidly believed that these offers of land and rank could not "provoke other than a feeling of disgust." But he was mistaken.[13]

It is impossible to determine how many Americans read these appeals and decided to leave the army and go home, but between two and three hundred soldiers did wind up in the Mexican army. Mexican officials formed these men, along with some foreign-born residents of Mexico, into the *Legión de Extranjero*, or Foreign Legion. The legion took as its insignia a green flag with an Irish harp on one side and a depiction of Saint Patrick on the other. This may have been in deference to the number of Irish-born deserters in its ranks, and it may have been intended to entice still more such soldiers from the American army. Whatever the reason, this flag caused Americans to refer to this unit as the Saint Patrick's, or San Patricio, Battalion.[14]

While large numbers of soldiers illustrated their unhappiness with military life by deserting, there were others who chose another way to show their displeasure—they mutinied. Mutiny was as old as armies themselves. There had been several such uprisings among George Washington's troops, but the conditions leading up to them were different from those prevailing during the Mexican War. As the Revolution continued the level of discontent rose throughout the American army, but it was due to circumstances among the civilian population that actual mutinies occurred. The long-suffering Continentals objected not to the amount of privations that they endured in the cause of liberty but to the apparently complete lack of any similar patriotic losses among private citizens and the inability of Congress to alleviate shortages of food, clothing, and pay. They rebelled at the thought that the very nation whose existence they were struggling to ensure had turned its back on them. There was at least one mutiny among Federal troops during the Civil War, but it was racially motivated. Black troops objected, and rightfully so, to receiving less pay than white soldiers. A century later, during the Vietnam War, there were many reports of platoon or company-size mutinies. These were often due to a mixture of civilian opposition to the war and the racial tensions enveloping the United States at the time.[15]

Even though the Mexican War faced significant political opposition at home, Congress routinely voted military appropriations to keep the army well supplied. The relative brevity of the war, as well as its unequaled tactical successes, prevented popular opposition from reaching critical levels. And since there were no known blacks in the American army at that time, there was not the sort of racial friction that appeared in later wars.

The Articles of War were very specific when it came to condemning those soldiers who instigated, took part in, or failed to try to suppress a mutiny, but they offered no precise definition of the crime. Consequently, various officers labeled a wide range of infractions as mutinies. In an Illinois regiment, three men sent a petition to their colonel asking him to allow their company to elect replacements to fill some vacant company offices. This incensed their captain, who wanted to be able to appoint the new officers, so he arrested the men for mutiny.[16]

On a larger scale, when an entire company of Massachusetts volunteers refused to accept a new issue of uniforms, Gen. Caleb Cushing imprisoned them as mutinous. Accounts vary as to the details of this event. An Ohio volunteer reported that the New Englanders resented being forced to pay for more clothing when the uniforms they had were still serviceable. Perhaps they resented conformity to dress regulations as much as the soldiers of the Second Rhode Island Regiment who had similarly rebelled back in 1779. A regular army officer embraced this view of the Bay Staters when he wrote that they refused to wear the new, government-issue uniforms because they wanted distinctive clothing that would set them apart from other troops. "This was entirely unnecessary," he continued, "as they were easily to be distinguished from all others . . . by their 'General rowdy appearance,' and ignorance of a *Soldier's duty.*"[17]

Although these two instances might appear to stretch the definition of mutiny, there was a very real example of that crime in the camp of the North Carolina volunteers in the late summer of 1847. Many of the men and some of the officers in this regiment had long chafed under the authoritarian rule of their colonel, Robert T. Paine. Most recently, Paine had had a large wooden horse erected near his tent. He intended to sentence soldiers guilty of minor infractions to straddle its sharp, narrow back for varying periods of time. This particular form of punishment was not only physically discomforting but also very demeaning. And it appeared to be what touched off the mutiny.

The North Carolinians were brigaded with the Virginia Volunteers and with the Second Mississippi Volunteers. There was much friendly intercourse among the three regiments, so the existence of the wooden horse quickly became known throughout the brigade camp. None of the soldiers liked it, but the men in Paine's regiment seemed reluctant to do anything about it. The others were afraid that this particular mode of punishment might find its way into their own camps, so they decided to destroy it.

On the night of August 14, 1847, about a hundred Mississippi and Virginia volunteers, with most of them being from Virginia, entered the North Carolina camp and proceeded to hack apart Paine's wooden horse. Colonel Paine was not in camp at the time and was unable to fix the blame on any particular individuals.

The next night a group of some fifteen to twenty unruly soldiers returned and shouted insults at Colonel Paine as they passed his tent. He followed them back to the Virginia camp and decided to arrest the apparent leader of the group. As he was about to do this, another Virginian made some comment about having been present when the wooden horse was destroyed, so Colonel Paine grabbed both of the troublemakers by the collars and marched them toward the tent of John F. Hamtramck, the colonel commanding the Virginia regiment. Colonel Hamtramck immediately sent one of the culprits to the guard-house, but the other managed to lose himself in the crowd that was milling about. Colonel Paine then addressed himself to this crowd and warned them not to return to his camp that night.

About thirty minutes later, however, a handful of troublemakers came back, throwing rocks at the colonel's tent. He chased them for a short distance but was unable to catch any of them. A few minutes later he chased two more men out of his camp.

To forestall any further attempts to injure him, the colonel ordered his regimental sergeant major to post an eight-man guard around his tent. Two of the soldiers detailed for this duty refused to obey. When Paine investigated he found that the entire company to which these two recalcitrants belonged was in a state of near mutiny. He arrested a couple of the ringleaders and hoped that the issue was finally settled. When he returned to his tent it was again pelted with stones, this time coming from within his own regiment.

By this time, some Virginians had returned and were milling about near the quarters of Paine's lieutenant colonel, who was confined to his tent because of illness. Paine immediately ordered one of his officers to bring up twenty men to disperse the Virginians as he began walking toward the disturbance. As he approached within a few paces of the rebellious soldiers, they split up into two groups and began to head back toward their own camp. Paine yelled at them to halt or he would fire. One of the rebellious troops, probably not believing that the colonel would shoot American soldiers, called over his shoulder, "Go to hell, God damn you." And another called out, "Shoot and be damned." Colonel Paine fired once. His bullet killed a North Carolina soldier and wounded one of the Virginians in the hand.

Meanwhile, the twenty-man detail he had called for was nowhere in sight, so he ordered out his entire regiment. As he traveled through his camp's company streets, he saw that his troops were not respond-ing to the call and that there were still large numbers of soldiers from other regiments in his camp. One of his captains urged him not to go any farther because his life would be in jeopardy if he did. By this time, the commotion in the North Carolina camp, occurring as it did after all the soldiers were supposed to be asleep, had drawn the attention of brigade commander Gen. Caleb Cushing and Gen. John Wool. The generals immediately posted a line of sentries between the North Carolina camp and the Virginia camp to prevent future problems in the night.

Peace finally returned, but problems still existed. Twenty-five of Paine's officers signed a petition the next day asking him to resign. Meaning to end the contretemps without further repercussions, General Wool immediately issued dishonorable discharges to the two officers whose names appeared first on the petition and threatened to discharge the rest of them unless they recanted. Two of the enlisted men who were involved suffered the same fate, and the soldier who had been killed was denied a military funeral.

When word of these events reached Washington, President Polk disapproved of how General Wool had handled the situation. He had dismissed four men from the service without benefit of a fair hearing. Consequently, the president instructed General Taylor, through Secretary of War William Marcy, to hold a court of inquiry concerning the mutiny and homicide. The court met in early 1848, and, after almost two months, decided that a mutiny had indeed occurred, and that Colonel Paine had acted entirely within his rights when he fired upon the mutineers.[18]

This mutiny provided an example of volunteers from three different states acting in concert, but usually there was a considerable amount of interstate rivalry among the citizen soldiers. Members of South Carolina's Palmetto Regiment did not get along well with the New York volunteers, and their officers sought to be brigaded with other regiments from the South. At one point the South Carolinians even relocated their quarters so they would not be near the New Yorkers. There were also several individual encounters, such as when an Indiana soldier "cut one of the Georgy volunteers with a nife." On another occasion, a sentry from one of the Indiana regiments shot and killed an Ohio volunteer who had refused to halt when challenged.[19]

An Ohio soldier described how he and his companions took on a Tennessee battalion, apparently for no more reason than that the Tennesseans had claimed that they had never been whipped "and could not be whipped by anything that lived." The Ohioan was proud to say that upon their leaving, almost every one of the Tennesseans "had a bruised or blacked eye, or a smashed nose."[20]

Although some of these encounters seem to have presaged the greater sectional dispute that resulted in the Civil War, the major impetus was probably the high level of state pride among these young men. The interregimental rows were just as likely to occur between units from the same region of the country—Pennsylvanians versus Ohioans, or Pennsylvanians versus New Yorkers, for example—as between northern and southern regiments. The practice of raising volunteer regiments composed entirely of men from the same states fostered a unit pride that was of considerable benefit. But it also reinforced the strong attachments Americans already felt toward their states and led more easily to friction between the regiments.

Nor did all such incidents involve men from different states. A Kentucky volunteer reported that he and his companions were so disappointed at not being able to engage in battle with the Mexicans that they "Commenced Among Themselves: their was Not Much Damage Done." Perhaps the most notable internal squabble involved the Georgia volunteers.[21]

Trouble began on August 30, 1847, as four companies of Georgians were preparing to take a steamboat from their camp near Matamoros up to Camargo. Among these companies was one from Savannah called the Jasper Greens, made up predominantly of Irishmen. Another was the Kennesaw Rangers from northern Georgia. A member of the Greens got into a scuffle with another man and found himself bested. When the Irishman's brother, also a member of that company, failed to come to his assistance, one of the Rangers hooted derisively. Another member of the Greens, a Scotsman, then entered the fray and was rewarded with a wine bottle to the head. Before the fight could escalate further, the captain of the Jasper Greens stepped in and stopped the fisticuffs, at least temporarily.

The next day, as the Georgians were preparing for their trip upriver, several of the Rangers made disparaging remarks about the Scotsman as he carried his baggage to the dock. They said that he must be a jackass, since he was loaded down like one, and they also called into question his ancestry. The Scot put down his load and offered to take on any one of the Rangers. But once again, before the situation got out of hand, a mediator stepped in and restored peace.

Nothing else transpired until that night after the Georgians were aboard the ship. Then, for some unknown reason, a man cried for help. It was as if this were the signal that both companies had been waiting for as they set upon one another in the dim light. Officers promptly stepped forward to try to restore order, and they might have succeeded but for the well-intentioned intervention of some Illinois volunteers who were returning from a burial detail nearby.

Col. Edward D. Baker of the Fourth Illinois Volunteers heard the commotion on the steamer and rushed forward with some of his troops. In the darkness, Captain McMahon of the Kennesaw Rangers mistook the advancing Illinoisans for members of the Jasper Greens and immediately offered resistance. A few shots rang out and swords and bayoneted muskets were freely wielded. Within a few minutes it was all over. One of the Jasper Greens lay dead, and Captain Mc-Mahon and Colonel Baker were both wounded. Later, captains of both of the Georgia companies agreed that illegally obtained whiskey was the main cause of the melee. They also blamed Colonel Baker's intervention for making the situation worse than it needed to be. This encounter between the Georgians and Illinoisans was far broader in scope than any other interstate hostilities during the Mexican War, but it was not unique in American military history. Pennsylvania soldiers severely wounded several Massachusetts troops with musket fire in 1776 in the aftermath of an altercation between officers of the respective units.[22]

The most enduring friction between any groups of soldiers during the Mexican War, however, was the rivalry between the volunteers and the regulars. The majority of enlisted men in the regular army came from the lower strata of society. In most cases they were in the army because that was the only way they could make a living. The volunteers, on the other hand, tended to come from the middle classes or higher and looked down upon the regulars.

But there was a deeper reason why the volunteers detested the regulars. It was an age-old fear of a standing army—which the regulars comprised. Over 160 years earlier, an unknown English author had expressed a sentiment still current in the 1840s: "Whether our enemies shall conquer us is uncertain. But whether a standing army will enslave us, neither reason nor experience will suffer us to doubt." Just after the Revolutionary War, Congress had resolved that "standing armies in time of peace are inconsistent with the principles of republican government, dangerous to the liberties of a free people, and generally converted into destructive engines for establishing despotism."[23]

On the other hand, defenders of the regular army thought that the American people were misplacing their trust when they insisted that the volunteers could win the war with little help from anybody else. They recalled George Washington's unhappy experience with volunteers during the American Revolution: "They come in, you cannot tell how; go, you cannot tell when, and act, you cannot tell where, consume your provisions, exhaust your stores, and leave you at last in a critical moment." One young West Pointer summed up his feelings rather concisely when he said, "A more heterogeneous, undisciplined compound of material called soldiers, I am sure never before was brought together in any Army. . . . The majority of officers are more ignorant and difficult to instruct in their duties than privates." Similar sentiments were repeated over and over again in extant letters and journals of regular army officers.[24]

Regular officers abhorred the lack of discipline among the volunteers, even though one regular army enlisted man wistfully commented that he would give ten years of his life to finish his term of enlistment in a volunteer regiment. One lieutenant complained that the volunteers had no sense of their proper duty, that they did not realize that there was more to a soldier's life than battles and glory: "Gentlemen from Louisiana, owning plantations and negroes, came here as common soldiers, and then revolt at the idea of drawing their own water and cutting their own wood, and in fact, they expect the regulars, who have to take care of themselves, to play waiters to them." Another officer had great difficulty getting the volunteers in his command to help in the construction of a fort. He found that "the volunteers will scarcely work; daily labor was not embraced in their conceptions of war."[25]

Even some of the volunteer officers recognized how difficult it was to keep their men in line. An officer of the First Mississippi Regiment seemed almost despondent when he wrote,

One who has never commanded a company of voluntiers can form no idea of the unpleasantness of the life. Voluntiers I am satisfied will never do for an invading army. They will do well enough to defend their own firesides, but they can not endure the fatigue incident to an invading army, besides to keep them under proper discipline they should be under excitement.[26]

Adding to the rivalry was the fact that some volunteer officers were convinced that "all the Regular officers feel a jealousy of the volunteers which they cannot conceal." And there *was* a certain amount of jealousy. Lt. George B. McClellan, only recently graduated from West Point, rankled at the thought that he had spent several years at the Military Academy acquiring the skills of a second lieutenant, only to find that a great number of the volunteer officers had no formal military training at all. Wrote McClellan, "I found that every confounded Voluntario in the 'Continental Army' ranked me—to be ranked and put aside for a soldier of yesterday, a miserable thing with buttons on it, that knows nothing whatever, is indeed too hard a case."[27]

This rivalry occasionally had its lighter moments, such as when a regular officer was watching the artillery practice of some of Col. Alexander Doniphan's Missourians. "Pretty good shooting for civilians," he rather haughtily observed. At this, one of the volunteer officers remarked that he had "never seen it excelled in four years at West Point." The first officer, feeling properly chastised, never realized that the only reason the volunteer officer's comment was true was because he had never been to West Point.[28]

Two other common complaints about the volunteers were that they claimed a disproportionate share of the credit for victories and that they committed undue outrages on the Mexican civilians. Both charges were true. One volunteer matter-of-factly told his wife, "The regular army is no account. They are cowardly dogs and will not fight. The volunteers are the men upon whom the country has [to] rely." Another man, describing the Battle of Monterrey to his mother, wrote, "The Mississippi and Tennessee Volunteers done all the fighting. . . . The Regulars could not be found at any place." An officer of the regular army found it disconcerting when, after the siege of Puebla, the Pennsylvania volunteers claimed that their deeds of valor "had not been equalled since the days of Napoleon." Capt. Robert E. Lee echoed these sentiments, although without pointing any accusatory fingers, when he said, "We are our own trumpeters, & it is so much more easy to make heroes on paper than in the field. For one of the latter you meet with 20 of the former, but not till the fight is done."[29]

Many of the regular army officers who so despised the volunteers had another opportunity to vent their displeasure when the Civil War called forth several hundred thousand more such troops. The longer enlistments and the greater length of this conflict, however, combined to make the volunteer soldiers every bit as well trained and effective as their regular army counterparts by the second half of the war, so intense rivalry tended to be short lived.

Ironically, the United States Army tended to institutionalize such rivalry in the twentieth century by assigning serial numbers to soldiers based upon their condition of enlistment. Prior to 1970, regular army enlistees had numbers with an "RA" prefix while latter-day militiamen in the national guard had the prefix "NG." Thus, even though both classes of soldiers might serve together at times, their serial numbers made it plain that they were not equal, and some turmoil resulted.

A great deal of the disciplinary problems facing the American army in Mexico had to do with crimes against civilians. It almost seemed as if the mere fact of donning a uniform or being sworn into military service caused men to alter their morals. The same citizens who would have been appalled at being victimized by an unruly soldiery became larcenous themselves upon taking the oath of enlistment. Nor did this transformation wait until they were on enemy soil before manifesting itself. At a rendezvous camp for Ohio volunteers many of the recruits made an extra effort to get up early enough in the morning to get to the neighborhood herds of dairy cows before the milkmaids did. There were sometimes as many as four men, each with his tin cup in his hand, milking the same cow. Likewise, a group of regular army recruits found themselves amid orchards of apples and peaches when their train broke down between Providence, Rhode Island, and Boston. One of their number later rationalized the fact that they helped themselves to the ripe fruit:

Soldiers, especially on the march, seem to have exceedingly imperfect and confused ideas on the subject of *meum* and *teum*. On the present occasion, I believe the most conscientious among us considered ourselves completely exculpated by the fact, that being hot and thirsty, we could find no good water to drink.[30]

Officers of the regular army were quick to note that volunteers committed a large majority of these crimes. One of these officers wrote in his journal that the volunteers were taking everything they could get their hands on, and that "the only thing a volunteer is distinguished for, is stealing from market women." Even young Lt. Ulysses Grant, who seemed much more willing to accept the volunteers than most of his colleagues, described events in Matamoros to his future wife: "Some of the volunteers . . . seem to think it perfectly right to impose upon the people of a conquered City to any extent, and even to murder them where the act can be covered by the dark. And how much they seem to enjoy acts of violence too!" Even one disillusioned volunteer sadly noted that "not a day passes but what some outrage, some crime is committed by the American soldier, whose victims usually are Mexicans."[31]

Just as most of the soldiers committing these crimes would never have considered doing the same thing to whites, racism also played a part in how army authorities dealt with these cases. In one instance, an American soldier appeared before a court-martial on charges of raping a Mexican woman of about sixty years of age. One of the officers on the court—who had expressed to his wife his opinion of Mexican womanhood as "the most revolting, forbidding, disgusting creatures in the world, not even excepting our own Indians"—thought the charges ridiculous. "The very idea," he wrote, that an American soldier would commit such an outrage on one so ugly "was enough to make one throw up a breakfast which had been on the stomach for several hours."[32]

In spite of such attitudes on the part of American leaders, justice— or retribution—was sometimes swift, such as when Mexicans set upon unwary American soldiers who ventured alone into darkened Mexican streets. When Mexicans wounded a couple of American soldiers who had molested some local women in Monterrey, an American officer displayed a surprising mixture of racism and empathy when he wrote, "It is true there is probably little virtue among their women, but if there is any virtue it should not be violated." Most soldiers, however, were not so understanding of the Mexican acts of vengeance.[33]

Occasionally the military courts meted out formal justice in cases involving crimes against Mexican civilians. A court in Matamoros found an army private guilty of stealing a billiard ball from a Mexican civilian and sentenced the culprit to thirty days of hard labor. The same court had earlier found two other soldiers guilty of breaking into a Mexican's house and stealing approximately six dollars. In addition to the thirty days of hard labor that the other thief received, these men were to spend their nights in a hole dug in the ground for such use. Then, as if that were not enough, they were to have twenty-five pails of water per day poured on their faces during the final week of their sentence.[34]

Not all the criminals paid for their crimes against the Mexicans. In the spring of 1848, for instance, in a Mexico City gambling hall frequented by American soldiers, accusations of cheating led to a free-for-all. A dozen or more shots were fired in the darkened room, and when it was all over a Mexican banker lay dead and several Americans —including two lieutenants from a Pennsylvania regiment—were under arrest. A military court found these officers guilty of killing the Mexican civilian and ordered them to be hanged. Timing was on the side of the accused, however, because by this time the American army in Mexico was merely marking time, waiting for the Mexican government to ratify the terms of the Treaty of Guadalupe Hidalgo so they could return to the United States. Under these circumstances it would be very difficult for army officials to face the American public if they had these men executed a mere week or so before the end of the occupation. Instead, Gen. Robert Patterson assured the two Pennsylvanians that their convictions were merely to assuage the Mexicans and that they should not worry that their sentences actually would be carried out.[35]

Sometimes the crimes were wholesale, as in a case involving the Arkansas cavalry. The Arkansans, whom General Wool contemptuously called "Colonel Yell's Mounted Devils," were camped near Agua Nueva, waiting for Santa Anna's troops to march north from

San Luis Potosí. In the meantime, these troops did little to engender kind feelings between themselves and the local populace. They eventually pushed the Mexicans too far, and the civilians retaliated with the murder of one of the soldiers in early February 1847. The mistreatment of civilians was apparently acceptable to the soldiers, but it was quite a different matter when one of their own suffered.[36]

The next day, two companies of Arkansans rode out of camp in search of their companion's killers. They came upon a group of Mexicans trying to get away from the anticipated battle between Santa Anna and the Americans. One of the soldiers found a piece of property belonging to the murdered American in the possession of one of the refugees, and the cavalrymen opened fire. The civilians fled to the protection of a nearby cave, where the massacre continued. By the time the sounds of the conflict reached the American camp and General Wool sent other troops to investigate, some twenty or thirty Mexican civilians lay dead.

The resulting official investigation failed to identify individual Arkansans who participated. Instead, General Taylor ordered both companies to return to the mouth of the Rio Grande, where they would be unable to share in the glory of the coming battle. For some reason, Taylor did not seem able or willing to implement the necessary disciplinary measures that would halt such outrages as that committed near Agua Nueva.

While the Arkansans came in for a large amount of censure for this incident, no single group of volunteers was so universally condemned for its conduct toward civilians as were the Texans. One officer told how "they come here with the sores and recollections of wrong done, which have been festering in them for ten years, and under the guise of entering the United States service, they cloak a thirst to gratify personal revenge."[37]

Sometimes these feelings manifested themselves in theft or destruction of Mexican property. Late in the war, while they were on a patrol after some Mexican guerrillas near Mexico City, some Texans camped for the night near a rather large hacienda—complete with its own small church. One of the Americans stumbled onto a barrel of wine near the little chapel and he and his companions immediately helped themselves to its contents. The *hacendado* complained that he was a poor man and now these Texans were drinking all of his wine, but they assured him that they would pay for it. The owner was apparently more concerned about the loss of the wine itself than he was about being repaid for it, as next he told the assembled drinkers that the wine was not really his but belonged to the priest. This change of tactics did not have the desired effect of shaming the Texans into sobriety—they merely offered to pay the priest for the wine rather than the landowner. Growing more and more frustrated as he watched the ever-sinking level in the wine barrel, the landlord tried one more time when he told the tipplers that this was consecrated wine. The Texans proved just as tenacious, however, when they responded that if that were the case they would not pay for it at all, but would simply "drink it for the love of God."[38]

Unfortunately, a fair number of such encounters did not end so harmlessly. One of the Texans later wrote, tongue in cheek, how they flaunted the regulations with regard to the Mexican populace:

Our orders were most strict not to molest any unarmed Mexican, and if some of the most notorious of these villains were found shot, or hung up in the chaparral . . . the government was charitably bound to suppose, that during some fit of remorse and desperation, tortured by conscience for the many evil deeds they had committed, they had recklessly laid *violent hands upon their own lives!*

A regular army surgeon mentioned the case of eight Texans who rode up to a Mexican ranch and began helping themselves to pigs and chickens. When the owner came out of the house with his small son to complain, they shot them both and then killed two servants. Commenting on the fact that army officials had not punished these men, but had instead sent them home, the doctor wrote, "All this is quite strange. Genl. Taylor has much to answer for." In response to a query about the Texans' depredations, General Taylor merely wrote, "I have not the power to remedy it, or apply the corrective, I fear they are a lawless set."[39]

General Taylor, and virtually all other regular army officers, found it easy to blame all the lawlessness on the volunteers, and it does appear that these troops committed more acts of violence on Mexican civilians than did the regulars. Taylor and his contemporaries tended to ascribe such behavior to the fact that the volunteers had not been subjected to the rigorous discipline required of regular troops, but there now appears to be more to it than that. Psychological studies of soldiers accused of murdering civilians in later wars show certain patterns that, by extrapolation, also seem to apply to the soldiers of the Mexican War. For instance, a large percentage of these men had had an older brother killed before they committed their crimes. The thirst for vengeance that followed such a loss may easily be seen among the volunteers during the war with Mexico too.[40]

Some of the Texas volunteers had fought in the Texas Revolution or had helped to stop the Mexican incursions of 1842. Others had taken part in the unsuccessful mission to Santa Fe or, like Capt. Sam Walker, had spent time in Mexican prisons as a result of the ill-fated Mier Expedition. They had not always suffered the loss of brothers, but they had seen friends die and had often suffered personally at the hands of Mexican soldiers. Many volunteers from other states had similar reasons to hate the Mexicans. They, too, had seen an older brother, a favorite cousin, or perhaps a father go to Texas in the mid-1830s and not return. Then, ten years later, it was these brothers, cousins, and sons who found themselves in a position to exact some measure of revenge for their losses. A few of the regular army troops may also have suffered the loss of a loved one in the earlier Texas fighting. The fact that European immigrants constituted a large proportion of the regular army, however, indicates that this number cannot have been very high.

Modern-day psychologists have noted another circumstance that may also help to explain the atrocities committed by American soldiers in the 1840s. Research has shown that when soldiers were actively engaged in combatting the enemy, their fervor cooled somewhat. Those, however, who remained out of the fighting and could only hear about it from others sought outlets for their passion: "In other words the men who, through lack of skill or opportunity, have not done their fair share of killing (say) will remain more worked up than those who have." This phenomenon may explain the unnecessary violence perpetrated by the volunteers who arrived in Mexico in the wake of the major campaigns. Quite a number of volunteers never took part in a battle. Their military experience consisted of guarding supply bases and watching helplessly as their comrades died of disease. They chafed at being assigned such tedious duties, particularly when other volunteers—often members of other regiments from their own states—were earning laurels on the battlefields. For some of these men the indignity of being relegated to a backwater of the war was too much. They had volunteered for the army to avenge Texas and gain personal glory by killing Mexican soldiers. When legitimate opportunities proved so limited some of them accomplished their goal by murdering innocent Mexican civilians. Indeed, some of these late-arriving volunteers may have been under the dual pressure of trying to avenge the death of a relative and of not being allowed to do so in legitimate battles.[41]

CHAPTER 8

___

The Volunteers Take the Field

The natural inclination when thinking of war—any war—is to recall glorious scenes of the battlefield, and these are exactly the scenes to which the volunteers looked forward so eagerly. Yet the battles of the Mexican War, as in most wars, occupied only a very small percentage of a soldier's time. During the eighteen months or so of active campaigning there were only about a dozen pitched battles. Regular troops fought the first two battles, and volunteers took part in all the rest.

Active campaigning ceased for a time following the battles of Palo Alto and Resaca de la Palma as military leaders in both countries planned their next moves. The Mexican army had abandoned Matamoros to General Taylor and had moved westward to Monterrey, the capital city of the Mexican state of Nuevo Leon. The American army moved too, but slowly.

The volunteers had little patience with the drudgery of camp life. They were anxious for combat. A Virginia volunteer, writing to his father early in 1847 from his regiment's rendezvous point at Fortress Monroe, voiced a sentiment that was echoed by thousands of young men at the start of another war a scant fourteen years later when he wrote, "I am very anxious to get off, fearing that we might not arrive in time for the first great battle, and I believe the last." He apparently did not think the actions he had already missed out on—Palo Alto, Resaca de la Palma, and Monterrey—significant enough to be called battles. And he was equally mistaken as to the number of battles remaining.[1]

The Americans who went to war in the mid-1840s were nothing if not confident of success. In this time of no conscription these men believed in the reasons, so far as they understood them, for which their country had gone to war. There were no soldiers drafted against their will to fight a war in which they did not believe. An Illinois volunteer wrote, "If I Dye in the war with mexico I donte want you to say he was perswaded into it but that he volenteered of his own accord and died in defending the riches of his cuntry."[2]

The volunteers were cocky and seemed to feel a certain invincibility that all young soldiers experience at first. This sentiment, born of an ignorance of what war is really like, was nurtured by the success of American arms in the early battles. It was heightened by a correspondingly low opinion of the Mexican soldiers, which was part nationalism and part racism. One soldier, as yet unbloodied by actual combat, expressed both feelings with a single-sentence entry in his journal: "There would be no use for us after we had been in one battle for we would so completely annihilate the Mexicans that they would not think of meeting us but once."[3]

In spite of such displays of bravado, most soldiers experienced varying degrees of fear as a battle was about to start. This anxiety usually passed very quickly once the shooting actually began, and "the primitive man asserted himself in a mad fury to kill." Some men entered combat with the fatalistic view that they would not survive. Capt. William Alburtis of the Second U.S. Infantry was one such person. Just prior to the landing at Veracruz, he expressed misgivings, but he was a professional soldier and would not let his anxiety stand in the way of his duty. He died the next day, one of only thirteen Americans killed during the siege of Veracruz. For many troops, this feeling of impending doom manifested itself in the urge to prepare their wills. An officer of the Mounted Rifles did this right before each of his first two or three battles, but gave it up when he kept surviving. He lived past his seventy-fifth birthday.[4]

Most, of course, would not admit to feeling fear, and instead employed various euphemisms when describing what was going through their minds at such times. "It was not fear," wrote an Illinois volunteer, "yet it was more like fear than any thing I ever felt during the heat of the action." An Ohioan admitted to feeling a bit squeamish, "queer" in the parlance of the 1840s, when his unit received orders to load its muskets before going into action for the first time. "After we had loaded our guns and got started into town I did not feel so badly excited," he explained.[5]

Another Ohio volunteer later remembered experiencing the same sort of foreboding, but his premonitions only lasted a few moments. He claimed in a book published just after the war—and in a vein no doubt calculated to bolster his own image—that these feelings passed when he recalled that he "had voluntarily offered myself a sacrifice to my country." A Mississippian, however, should probably take credit for the most understated expression of prebattle jitters when, describing a recent battle to his brother, he confided, "I did not feel as pleasant as I would had I been at home, but it was fight or die and I was ready for battle."[6]

Although the men generally controlled their anxieties at the approach of battle and performed their duties properly, there were some for whom the noise and fury of combat became too much to bear. The numbers of such soldiers, who in later wars were diagnosed as suffering from combat fatigue, is difficult to document. Since most people regarded an inability to perform in combat as nothing but cowardice, those who thus broke under the strain were not prone to record these experiences. Some ran away from battle. Others cowered on the battlefield, frozen in fear and unable to move forward or back. During one engagement, later in the war, a soldier was seen mechanically loading his musket and firing it into the air. His nerves may have cracked over being in one too many battles, or it may have been his very first, and the carnage and destruction all around him was just more than he could handle. Unfortunately, there were no army psychologists to investigate such cases as this, and most such behavior was chalked up to abject fear.[7]

It should come as no surprise that many soldiers during the Mexican War found actual combat to be very disconcerting. Nothing in their brief training had prepared them for the realities, and horrors, of battle. Occasionally, due perhaps to inferior gunpowder, Mexican cannonballs were rolling and bouncing along the ground by the time they reached the enemy positions. The Americans made a game, then, of hopping out of the way, and it gave them—especially if it was their first battle—unrealistic expectations. Before long, as the American infantry advanced, the Mexicans filled the air with musket balls and canister shot until they were "so thick one could not help feeling like putting his hand before his face as if it were hail."[8]

Before the volunteers could test their mettle against the enemy they had to do a considerable amount of preparatory work. It took a month for General Taylor to concentrate his army at Camargo and establish a permanent supply base there. When the next leg of the campaign for Monterrey began, on August 19, 1846, the constantly growing lists of sick soldiers made this movement very difficult. For example, when the commander of the First Tennessee Regiment received orders to pick his best five hundred men to go to Monterrey—his regiment had left Tennessee with one thousand recruits—he had trouble finding the requisite number of troops who were even well enough to march. It took about a month for the entire army to make the transit, but by September 12, the final move was underway. A week later the Americans camped within sight of Monterrey.[9]

The city itself was well suited to resist attack, and the Mexican soldiers had had three months in which to strengthen its defenses. General Taylor proposed to attack the city from two directions in a giant pincers movement. On the morning of September 21, therefore, while a smaller force attacked from the west, the bulk of the army struck the northeast side of the city.

As the main assault force, under Lt. Col. John Garland, neared the city it encountered a virtual hornet's nest of resistance. Mexican cannons raked the American formation, and every house seemed to shelter enemy infantrymen who added their fire. A Mexican cannonball decapitated a young volunteer, and a nearby regular, upon seeing the unfortunate man's brains splattered on a wall, mused that it was hard to imagine "that a man that had so many brains could be fool enough to volunteer to come to such a place as this."[10]

In spite of heavy losses and the complete demoralization of some of the volunteers in his command, Garland's men gained the streets of the city. When General Taylor saw how far they had advanced he sent other troops to their aid. The Mexican resistance in the city proved too powerful for Garland's force, however, and he withdrew before the reinforcements reached him.

Most of those in the relief force were volunteers, eager to prove their valor, and when they attacked they suffered very heavy losses. At one point, as some Tennesseans were marching toward the action, a single Mexican cannonball raked their line and left four dead and three wounded. The losses might have been even higher but for an unusual turn of good fortune. Mexican troops had used cheap cotton bags filled with sand to build up a protective barricade on the roof of one of their positions. They soon discovered, however, that when they leaned forward across this parapet to fire their muskets, sparks that escaped from their priming pans ignited some of the sandbags. The resulting smoke and flame then made it impossible for the defenders even to approach their own breastworks. They could not return the American fire with any degree of accuracy.[11]

Finally, about noon, the Fort de la Tenería fell, with help from a small group of Garland's regulars who had not fallen back with the rest of his force. One of the Tennesseans proudly wrote to his wife about his part in the capture of this Mexican strongpoint. He told her he was the first one over the rampart, a claim that was no doubt made by quite a few others, and went on to describe what happened next: "I discharged my pistoll at a mexican and (*guess nothing but the Bell & bones was found*). he instantly fell. he was trying to lode the cannon but he was two late. I sent him to a nother wourld."[12]

It was while the Americans were struggling for a foothold in this sector of the city that the much-vaunted enemy lancers made their appearance. Many considered them to be the elite of the Mexican army and their arrival now caused at least one awestruck Ohioan to observe that they "appeared as if they covered ten acres of ground. It was the prettiest sight I ever saw." A few moments later, when he witnessed the lancers deliberately killing the American wounded, his opinion changed: "Oh! how I could have buried the assassin's knife in their murderous brests if I had of had an opportunity. I don't blame the Texians for wanting to kill every one they come a cross."[13]

By nightfall, after much heavy fighting, the Americans still held only the Fort de la Teneria at the eastern edge of Monterrey. During the night of September 22–23, Gen. Pedro Ampudia, who had resurfaced as the commander of the Monterrey defenses, abandoned most of his outlying works and consolidated his troops in the city itself.

When the Americans at the Tenería awoke the next morning they could scarcely believe this turn of events. Pushing forward cautiously and entering the city before noon, they quickly learned that street warfare, which they now faced, was a very vicious activity. Every house, with its thick walls and parapeted roofs, was a virtual fortress.

As the fighting progressed from house to house and street to street, General Worth heard the gunfire and decided, without orders, to join in. Both American forces, like the jaws of some giant blue vise, slowly closed on the city. In the streets of Monterrey the fighting was fierce. The two sides shot at each other from windows on opposite sides of streets. Soldiers in courtyards fired at those on the rooftops. Sometimes soldiers of the two sides fought at what a Mexican soldier later described as "burn-clothes distance," so close that the soldiers' uniforms were singed by their opponents' muzzle blasts.[14]

For the Americans to expose themselves in the streets was to invite a hail of gunfire, so they adopted a different way of advancing. They entered the houses and used pickaxes, crowbars, and lighted cannonballs to blast their way through the common walls and into succeeding houses. In this way, they gradually approached the main Mexican force in the Plaza Mayor. When they had to cross streets, which enemy artillery swept, they waited for the cannons to fire and then scampered to safety while the Mexicans reloaded. That afternoon General Taylor inexplicably halted the American advance before it reached the main plazas.

Late that night—it was actually early on the morning of September 24—General Ampudia offered to surrender the city if his army were allowed to withdraw. Taylor refused and demanded the surrender of both the city and the army. The agreement, to which both sides finally consented, allowed the Mexican soldiers to pull back to a designated location from which they could not advance for eight weeks. Taylor likewise promised that the American army would not go beyond a certain line during that period unless either government disallowed the truce before its expiration. The city of Monterrey thus became a major American base for the rest of the war.

Col. Jefferson Davis, who had helped draw up the armistice, expressed his unqualified approval of it, saying, "they were whipped, and we could afford to be generous." Most Americans in the ranks, however, mourned the loss of their comrades and believed that the terms of the armistice would ultimately mean they would lose more friends in future battles. An Ohioan summed up his feelings in one short sentence: "Damn the armistice!"[15]

Nevertheless, the defenders of Monterrey marched out unmolested. One observer seemed surprised that the Mexican soldiers were not brutish oafs. Instead, they were not much different in appearance from the Americans. In fact, one regiment "was composed of the finest looking body of men I ever cast eyes on in perfect discipline and well armed." Another onlooker shared these sentiments, finding the enemy troops to be "a remarkably fine looking swarthy set of fellows, well dressed and martial in appearance." Lt. Ulysses Grant, however, disagreed: "My pity was aroused by the sight of the Mexican garrison of Monterey marching out of town as prisoners. . . . Many of the prisoners were cavalry, armed with lances, and mounted on miserable little half-starved horses that did not look as if they could carry their riders out of town. The men looked in but little better condition."[16]

Upon examining Monterrey's defenses after the armistice, American soldiers were amazed that the city had not held out much longer. They called it a veritable Gibraltar. Near the Tenería, one regular noted, "where so many of our brave fellows fell, my wonder is that *any escaped*."[17]

In an unusual display of bipartisanship, Maj. Gen. William O. Butler served up equal portions of praise for both the volunteers, of which he was one, and the regulars. "Never, I believe, did troops, both volunteers and regulars, behave with more calmness and intrepidity, and I do not believe that, for downright, straight-forward, hard fighting, the battle of Monterey has ever been surpassed." General Butler was pretty close to right. Not only was the fighting hard, but it was costly. The Americans lost 120 men killed, 368 wounded, and forty-three missing. Mexican losses were lighter.[18]

The Battle of Monterrey was an important victory for General Taylor's army. It was the first battle of the war in which large numbers of volunteer soldiers had participated, and they had performed well. Perhaps they had performed too well, since the result of their baptism of fire was a heightening of their self-confidence at the expense not only of the enemy but of their own regular army comrades as well.

Their letters home to families, friends, and local newspapers were so full of self-promoting flattery that a veritable war of words threatened to erupt among the partisans of the various volunteer regiments.

The American soldiers often expressed inflated opinions of their own martial prowess in terms of sectional pride. They were not just proud to be American soldiers. They meant to uphold the honorable names of their communities or home states. A member of Kentucky's Louisville Legion assured his wife that, should an anticipated clash with the enemy develop, "we will have the chance of shewing Kentucky spunk and if I am not mistaken . . . the boys of Louisville will not disappoint the expectations of their friends." An Indiana soldier wanted his friends to know that if he were killed in Mexico or, as he put it, "if I should accidentally fall a victim," they should not grieve. His main concern in such an event was that he should not have "disgraced my own native Hoosier State—But that in defence of my country's right I died." Another soldier, a member of another regiment from the same state, definitely had dreams of glory when he observed that "the Volunteers are impatient to have active service, where they may exhibit more observable acts of patriotism, and that Indiana's Chivalry in this Campaign may have an honorable page assigned her, in the future history."[19]

A young Mississippian aptly illustrated the lack of esteem with which the Americans held the Mexican soldiers when he wrote his mother after the Battle of Monterrey. He reassured her that he had been in no real danger during the fighting because his regiment was "only opposed by small arms for which by this time the most of us had conceived the most sovereign contempt." The still relatively inexperienced American soldiers almost invariably shared the opinion of a regular army officer who thought that, even though some of the Mexican officers were capable, their troops were sadly deficient. He hinted at a feeling of Mexican racial inferiority when he wrote his wife that the people from whom the Mexican soldiers were conscripted were "bad at the beginning and length of service does not appear to benefit them much. They fight not for principle but from compulsion." Another American officer found the Mexican army to be just as ineffective, but laid the blame upon the officers instead of the rank and file. Young Ulysses S. Grant believed that the Mexican soldiers quickly became dispirited in a battle and simply gave up, and this he blamed on their officers: "Poor fellows; if they were well drilled, well fed and well paid, no doubt they would fight and persist in it; but, as it is, they are put to the slaughter without avail."[20]

The American soldier of the 1860s, whether he wore blue or gray, considered his opponent initially in much the same way as the American soldier had thought of the Mexican *soldado* in 1846. There was not nearly the racial difference between the Civil War armies, of course, since their troops were all products of the same ethnic strain. Nevertheless, they each regarded the other as having apparently undergone some sort of cultural mutation that left them despicable beings of some lower order. This depravity manifested itself on both sides, at least according to reports early in the war, in such actions as the wanton murder of the wounded, the use of poisoned or exploding bullets, and the desecration of enemy bodies. If these reports were true, parallels occurred in Mexico, where Americans observed enemy lancers as they rode over the battlefields at Monterrey or Buena Vista and killed Americans who were already wounded.

So far this comparison has only served to point up commonalities between the two wars. But soldiers in the later conflict changed their opinions of their foes, and this change related to the fact that they were engaged in a civil war—not a foreign war—and that the war had not been so one-sided as to be over in a year's time. In Mexico, it was easy for the Americans to maintain a high degree of animosity toward the opposing army because of their feelings of racial and martial superiority. By the second year of the Civil War, in contrast, many had begun to see how very similar the soldiers of the two sides were. They all, for the most part, spoke the same language. They all celebrated Washington's birthday and the Fourth of July.

One thing that furthered this mutual realization was the fraternization that went on between the lines. Although such behavior was certainly not universal, it was also by no means a rarity. Troops from opposing sides sometimes arranged informal truces and visited one another peacefully. For a short time they were able to forget that they were in the midst of a fratricidal war and instead talk of home and, perhaps, trade southern tobacco for northern coffee. For the most part, officers on both sides condemned these gatherings, but the men involved had a chance to realize the humanity of their enemy. This sort of interarmy camaraderie was virtually unheard of during the Mexican War, due in large part to the language barrier that was not a problem in the Civil War. Even without linguistic difficulties, however, it would have been more difficult for the American soldier in Mexico to have put aside his racist feelings long enough to concede that his counterpart might have the same range of emotions as he did.

As the Civil War moved into its second, and third, and fourth years, the soldiers got farther and farther away from their original impressions of their enemy. Where early in the war, each side regarded the other as cowards who would run at the sight of a real army, as time passed they became more likely to hold the other side in grudging respect. In contrast, only rarely did an American soldier in Mexico ever express any admiration for the bravery of Santa Anna's troops. Nor was this entirely due to racism. Union and Confederate soldiers had all been involved in both winning and losing battles, and they had gained a certain admiration for their opponents. In Mexico, this did not happen. Even though in some battles, such as Buena Vista and Molino del Rey, the Mexican troops fought with a ferocity and bravery unexcelled by the Americans, they still lost. It is very easy to take lightly any opponent that has never been victorious.

Both wars saw Americans perform acts of kindness that seemed somehow out of place in a war. American doctors routinely treated the wounded of the enemy along with their own, and soldiers often offered water to wounded enemy troops. On the battlefield itself, though, the enemy received different treatment in the two wars. During the Civil War, the soldiers recognized enemy bravery in the midst of the fighting by sparing the life of a foe who exhibited it. Such was the case when Confederate Sgt. Richard Kirkland risked his life to minister to the wounded Federals in front of the Confederate breastworks at Fredericksburg. There was also the unnamed Union infantryman who grabbed up his regiment's fallen battle flag within a few yards of the Confederate works at Pickett's Mill and carried it off unmolested. These were cases, however, that occurred later in the war, after the men in the trenches had learned to recognize and reward such valor. Such recognition did not occur in Mexico. The war did not last long enough, nor were Mexican forces successful enough, for this to occur with any regularity.[21]

Meanwhile, as General Taylor's army moved on Monterrey, the second prong of the American offensive into northern Mexico was taking shape at San Antonio, Texas. Brig. Gen. John E. Wool, the army's third-highest-ranking officer, was to lead a mixed division of regulars and volunteers. Their target was the city of Chihuahua, two hundred miles south of El Paso and 350 miles northwest of Monterrey.

The volunteers came from Illinois—two regiments of infantry—and Arkansas—one battalion of cavalry. The infantry traveled down the Mississippi River to New Orleans, and then across the Gulf of Mexico to Port Lavaca, on the Texas coast. They then moved inland a dozen miles and set up camp. After drilling there for a week, they began the 160-mile trek to San Antonio about the middle of August 1846. For almost half the distance, their route remained in the coastal lowlands where the ground was often marshy and wet, and covered with tall prairie grass. The hot Texas sun only added to the usual list of discomforts associated with a long march. Complaining of sunburn, but still able to keep his sense of humor, one officer wrote that the skin on his nose had "already peeled off five times, & as often blistered again, & I fear that I shall suffer a great reduction of my proboscis during this campaign." After two weeks, the suffering soldiers finally reached the outskirts of San Antonio.[22]

San Antonio was an old city in 1846, more Mexican than American. The buildings were generally one-story structures with flat roofs and very few windows onto the streets. One soldier found the town to be "full of saloons, faro games, bowling alleys and billiard halls and many other ways for a man to lose his money." To the Illinoisans, the people of San Antonio were just as unusual as the city's architecture. The soldiers were quick to form opinions of them, and those opinions, as was the case wherever American soldiers encountered Mexicans, was not very high. One man noted rather cynically, "The more *respectable* portion of them consists of *scape-gallows* & *black-legs* from the States."[23]

Troops under General Taylor had already fought and won the Battle of Monterrey before General Wool's command was ready to leave San Antonio. At last, on September 26, 1846, the main body of his troops began moving slowly south toward the Rio Grande and Mexico. It took about two weeks to reach the Rio Grande, but by the middle of October, the troops were finally on Mexican soil.

General Wool took this occasion to remind his soldiers that the war was between the armies of the opposing nations. He cautioned them, under pain of severe punishment, not to abuse the Mexican civilians whom they would encounter: "We have not come to make war upon the people or peasantry of the country." He further warned against looting and enjoined them to pay liberally for any and all supplies that the Mexicans might furnish.[24]

By the time the small American army reached the city of Monclova on November 3, Wool received an order from General Taylor telling him that, in light of the armistice at Monterrey, he was to advance no farther. It seems odd that this truce had been in effect for six weeks before Taylor decided that Wool's force should also abide by it! Even more ironically, on the day before Wool received this information, a messenger arrived in Taylor's camp telling him that the secretary of war was abrogating the armistice. Nevertheless, Wool's troops remained in Monclova awaiting further orders from Taylor and anxious for a chance at the enemy. Any such chance, however, received another setback when word arrived that the Mexican garrison at Chihuahua had abandoned the city and fallen back toward San Luis Potosí, where Santa Anna was reportedly concentrating a large force.

The anxious American soldiers chafed at the inactivity and General Wool urged General Taylor to let him unite his men with Taylor's troops "and take part in *conquering a peace*." On November 19, Wool sent a messenger to Taylor with another plea for action. He seemed convinced that Santa Anna was concentrating a large army at San Luis Potosí, and unless Wool and Taylor joined forces, the Mexicans would fall first upon Taylor and then upon Wool and destroy them both. He also stressed the effect that idleness was having on the morale of his volunteers: "No serious depredations have yet been committed, although . . . I find it difficult to restrain them."[25]

Wool's command left Monclova on November 24, and marched a hundred miles deeper into Mexico to the town of Parras. On December 17, Wool received an urgent message from Brig. Gen. William J. Worth at Saltillo. Worth had information that Santa Anna was finally on the march, moving northward from San Luis Potosí. Since Worth had less than a thousand men in his command, he desperately needed help. Within two and a half hours of the receipt of this message, Wool's army was once again on the move, and by December 21, it had marched over a hundred miles and reached Agua Nueva, some twenty or twenty-five miles south of Saltillo. But the reports that Santa Anna was near at hand proved false, so Wool's men had to wait a little longer before doing any fighting.

Meanwhile, as the plans for a landing at Veracruz matured, Gen. Winfield Scott, who was to lead the invasion, began calling on General Taylor to send him seasoned regular army troops. Consequently, General Worth's regulars left Saltillo for the coast in early January 1847. Within days, Santa Anna was aware of the move and began planning to lead his army north to attack the weakened American garrison that remained. The territory between San Luis Potosí and Saltillo is rugged and unforgiving. General Taylor had felt that it presented too much of an impediment to a marching army for him to have tried to attack the Mexicans at San Luis Potosí. Santa Anna was willing to gamble, however, that his army could survive such a trek.

The Mexican army, concentrated at San Luis Potosí, now numbered well over twenty-one thousand men, but most of them were inadequately trained. Likewise, they were poorly armed and equipped and had had little time in service. There was no uniformity of weapons. Some of the infantrymen even carried muskets with leather thongs securing the barrels to the stocks. Many were without bayonets, and quite a number were about to enter their first battle without ever having fired a gun before. The long march that lay ahead of these soldiers undoubtedly caused some of them to question their patriotism. To counter any flagging spirits, Santa Anna promised them a chance to plunder the rich American camps after their inevitable victory on the battlefield. Of course, in case this was an insufficient motivator, he also promised to shoot all deserters.[26]

The Mexican troops began leaving San Luis Potosí on January 27, and by February 18, they began arriving at the village of Encarnación, approximately twenty-five miles south of the American outpost at Agua Nueva. They had marched 150 very treacherous miles in three weeks, and had lost over sixty-four hundred men along the way. In the meantime, American engineers realized that the American position at Agua Nueva was not a suitable spot in which to fight a battle. True, it was a pleasant, well-watered, and picturesque place to camp. But the mountains that surrounded it offered many routes by which the Mexicans could bypass the site and fall upon the American communications link to Saltillo and Monterrey. General Taylor therefore ordered his troops to fall back to Angostura, just over a mile south of Hacienda San Juan de la Buena Vista.

General Wool had selected Angostura two months earlier as a location, well laid out by nature, from which to fight a defensive battle. The road to Saltillo passed through a narrow valley there. To the west of the road—the American right flank in the coming battle—the landscape was so severely broken by deep and precipitous arroyos as to form a barrier against effective enemy movement. On the other side of the road the terrain was rugged, but passable to a determined enemy force. It was on this side of the road that most of the American troops took up positions.

There was some slight skirmishing between American mounted patrols and advance Mexican scouting parties on February 20, but the main battle began two days later. By 8:00 A.M. on February 22, the American soldiers were ready. It was George Washington's birthday, and partly to honor the first president and partly to inspire the men, the regimental bands struck up such patriotic airs as "Hail Columbia."

At about 11:00 A.M., Santa Anna sent an emissary under a flag of truce toward the American position. Under this flag, General Taylor received a note that read, in part,

You are surrounded by twenty thousand men, and cannot in any human probability avoid suffering a rout and being cut to pieces with your troops; but as you deserve consideration and particular esteem, I wish to save you from a catastrophe, and for that purpose give you this notice, in order that you may surrender at discretion, under the assurance that you will be treated with the consideration belonging to the Mexican character; to which end you will be granted an hour's time to make up your mind.

Santa Anna's army definitely outnumbered the forty-six hundred Americans, but perhaps Taylor recalled the massacre of Col. James Fannin's command after it had surrendered at discretion during the Texas Revolution. At any rate, he was not ready to surrender and his response to Santa Anna was short and to the point: "In reply to your note of this date, summoning me to surrender my forces at discretion, I beg leave to say that I decline acceding to your request." Both commanders then continued placing their troops.[27]

Finally Santa Anna was ready, and he began probing various points in the American defenses. An Illinois volunteer described the attacking Mexican infantrymen "in their long tall hats, bedecked with tinsel, & their Blue over coats streaming in the wind:—& what was more *interesting* to us just then, their long glittering muskets pointing directly at us as if they were really trying to *shoot us*." A Kentuckian was equally impressed with the gravity of the situation. In fact, he was near despair at the sight of the black flag of no quarter that the Mexicans were displaying: "All with whom I have spoken on the subject told me they expected to die there, and then."[28]

Even after the American army had performed well during the first day's fighting, General Taylor was not satisfied. He was afraid that his supply depot at Saltillo was still vulnerable to a Mexican cavalry raid and spent the night worrying about it. Nor did Santa Anna devote that same night of February 22–23 to peaceful slumber. Heartened by his army's progress, he decided to renew his push against the American left the next day and occupied a large part of the night shuffling infantry and artillery to various points on his line. His soldiers passed the cold, rainy night without the benefit of campfires for fear of revealing their positions to the Americans.

The Mexicans reopened the battle on February 23 by attacking along the mountainside on the American left, where they slowly forced the defenders back. The fighting was again fierce, but it was at such times that a grim sense of humor appeared among some men. For example, an American volunteer heard a Mexican soldier frantically calling for more cartridges. "I will give you one," muttered the volunteer, and promptly shot him.[29]

While Santa Anna's initial attack developed, other Mexicans also tested the American right, but with little success. When General Wool, who was Taylor's tactical commander during this battle, saw how this secondary assault was unfolding, he sent a message to Brig. Gen. Joseph Lane, who commanded the two Indiana regiments at the point of contact, to do his utmost to hold his position. These volunteers were eager to prove themselves in this their first battle. They were not content merely to hold, but instead enthusiastically went forward to meet the enemy. In the ensuing confusion, Lane ordered the artillery battery accompanying the Indianans into a more advantageous position. As the guns began to shift, the Second Indiana's Col. William A. Bowles misinterpreted the movement and thought the gunners were abandoning him, so he ordered his men to retreat. Some did so in good order. Many, after this brief exposure to the horrible reality of war, panicked and fled, along with four companies of Arkansas volunteers. Santa Anna's success in this area of the battlefield left the way open for his cavalry to move around the American battle line and head for the supply base in the rear.

Soon, when the Mexican horsemen bore down on the hacienda at Buena Vista, a mixed force of volunteer cavalry and regular dragoons was there to meet them. Many of the volunteers were unable to stand up to this onslaught and fled. But those who remained, along with the dragoons, pitched into the enemy with good results. They split the attacking force in two. One segment turned back and one continued on toward the hacienda, where it met the fire of a number of volunteers from the Second Indiana, who had rallied there after their initial panic had subsided.

The Mexicans were unable to dislodge the hacienda's defenders so they turned toward a position held by the Third Indiana Regiment and the Mississippi troops. By this time, these volunteers had formed in the shape of a giant obtuse V with the open end forward. As the enemy horsemen neared the mouth of the V, they met a blistering fire. The Indianans carried the standard .69 caliber muskets—which were certainly lethal enough—but the Mississippians used brand-new .54 caliber rifles that were capable of emptying saddles at much longer ranges. Those Mexicans who survived this slaughter quickly retired to the cover of a nearby ravine, from whence they escaped under the cover of a flag of truce.

Late in the afternoon, Santa Anna combined the remnants of several of his brigades and pushed them forward once more. While they were still out of sight of the Americans, Col. John J. Hardin, working under the assumption that the Mexicans were not only *not* attacking but were in fact retreating, led a force of eager Illinois and Kentucky volunteers forward. They met Santa Anna's troops head on. Bitter hand-to-hand fighting ensued in which both Colonel Hardin, of the First Illinois, and Col. Henry Clay, Jr., of Kentucky, received mortal wounds. American artillery tore gaping holes in the Mexican ranks, but still they came. Soon the weight of the Mexican attack began to tell. So many American cannoneers were down that two cannons had to be abandoned.

It was at this juncture that Capt. Braxton Bragg arrived with his artillery battery and asked General Taylor for instructions. The general told him that the position must not fall under any conditions. Then, as the battery prepared to go into action, Taylor quizzed Bragg:

"What are you using, Captain, grape or cannister?"
"Cannister, General."
"Single or double?"
"Single."
"Well, double-shot your guns and give 'em hell, Bragg."

Bragg commenced his work and the effect of his fire was immediate and decisive. The Mexican infantry just could not stand up to any more of the brutal American artillery.[30]

A rainstorm put the finishing touches on the day's fighting, and as darkness fell, Santa Anna ordered his army to retire to Agua Nueva. Not all of his men agreed with the decision to retreat. Many believed that they had acquitted themselves well so far, and that if their commander would only allow them, they could finish off the Americans on the next day. Nevertheless, Santa Anna was adamant, citing the fatigue of his soldiers and the lack of food with which to feed them.

A Mexican artillery officer later described the reactions he observed among the soldiers when they learned they would be falling back:

This disposition caused general and profound disgust among the troops; they saw with grief that they were going to lose the benefit of all the sacrifices that they had made; that the conquered field would be abandoned, and that the victory would be given to the enemy; and finally, to affirm the idea already general in the army—that it was impossible to conquer the Americans.

Another Mexican sadly noted that the combined effects of hard marching, severe weather, scant rations, fierce fighting, and now a demoralizing retreat had had devastating effects:

The army seemed made up of dead men: the miserable conditions to which the sick were reduced caused the skin of many to stick to their bones, and its shrinking exposed their teeth, giving to the countenance the expression of a forced laugh, which filled one with horror.[31]

This battle—fought almost entirely by volunteers on the American side—had been the most costly of the war so far. Both sides lost heavily. Taylor listed 665 as killed, wounded, or missing, while Mexican losses exceeded thirty-five hundred. The American volunteers seized upon this victory as proof of their inherent abilities as soldiers and as further verification of their already-low opinion of their enemies. One man recounted to a friend how he and many of his companions had retreated into a ravine to escape the fury of the battle. Mexican troops arrived and began firing into them, but "they are most miserable shots, or they would have killed every one of us, huddled as we were in the bottom of that narrow ravine."[32]

This was also a battle, however, that saw for the first time wholesale panic among volunteers, causing General Taylor to label members of the Second Indiana as cowards. Thereafter, the men of this regiment, and of the other Indiana regiments, tried very hard to convince themselves and all who would listen that they were just as brave as any other soldiers. Even soldiers who had not been in that battle were quick to take up for their fellow Indianans: "If we had been [in the battle] I believe the unjust charge of cowardice could never have been committed against the Indiana Volunteers."[33]

The Battle of Buena Vista was the fourth in an unbroken string of American victories in northern Mexico. In spite of these tactical successes, however, the strategical aim of forcing Mexican capitulation still proved elusive. After his repulse at Buena Vista, Santa Anna led his troops into central Mexico where, within a very short time, they would attempt to stop Maj. Gen. Winfield Scott's forces from capturing their national capital.

CHAPTER 9

The Army of the West

Government leaders in Washington selected Col. Stephen Watts Kearny to lead a force to New Mexico. A significant trade existed between the United States and Santa Fe, and it was important that it be protected. When that area was secure, Kearny was to push on to California to assist the few Americans there. The core of his force, which came to be known as the Army of the West, would be the First U.S. Dragoons. In addition, Secretary of War Marcy requested the governor of Missouri to furnish one regiment of mounted volunteers, two companies of volunteer artillery, and two companies of volunteer infantry.

About a week later, Kearny received further reinforcements from what many regarded as an unlikely source. The members of the Mormon church, after having been persecuted for their beliefs wherever they settled, most recently at Nauvoo, Illinois, had at last determined to pull up stakes and head west, far away from any nonbelievers. Such a move, however, required a considerable amount of supplies such as wagons, horses, and food. And there was the threat of molestation by unfriendly Indians along the way. Rather than giving outright aid to the Mormons for their trek, however, government authorities allowed Colonel Kearny to recruit five hundred to one thousand Mormons into his army. Also, to avoid friction between the Mormons and the other soldiers, these recruits would not join existing units but would form an all-Mormon battalion. In this way, at least some of the Mormons would be able to make their way west at government expense and draw wages at the same time. At the expiration of their one-year enlistments, they were to receive their discharges in California.

In spite of the advantages of such an arrangement, the plan met with some resistance among the Mormons. The same government that had been unable or unwilling to protect them from the mob actions of other citizens was now asking them to join its army. In addition, many of those who enlisted would have to leave their families to the care of other church members in the march through unknown and possibly hostile territory. One man vehemently denounced the request for volunteers and, referring to the entire population of the United States, said that "they may all go to hell together. I will see them . . . in hell before I will fire one shot against a foreigner for those who have mobbed, robbed, and plundered and destroyed us all the day long and now seek to enslave us to fight for them."[1]

Church leaders, however, looked at the request for volunteers as a possible blessing in disguise. Not only would several hundred church members be able to go west without placing a drain on the supplies of the main body, but the government in Washington might also finally realize that the Mormons were willing to be good citizens if they could expect reasonable treatment in return. Some even dared to hope that the government would reward their efforts at winning California from Mexico by allowing the Mormons to control it after peace came. When Brigham Young and other church elders talked to their flock and explained this reasoning, approximately five hundred volunteers came forward, answering the call of their church more than that of their country. Many shared the notion of one of their members who wrote, "It was against my feelings, and against the feelings of my brethren although we were willing to obey counsel."[2]

Colonel Kearny's command slowly began to take shape at Fort Leavenworth, along the Missouri-Kansas border. On June 6, Col. Alexander Doniphan's First Missouri Mounted Volunteers began arriving. Two companies of dragoons had left for Santa Fe on the previous day in response to rumors that New Mexico Governor Manuel Armijo had sent troops up the Santa Fe Trail to capture American wagon trains en route from the United States. Within a couple of weeks, the Missouri volunteers and the rest of Kearny's dragoons were also on the trail. The Mormon Battalion did not get organized and mustered into service until the middle of July, so they came later.

The initial excitement of the campaign faded somewhat as the soldiers moved through the wilderness. There were occasional breaks in the monotony, such as the soldiers' first look at a prairie dog town or the sweeping majesty of thousands of buffaloes. One volunteer described his first sight of the shaggy beasts: "Far over the plain to the west and north was one vast herd of buffaloes; some in column, marching in their trails, others carelessly grazing. Every acre was covered, until in the dim distance the prairie became one black mass, from which there was no opening, and extending to the horizon."[3]

Sometimes the men provided their own diversions from the boring routine of marching. Some of the Mormon volunteers formed a debate society to pass the evening hours. Two Missouri volunteers provided some relief of a different sort for their comrades after their detachment had stopped for the night. They wandered off a short distance from camp to see what they might be able to find of interest and came upon an aboveground Indian grave site. Then, mixing a rather macabre sense of humor with an utter disregard for Indian culture, they took the Indian's body to camp, where they supported it on long poles and, in the dark, made it appear to be moving under its own power. When they tired of this, one of them took the Indian's skull, which he planned to use for a soup ladle.[4]

The abundance of buffalo provided a ready source of meat, but other provisions were sometimes in short supply along the route of march. In fact, the two items most commonly lacking were wood for the cooking fires and drinking water. For long stretches of the journey there was virtually no wood available, and the men looked once again to the buffalo for sustenance. In this instance, aid came less in the form of the buffaloes themselves than in what they left behind. The soldiers quickly learned that well-dried buffalo dung was combustible and that a pile of "buffalo chips" made an excellent fire with which to cook. Thus, as they neared the end of each day's march, the tired troops drew the ramrods from their muskets and used them to skewer likely-looking chips along the line of march until the ramrods were full.[5]

Finding suitable drinking water was much more difficult. When the column reached a stream the thirsty soldiers could drink as much as they wanted and fill their canteens, but they might not find another source of water for several days. The desert winds and hot sun caused parched and blistered lips, and many found it difficult even to talk with their tongues swollen. Some tried to combat the effects of this extreme dryness by keeping musket balls in their mouths to promote salivation, but to little effect. Occasionally the soldiers would find small amounts of water in the ruts in the road or in buffalo wallows. This water was, however, as one Missourian observed, "muddy, filthy, and covered with green scum, which the horses of the mounted men refused to drink. Yet the men drank it with avidity; they suffered so much from thirst."[6]

After covering well over five hundred miles, the main body of the Army of the West reached Bent's Fort, a private fur-trading post in eastern Colorado, on July 29. Kearny decided to remain there for couple of days so his weary men and worn-out animals could regain their strength before beginning the next leg of their journey.

While at the fort, Kearny learned that Governor Armijo was making arrangements for resisting the American invaders. When the colonel made this known to his command, he received a very positive reaction. According to one of the volunteers, this news "seemed to cheer men who had walked 1,000 miles for this purpose. The battalion appeared to think it hard we should go back [to Missouri] without one [a battle], and expressed great anxiety for it to take place." It was also at Bent's Fort that a Mexican, claiming to be a relative of Governor Armijo, approached Colonel Kearny with information he claimed would guarantee an American victory when they met the governor's force. Even though the Mexican defensive position near Santa Fe was a strong one, he said, all that Kearny needed to do was to "fire five or six cannons, no matter which way, and he would ensure them [the Mexicans] all to run."[7]

In fact, Governor Armijo had chosen an ideal defensive position in Apache Canyon, twelve miles southeast of Santa Fe. But his troops, local levies for the most part, just did not have their hearts in it. Therefore, on August 16, he disbanded his forces and left for Chihuahua with a small escort of lancers. Later, as Kearny's troops passed through the canyon, they realized that it could well have been turned into a slaughter pen for them. Nevertheless, these men had marched over hundreds of miles of barren countryside for the sole purpose of gaining some measure of martial glory, and, as one wrote, "the prospect now is that we shall march into Santa Fe without firing a gun. This news throws rather a gloom over the spirits of the army. They are sadly disappointed at learning that we shall have no fighting." Upon sober, honest reflection, however, most of them probably agreed with the Missourian who admitted, "We all felt well satisfied to pass without being attacked. We had all felt very brave before; but we now saw how difficult it would have been to have forced the pass, and were glad to be beyond it." Another volunteer thought it "better thus to have obtained a bloodless victory by the terror of our arms than to have purchased it with blood and loss of life." Two days after Armijo abandoned Santa Fe, Kearny's column entered the town.[8]

The troops were quick to form opinions of the Mexican civilians they saw in Santa Fe. And, like their comrades in arms in other parts of Mexico, these judgments were usually not very complimentary. Most noted the obvious differences between themselves and the natives in language, clothing, and skin color. Some also remarked upon the apparently lower standards of hygiene among their hosts. One volunteer commented that "there is an universal presence of vermin on the bodies of all the inhabitants, and it is not unusual to see women and men stop suddenly, expertly hunt, and a sharp sound announces to you a death—while the next minute they handle fruit or cheese they are offering to sell you." A member of the Mormon Battalion cloaked his similar observation in euphemism: "All kinds of cattle are scarce here, except crawling cattle, which are so common that the Spaniards carry them in their heads and clothing." It was not long before the soldiers also became victims of the ubiquitous body lice. One Missourian was so moved by the experience that he composed a satirical poem about the "gentle and graceful movements of a Spanish *louse*, as he journeys over one's body!"

> Oft in the stilly night,
>   Ere slumber's chains have bound me,
> I feel the cursed creatures bite,
>   As scores are crawling round me.

O not like one who treads alone,
   The banquet halls deserted;
In crowds they crawl despite the groan
   Of him whose blood they started.[9]

Within five weeks of his arrival, Kearny, now a brigadier general, decided that pacification was nearly complete and he could push on for the Pacific. He instructed Colonel Doniphan to remain in Santa Fe until the Mormon Battalion and a second regiment of Missouri volunteers arrived. Then he was to take his men south and link up with General Wool in northern Mexico. On September 25, 1846, General Kearny's three hundred mule-mounted dragoons left Santa Fe for California. Also in the expedition were a handful of topographical engineers, some small mountain howitzers, and baggage wagons.

After a week and a half on the trail, Kearny met Kit Carson, about ten miles below Socorro. The famed mountain man and a score of companions were on their way east with news of the American seizure of Upper California. Upon hearing this, the general sent most of his men back to Santa Fe, since they would not be needed to fight in California. He kept two mountain howitzers and about a hundred men. He also pressed Carson into service to guide him on the rest of the journey. The terrain quickly became too rough for wheeled vehicles, so Kearny further trimmed his force by sending his wagons back and resorting to pack mules to carry necessary supplies.

The dragoons plodded onward, often short of food and water. They crossed into California on November 25 and, after an eleven-and-a-half week trek and two skirmishes with Californios, they finally reached the safety of San Diego on the afternoon of December 12.

While General Kearny and his dragoons were making their tedious way to the Pacific, the Mormon Battalion, the second military contingent to go overland to California, arrived at Santa Fe during the second week of October 1846. After a few days' rest it headed west under the command of Lt. Col. Philip St. George Cooke, a regular army officer, with orders to find a passable wagon route to California. Most of the handful of wives and families who had accompanied the battalion to Santa Fe did not continue with the men. Instead, they went to a Mormon winter camp in Colorado, near present-day Pueblo.

After leaving Santa Fe, the first part of the trek to California was relatively pleasant. The battalion marched along the Rio Grande River through several Mexican villages where they carried on a lively trade with the inhabitants. The villagers were more interested in bartering their foodstuffs for used articles of clothing than for cash. Since the Americans had almost no money at all, this was a welcome arrangement.

When the Mormon Battalion began its day's march on December 10, there were no outward signs that it would be any different from any other day on the trail. But it was, since on that day the Mormons had their one and only battle during their service. It was a battle not with Mexican soldiers, but with wild cattle.

As the men marched along the San Pedro River a herd of wild cattle, mostly bulls, began intermingling with the herd that accompanied the battalion. The army herdsmen, fearing the influence of this wild stock, drove them away. The bulls had not traveled far when they encountered the members of a Mormon hunting party, who opened fire and dropped five of the animals. The others panicked and fled for the river. Unfortunately, the rear of the marching column of men and wagons was directly in the path of the frightened bulls.

The Mormons had little time to react. For general safety they had been marching with unloaded muskets, and now they scrambled for cartridges so they could divert the stampede with gunfire. Before they could do that, however, they had to clamber for safety into the wagons or up trees. One man was caught away from such protection and tried to outrun one of the bulls. He quickly saw that it was an uneven match, so he threw himself headlong onto the ground, hoping for the best. This action startled the pursuing bull and he jumped over the prostrate soldier and ran on. Another volunteer avoided serious injury when a bull charged him and its sharp pointed horns passed harmlessly on either side of him, pinning him against one of the wagons.

While the soldiers had scarcely enough time to escape, the battalion's animals were not all so lucky. One bull attacked a saddle horse that was tied to the back of a wagon. The horse shied away at the last moment and the bull crashed into the wagon's tailgate with enough force to lift the two rear wheels off the ground. Another bull put his head down and charged broadside into a team of mules hitched to a wagon. He passed under one mule, tossing it effortlessly into the air, and disemboweled its mate with his sharp horns.

Some men finally were able to load their muskets and they began shooting at the bulls. Colonel Cooke observed one of his troops, apparently frozen in fright, while a big black bull charged straight for him. "Run, run, God Damn you, run," he ordered. But the soldier waited until the bull was nearly upon him when he fired, and the animal fell dead at his feet. The colonel then swore that "he'd be G——D——if that man was not a Soldier." [10]

This volunteer indeed showed remarkable presence of mind in the face of danger. Often, the bulls were not that easily dispatched. One soldier emptied all six shots from his revolver into an animal, two in the head, two in the lungs, and two in the heart, before it finally died. Another wounded animal fell near one of the command's butchers, who quickly ran out with knife in hand to cut the bull's throat. As the meatcutter bent to his task, but before he was able to use his knife, the bull got up, snatching the man's cap off on one of its horns, and ran off once again. The man chased after it and, after about seventy-five yards, the animal again fell. This time the butcher finished him off with his knife.

The stampede was soon over, but it resulted in a considerable amount of damage. Four of the command's mules lay dead, along with nineteen wild bulls. A bull had gored one soldier in the thigh, and one of the battalion's regular army officers shot the end of his thumb off when two bullets in his revolving-cylinder repeating rifle fired at the same time. [11]

A few days later, as the battalion neared the Mexican garrison town of Tucson, the Mormons began to hear rumors that it was heavily manned and that the Mexican troops there intended to give battle. Maybe now they would have a chance to test their martial courage on an enemy that could shoot back. On December 15, 1846, agents from Tucson arrived in camp with a message for Colonel Cooke. The note proposed that the soldiers at Tucson would not molest the Americans or hinder their advance toward California in any way if they would simply bypass their small community. Colonel Cooke refused to bargain. He expressed no wish to destroy the town, which he characterized as an "unimportant outpost of defense against Indians," but he intended to pursue as straight a line of march as he could, and that line ran through Tucson.[12]

The Americans marched with loaded muskets the next day but entered the town with no resistance. All of the Mexican troops and most of the residents had fled. The citizens who remained regarded the newcomers with timidity at first, until they saw that the invaders meant them no harm. The soldiers, on the other hand, were tired of the monotonous landscape through which they had been marching and were glad that there would be no enemy troops to contend with. As one person commented, "It looked good to see young green wheat patches and fruit trees and to see hogs and fowls running about and it was music to our ears to hear the crowing of the cocks." With such a relative bounty of foodstuffs surrounding them, the troops wasted no time in trying to supplement their army diets. Since most of them had little or no money, they again resorted to bartering extra clothing in exchange for such delicacies as flour, meal, beans, tobacco, and quinces.[13]

Although private property was scrupulously protected, the Americans did locate a cache of some two thousand bushels of wheat that belonged to the Mexican government. This they regarded as legitimate spoils of war and appropriated it for their own use. The famished animals were able to eat their fill while the battalion rested for a day. Many of the men boiled and ate some of this wheat, leading to a sudden increase in the incidence of diarrhea.

During the night of December 16, Colonel Cooke posted picket guards with instructions to sound the alarm if any of the absent members of the local garrison attempted to come back. About midnight, a couple of nervous sentries observed a party of civilians returning to town after having left in fear the day before. Mistaking them for Mexican soldiers, the guards fired and raced back to camp. After the alarm sounded the camp was immediately astir as sleepy men hurried to grab their muskets and form a line of battle. As one participant later wrote, "everybody were rubbing their eyes and looking out for Mexicans, but none came." When they realized how innocent the source of their excitement had been, they returned to sleep, and the next morning the Mormon Battalion pushed on once again.[14]

From Tucson onward the journey became exceedingly difficult. General Kearny had instructed the Mormon Battalion to carve out a wagon trail to California where none had existed before. Parts of this trail would be through long stretches of deep sand where the marchers would have to stack their muskets, unsling their knapsacks, and help the exhausted draft animals haul the wagons along by ropes. In the San Bernardino Mountains, the battalion faced a passage that was too narrow for the wagons to fit through—one foot too narrow. Colonel Cooke ordered two wagons unloaded and dismantled. The men then carried them through the passage, reassembled them, and reloaded them. This, however, was not a permanent solution to the problem because the instructions had been to find a wagon route to the Pacific Ocean. So even while the first two wagons were being unloaded, the colonel set men to work chipping away at the rock until they had widened the opening enough for the wagons to roll through in normal fashion.[15]

It was also on this stage of the trip that food became scarce. Within a week of leaving Tucson, the battalion visited the village of some friendly Pima Indians. Here the soldiers again found willing trading partners who would accept extra clothing for food, or, as one Mormon volunteer wrote, "we purchased some meal and beans and sold our clothes off from our backs to do that." One of his comrades was a little more philosophical, as he simply wrote that "we all thought more of the Belly than the Back." Even with these supplements, however, hunger continued to be a serious problem. By the end of the second week of January, a hungry volunteer wrote, "Provisions are nearly out & we have more than a 100 miles to go before we can get relief." Four days later, Colonel Cooke walked through the camp as the men were at breakfast. He noted that "they were eating their last four ounces of flour; of sugar and coffee, there has been none for some weeks." Perhaps the dire straits to which the troops found themselves reduced may best be illustrated by the fact that some of them removed the sheepskin pads from beneath the pack saddles, pulled the wool off, and then roasted and ate the hides.[16]

To add to the misery of the marchers, the desert sands and the hard rocky ground over which they traveled soon wore through the soles of their shoes, making a difficult journey even more so. They had brought no spare shoes with them, so they had to improvise as best they could. One quick solution was to wrap their feet with strips of worn-out

clothing, but the state of their wardrobes was such that extra clothing
—worn out or otherwise—was quite scarce. When one of the expedition's oxen died, the men skinned it and wrapped their feet in pieces
of its hide. This provided some protection against the burning sand
but was, at best, merely a stopgap measure. Some troops learned that
they could fashion some oxhide footwear that was a little more suited
to the purpose if they used the skin from the gambrel joint of the leg.
They cut a ring above and below the joint and then stripped the skin
off without splitting it lengthwise. They then sewed up one end of the
resulting tube so the natural bend at the joint corresponded to the
placement of their heels.[17]

The members of the Mormon Battalion, shoeless, hungry, and
nearly naked, finally struggled into San Diego over the last three days
of January 1847.

Some months earlier, before the Mormons had even arrived at Santa
Fe, General Kearny had decided he did not need his entire force to go
to California, and the number of troops remaining in New Mexico
seemed more than enough to handle local Indian problems. He also
knew that another regiment of Missouri volunteers was already on the
trail to Santa Fe. Therefore, he ordered Colonel Doniphan to take his
First Missouri Mounted Volunteers deeper into northern Mexico to
link up with General Wool at Chihuahua.

Alexander Doniphan was an impressive physical specimen and was
well liked by his troops. He was well over six feet tall and possessed a
large, athletic frame. One contemporary noted that Doniphan was "in
the habit of interlarding his language with strong expressions which
many eastern men would call something like swearing." This earthy
habit no doubt further endeared him to his men.[18]

The Missouri colonel augmented his force with about a hundred
volunteers from the other Missouri command, and he also decided to
take along Maj. Meriwether Lewis Clark's artillery battery, although
the cannons did not join him until after he had reached El Paso.
Anxious to get under way, and no doubt tired of the cold winter in
Santa Fe, Doniphan started some of his men toward El Paso on
December 14, 1846. The rest of his little army followed at two-day
intervals, and at Dona Ana a caravan of traders joined it.

The Americans reached a place called Temascalitos, on the Brazito

River, about thirty miles northwest of El Paso, at midday on December 25. As they unsaddled their horses and set about making themselves comfortable, the advance guard hurried into camp with word that a Mexican force was approaching rapidly from the south. Colonel Doniphan, who had already settled down to a game of cards, rallied his Missourians into a battle line where they watched to see what would happen next.

The five hundred Mexicans—lancers and infantry with one howitzer—took up a position on a hill about a quarter-mile from the Americans. Their commander, Maj. Antonio Ponce De León, then sent a courier forward with a black flag bearing two white skull-and-crossbones on one side, and the words *Libertad o muerte* on the other. The messenger halted within a hundred yards of the American lines, and Colonel Doniphan sent forward his interpreter to find out what he wanted. The Mexican declared that De León demanded that the American commander should come to the Mexican camp to talk. The interpreter replied that if the Mexican leader wanted to talk to Doniphan, he should come to the American camp. The messenger took this as an insult and promised that the Mexican troops would attack and take the American colonel by force. And when they attacked, it would be under the black flag of no quarter.[19]

In trying to back up these brave words, however, some of De León's troops seemed hesitant to commit themselves to battle, so he rode out in front of his line to lead by example. The Missourians bided their time as the enemy opened an ineffective fire from a range of about four hundred yards. On the right of the American line, the men all knelt down in the grass just as the first Mexican volley came flying toward them. They stayed down as the Mexicans fired two more times, causing De León's troops to think that they had mowed down their enemy. When the Americans finally rose—as if from the dead—and fired, it was with lethal effect. One observer sardonically wrote, "Some of our men got as many as half a dozen shots at Mexicans; but most of the latter had such pressing business somewhere else, that it was difficult, after two volleys, to get a fair sight at them." A score or so of Doniphan's men were still mounted, and they drove away most of the enemy lancers, while the civilian teamsters, pressed into emergency service, fought off some others.[20]

The entire fight only lasted about thirty minutes and, in spite of De León's report that his troops had killed many of the enemy, there were only seven American casualties, none severe. The Mexicans had lost eleven killed and seventeen wounded. It astonished the Missourians to find a woman among the Mexican casualties, killed while performing her duties with the howitzer. The employment of women in the ranks was not common in the Mexican army, but the instance noted here was certainly not unique either. During a small engagement at Taos, an American dragoon unknowingly almost killed a Mexican woman soldier. She was only able to avert death at the last moment "by an act of the most conclusive personal exposure."[21]

Early the next morning Doniphan's troops, still in a celebratory mood after their first real contact with the enemy, were again on the move. They had divided up some of the goods captured from the Mexicans and presented an interesting appearance: "One had on a Mexican dragoon cap, another a blanket, some beads and crosses, and almost everyone something."[22]

Two days after the battle, Doniphan's command reached and captured El Paso, where it also confiscated four small cannons, several hundred muskets and lances, and five tons of gunpowder. A few days later, the men welcomed the arrival of additional American troops with an artillery salute from one of the captured pieces. The usual procedure when firing salutes was to pack some wadding down tightly over the powder before firing. In their haste, the cannoneers did not have time to find proper wadding, so one soldier volunteered a pair of his socks. The ensuing salute saw the socks sail through the air and strike one of the newcomers squarely in the face. Although he was not injured, he declared, "I'd rather be shot with a solid ball than with a pair of socks worn from Fort Leavenworth to El Paso, without a change for eight months."[23]

By the time Major Clark's artillery battery finally arrived, a month had passed and Colonel Doniphan had learned that General Wool had aborted his planned march on Chihuahua. Nevertheless, anxious for more action against the Mexicans, he decided to continue with his original orders. On February 8, 1847, his column, escorting a large caravan of merchants anxious to reach Chihuahua, left El Paso. Colonel Doniphan organized the three hundred or so civilians into an informal battalion. This increased the total American force to just over twelve hundred men.

The terrain between El Paso and Chihuahua was forbidding, composed primarily of barren desert. To make matters worse, a prairie fire threatened to destroy the entire expedition when it was about two hundred miles from El Paso. Luckily, the troops were able to start some back fires to protect themselves, and they camped on a small lake into which they drove some of the wagons to protect them. A couple of days later, Doniphan learned of the Mexicans' intent to offer battle at the Rio Sacramento, fifteen miles north of Chihuahua.

The Mexican defenders outnumbered the Americans by greater than a three-to-one margin, but the quality of these troops was questionable. Nevertheless, the Mexican defensive position, near where the El Paso road crossed the Sacramento River, was very strong. The Mexicans were also very confident that they could defeat the invaders. They even brought along iron shackles and short pieces of rope with which to secure all the prisoners they were sure of capturing.

As the Americans moved toward the Mexican defenses on the last day of February, Colonel Doniphan surprised his opponent by maneuvering the Missourians around the Mexican left flank. The enemy response was a mounted attack, but as the lancers approached the American position, Major Clark's cannons opened up and drove them away. Mexican cannons arrived and began firing, but with little effect —due, probably, to inferior gunpowder. Whatever the reason, the American troops were able to watch the approach of the enemy cannonballs and then dodge them with relative ease. Some men even made bets with one another as to where particular projectiles might land.[24]

As this indecisive artillery barrage continued, Doniphan decided to force the issue. The Missourians then charged the Mexican works, and a bitter hand-to-hand struggle ensued. Several of the mounted volunteers had their horses shot out from under them and continued on foot. One of these men spied a Mexican lancer bearing down upon him just after he had fired his rifle and before he had time to reload. Thinking quickly, he picked up a heavy rock and threw it, knocking the attacker from his horse. Then, before the lancer had time to come to his feet, the Missourian clubbed him to death with his rifle butt. Shortly thereafter the Americans captured the Mexican earthworks and the battle was over.[25]

During this battle some of the servants, most likely slaves who had accompanied the Missourians, also attempted to take part in the battle. About a dozen of them formed themselves into a company and elected one of their own to be their captain. They were full of fighting spirit, but they were also totally lacking in military training or discipline. When the shooting actually began they realized how unprepared they were, and in spite of their good intentions, they stayed as safely hidden among the wagons as they could until the fighting ended.[26]

The battle lasted for several hours, but the Americans lost only one man killed, the commander of the teamsters' battalion, and eight men wounded. Doniphan claimed that his Missourians had killed about three hundred and wounded a like number. The Americans captured seventeen pieces of artillery, thousands of small arms, and the same death's-head pennant under which the Mexicans at Temascalitos had demanded Doniphan's surrender two months earlier. Perhaps more important to the seemingly always-hungry soldiers was the fact that they also seized nine wagons full of hard bread, eight tons of dried meat, "several thousand head of cattle, and ten *acres* of sheep."[27]

On March 2, 1847, the Missourians marched triumphantly into Chihuahua. They had not received any pay since leaving Fort Leavenworth. Their clothing was becoming more and more ragged, and it was difficult to procure replacements without money. In one of Doniphan's companies, and it was undoubtedly typical of all the others, "no two pair of pantaloons were of the same hue; and there being few who owned a jacket, the red flannel or checked shirt made up the 'uniform.' Shoes were a luxury, and hats a very doubtful article."[28]

Colonel Doniphan worried about the depleted condition of his men's wardrobes and pocketbooks, but he also entertained a more serious concern, which he conveyed in a letter to General Wool asking for instructions. He was in charge of a small force, deep in enemy country, whose enlistments were due to expire in just three months' time.

In the meantime, the men made themselves as comfortable as possible. Some enterprising soldiers began to publish a newspaper, the *Anglo Saxon*, and a great many of them partook of such local entertainment as bull fights, fandangos, and card games. Of course, with time dragging by, they also created their own amusements. They filled two of the captured cannons with powder, plugged the muzzles, and blew them up just to see what happened. They also detonated several barrels of captured gunpowder. Sometimes they would round up numbers of stray dogs, only to turn them loose in the crowded streets with lit strings of firecrackers attached to their tails.[29]

On April 23, Colonel Doniphan finally received orders from General Wool to move his command to Saltillo, over five hundred miles away. The trip took almost a month. On May 23, after being reviewed by General Wool at Buena Vista, the First Missouri Mounted Volunteers headed once again toward the Rio Grande. They reached Reynosa on June 1, where they boarded steamers for the trip to the mouth of the river. From there they sailed to New Orleans, where they received their discharges. The war, for them at least, was over.

Colonel Doniphan's Missouri Mounted Volunteers had ridden over thirty-five hundred miles and won both their battles with the Mexicans. The public lionized them and the poet William Cullen Bryant compared their march to that of Xenophon, but their campaign had only a negligible effect on the outcome of the war. By the time the Missourians headed up the Mississippi River toward home, Maj. Gen. Winfield Scott's army had already begun the decisive phase of the war —the push toward Mexico City.

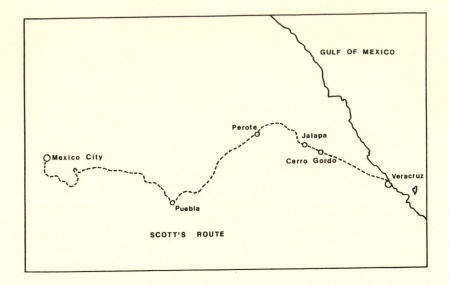

GULF OF MEXICO

Perote

Jalapa

Mexico City

Cerro Gordo

Veracruz

Puebla

SCOTT'S ROUTE

CHAPTER 10

To the Halls of the Montezumas

America's leaders had hoped that the war with Mexico would be short. They were even optimistic that, after the battles of Palo Alto and Resaca de la Palma, the Mexican government would see the folly of continued resistance and sue for peace. Yet when Mexican authorities continued to fight even after losing Monterrey, the president and his advisers decided that the time had come to strike more directly at the heart of Mexico. Soldiers in the field also recognized the need for more drastic efforts, since Mexican leaders were unwilling to give up all the land that the United States demanded as a part of any peace settlement. The commander of the First Tennessee Regiment summed up the situation in a letter to his cousin: "They cannot submit to be deprived of California after the loss of Texas, and nothing but the conquest of their Capitol will force them to such a humiliation." [1]

For General Taylor's Army of Occupation to march south toward Mexico City would have meant taking an extremely long route through territory that was both militarily and geographically hostile. Instead, this army would hold on to territory it had conquered while a second —as yet virtually nonexistent force—would land on the lower Mexican coast and march inland. One plan was for American troops to disembark at Tampico and then advance toward San Luis Potosí, a main marshaling point for the Mexican army. Another plan, and the one subsequently adopted, was for the landing to take place near the fortified city of Veracruz. Then, after capturing the garrison there, the Americans would march for Mexico City, some 250 miles inland.

Maj. Gen. Winfield Scott, commanding general of the United States Army, would lead the invasion force. He would draw a considerable portion of his troops from Taylor's army, and he would need fifty large ships to carry his expeditionary force to Veracruz. Once he reached the Mexican coast, however, he still faced the task of getting men and equipment ashore. Amphibious operations of this type were something new, and no suitable landing craft of any kind existed in America's munitions inventory. A navy lieutenant solved this problem by designing a wide, flat-bottomed boat carrying a crew of eight and capable of delivering forty men at a time to the beaches. In order to save space aboard the transport ships, he further specified that these craft be built in three different lengths so they could be nested when not in use. Not all such innovations were as acceptable as these surf-boats. One erstwhile civilian aeronaut suggested constructing a "balloon of common twilled muslin, of 100 feet in diameter, well coated with varnish." From this balloon, which he proposed to anchor with a five-mile tether, he would then be able to bombard the city of Veracruz as well as the harbor-protecting island fortress of San Juan de Ulúa.[2]

Scott's plans continued apace as troops from Taylor's army as well as recruits from the states began to assemble at Tampico. Upon observing the American flag being raised over this city for the first time one old resident commented mournfully,

That flag has been my ruin. I came from Spain, and I was then young, and was sent into Louisiana; that flag came and I then went into Florida; in a few years the same flag came, and I then came to this place expecting never to be disturbed by it again. But there it is—the same flag, the same people.[3]

While the buildup at Tampico continued Scott optimistically hoped to begin the investment of Veracruz by the middle of February, well in advance of the onset of fever season, but unforeseen delays pushed this date further away, and the invasion fleet did not set sail until March 2.

Scott had selected a satisfactory landing site two and a half miles south of Veracruz, near the island of Sacrificios, and he wanted the landing carried out as soon as possible for several reasons. No Mexican troops were on hand to hinder his assault, but that could change rapidly. The weather was good, but that too could change, and the ships, tightly packed together in the small anchorage, could be devastated by a norther. And finally, the longer they waited, the more likely that American troops would be caught in the yellow fever zone when that disease struck in its annual cycle.

As the soldiers waited aboard the ships none of them could know what lay ahead. A great many were new recruits, but even those who had seen some combat had not experienced an amphibious landing before. The men in the various regiments already knew their positions in the landing sequence, and they were now left to their musings as they waited for the operation to begin. Some used this time to write letters home, some composed their wills. Much of the bombast so common before was absent as the time for action drew nearer. As one man later admitted,

I cannot say that I felt in the slightest degree inclined to earn high fame or distinction, by any very decided demonstration or extraordinary exhibition of personal prowess and heroic valour on the present occasion; neither did I overhear any very strong expressions of regret amongst my comrades, at the circumstance of our regiment not being the first party who were landing.[4]

The landing took place on the afternoon of March 9, 1847. Even though there was no opposition, the operation did not go unobserved. Several European warships were anchored at Veracruz and their officers and crews crowded the rails and filled the rigging to get a view of what was happening. American sailors, too, those who were not actively employed in support of the landing, climbed high into their ships' rigging for what amounted to a bird's-eye view. A Pennsylvania volunteer said that it reminded him of "seeing so many robins or black birds on a wild cherry tree, or crows on trees watching the dead carcass lying beneath."[5]

A regular army artillery officer, writing later, echoed the feelings of most of those in the surf boats: "It was a moment of intense excitement, for as yet we did not know whether we would meet with any opposition from the enemy." Most were more than willing to cross swords with the enemy on dry land, but they knew that well-served Mexican artillery could make their landing very difficult. There was nothing they could do in the event of such a defense except hope that they could make it ashore before being blown out of the water. As it turned out, some Mexican cavalry did appear among the sand dunes behind the beach, but did not stay around to contest the landing. By eleven o'clock that night, eighty-six hundred American soldiers had reached shore without losing a single person.[6]

Getting his army ashore as easily as he did was certainly a relief to General Scott. But he knew that landing a force on an undisputed beach was not the same as capturing the enemy city. A fifteen-foot-high wall surrounded Veracruz, and two forts provided additional security for the fifteen thousand inhabitants and the 3,360 soldiers commanded by Brig. Gen. Juan Morales. On the seaward side was the fortress of San Juan de Ulúa, situated about one thousand yards offshore on the edge of Gallega Reef. The fort contained another eleven hundred men and mounted 135 cannons. Veracruz appeared, at least on paper, to be invincible.

Nevertheless, General Scott lengthened his line of troops until it completely encircled the city. Time was a very important factor in Scott's plans. The yellow fever season, which usually commenced in March or April, had nearly begun, and he desperately wanted to capture the city and get most of his troops inland to higher elevations and away from the dread disease. His army contained a high percentage of untrained volunteers, and he had no way of knowing how they would perform in action. Also, even had all his troops been seasoned regulars, Scott still had to deal with the enemy's fortifications and the fact that General Morales had over one hundred cannons in the city itself. These factors tended to rule out a direct assault because, even though an all-out attack offered the quickest way to victory, it would mean heavy losses. The other plan—a siege—was slower but more likely to be successful.

The Americans spent the next couple of weeks digging trenches and placing their siege guns. Before beginning the bombardment of the city, Scott offered the Mexican commander a chance to surrender, but he refused. Late on the afternoon of March 22, therefore, seven ten-inch mortars opened fire from a position about seven hundred yards south of the city. Two navy steamers and four schooners proceeded to a point about a mile offshore and added their combined firepower until they ran out of ammunition. A Pennsylvania volunteer described the bombardment: "I laid down on a sand hill . . . and saw one hundred ten inch bombs, thrown into the very centre of the town, in a very short time—every one of which exploded."[7]

Nor were the Mexican batteries silent. Though their shells caused relatively little physical damage, the Mexican gunners worked their cannons feverishly and caused considerable emotional distress among the entrenched Americans. Their cannons threw such heavy projectiles that their sound could almost be felt as well as heard—or, as one soldier with a poetic bent put it, "Perhaps Milton's description of the harsh, thunder-grating of the hinges of the infernal gates approaches to a faint realization of the indescribable sound."[8]

One of the city's defenders, in the hurry and commotion of battle, cut a fuse a little too long and the shell slammed into an American artillery position without exploding. A Pennsylvanian—one who was not particularly discomposed by the fury of the Mexican cannonade—calmly plucked the sputtering fuse from the projectile, rendering it harmless, and used it to light his pipe.[9]

As the bombardment continued the list of Mexican casualties grew. Some of the injured were taken to a makeshift hospital hurriedly set up in the Convent of Santo Domingo, but even there they were not always safe. An American shell exploded in the convent while doctors were operating on a wounded man, and the concussion blew all the lights out. Fresh lights showed that the patient had been torn to pieces by the blast. Other hospitals in the city suffered similar fates, including a women's hospital where seventeen died.[10]

Finally, on March 27, the Mexican commander agreed to surrender terms that permitted his officers to retain their sidearms and personal property, such as their horses. The soldiers, instead of being imprisoned, would be released after signing paroles promising not to take any further part in the war.

The surrender provided the first chance for a close observation of the Mexican soldiers for most of the American troops, and their opinions varied. A Pennsylvania volunteer thought they gave the appearance of well-drilled soldiers, while a regular army officer had just the opposite impression. The latter observer qualified his evaluation by pointing out that the Mexicans "were, however, a conquered army, and, of course, could not have felt or exhibited much of the haughty pride of the soldier."[11]

In spite of intense Mexican artillery fire during the siege, American casualties were surprisingly low. General Scott lost thirteen men killed and fifty-five wounded. Although estimates of Mexican losses vary, and go as high as one thousand, even the lowest figures claim almost two hundred deaths. As a result of the hundreds of tons of shot and shell that the American army and navy rained onto the city, more than half of the Mexican dead were civilians.

Most American soldiers quickly learned to view dead enemy soldiers with a certain amount of stoicism, but the large numbers of civilians killed at Veracruz was very unsettling to them. One volunteer described the city as being "almost a perfect ruin. Magnificent houses splendidly furnished torn all to pieces—with many of the inmates killed." He told of the streets littered with the bodies of dead animals —dogs, cats, and horses—and of grief-stricken Mexican civilians trying to cope with the loss of family members. "I cannot relate to you all [that I have seen]; my heart sickens in the attempt, what a horrible thing is war!" Captain Lee, who was himself a devoted family man, gave voice to similar feelings even before the city capitulated. As he watched the havoc being wrought by the naval battery he was well aware of the likely effects in the city: "My heart bled for the inhabitants. The soldiers I did not care so much for, but it was terrible to think of the women and children."[12]

General Scott was proud of his victory but could not allow himself to rest on his laurels. He had to complete plans for moving the bulk of his force toward the Mexican capital immediately. At the same time he had to see that the Americans occupying Veracruz behaved themselves. He reiterated an earlier order, one that he had issued before leaving Tampico, which admonished the men to be on their best conduct. Even though the Articles of War did not cover certain offenses outside of the United States, General Scott made sure that his soldiers knew that he would not tolerate criminal behavior from them. Military commissions would try any soldiers accused of rape, robbery, murder, desecration of Mexican churches, and a number of other crimes. As if to emphasize the commanding general's sincerity in this regard, a military commission tried an American civilian, traveling with the army, on charges that he had raped and robbed a Mexican woman. The commission found him guilty and he was quickly hanged.

Although Scott's army had successfully dealt with many logistical problems connected with the siege of Veracruz, the general soon found that the needs of an army on the march also caused headaches. Quartermaster General Thomas S. Jesup made calculations based upon a proposed twenty-five thousand-man army moving from Veracruz to Mexico City. Such a campaign, he reasoned, would require almost three million pounds of supplies, for the transportation of which he would need ninety-three hundred wagons and over seventeen thousand pack mules. To sustain both men and beasts, these supplies would include five hundred thousand bushels of oats and corn, three hundred thousand iron shoes for the horses and mules, and one hundred pounds of blister ointment for the soldiers' feet. Jesup also saw the need for a half-ton of office tape. This was not the adhesive variety but was of red cotton or linen and was used to tie around bundles of official documents, hence the modern term "red tape," used derisively when describing bureaucratic slowdowns.[13]

In the meantime, Santa Anna had returned to Mexico City and then hurried off on April 2 with seven thousand fresh troops to join the Army of the East at Jalapa, where he also forced a number of Veracruz defenders to break their paroles and rejoin the army. The area around Jalapa was very important geographically for it marked the transition from the yellow fever zone to the higher and cooler elevations that were relatively free from the disease-carrying mosquitoes. It was therefore paramount that Scott cover the sixty miles to Jalapa to preserve the health of his command. For the same reason, it was essential to Santa Anna that his forces deny the Americans access to Jalapa. He knew that if he could keep them penned up along the coast the yellow fever would have the same effect as several battle-hardened Mexican regiments. He therefore chose to defend the road to the capital at a narrow mountain pass near the village of Cerro Gordo, ten miles east of Jalapa.

By April 12, the leading division of the American army had arrived before the stout Mexican defenses. When General Scott learned the extent of the Mexican works, he hurried forward with the rest of his army. By the evening of April 16, with the bulk of his army at hand and after his engineers had thoroughly reconnoitered the area, Scott decided to challenge the Mexican position.

His troops were quieter that night, less given to joking or loud talking than usual. "It was no great wonder either," according to a regular artilleryman, "that the men were rather more reflective than usual, considering that very few of our number had ever been close in front of an enemy before, and we were approaching fortifications which we should have to carry by assault, at whatever sacrifice of life." [14]

The next morning the American assault began. As one of the division commanders gave his men the command to charge up a hill toward the enemy, one of his captains, displaying a glaringly deficient grasp of the tactical situation, inquired, "I beg pardon, General, how far shall we charge them?" At this the exasperated general roared, "Charge them to hell." The eager Americans needed no further urging and easily captured the hill. [15]

The Battle of Cerro Gordo lasted until midmorning of the next day. One American decided that the fighting he experienced here was so terrible that it was "beyond the power of my pen to describe." Another described a brief flurry of hand-to-hand fighting and declared that it was the kind of combat that he hoped "never to see again. It seemed like murder to see men running bayonets into each other's breasts." [16]

Sixty-three Americans died during the battle, and 368 suffered wounds. As with most battles during the Mexican War, Mexican losses are difficult to determine. One definite statistic, however, illustrates well the decisiveness of the battle. General Scott's forces captured over three thousand Mexicans, including almost two hundred officers. The Battle of Cerro Gordo was a blow from which the Mexican army did not soon recover.

The Mexican defeat badly dispirited Santa Anna's army. A government official in Mexico City was just as depressed when he wrote of the loss, which he termed "as complete as it was shameful. Everything was lost. Absolutely nothing was saved, not even hope." He thought it would now be only a matter of time before General Scott, following in the footsteps of Hernando Cortés, reached the capital city. [17]

The results of this battle, merely the most recent in an unbroken string of such victories for the American army, reinforced the feelings of invincibility that most Americans entertained. The low esteem with which the soldiers held their adversaries continued unabated, and this, in turn, fed the pattern of ethnocentrism. A Tennessean, touring the enemy position after the battle, found it "difficult to conceive a position which nature has more strongly fortified than Cerro Gordo." It was equally inconceivable to him that the Mexican army had been unable to hold this natural strongpoint against the Americans. A Pennsylvanian heaped opprobrium on enemy leaders after this battle when he wrote that the Mexican soldiers "are essentially cowards, and this is more true of the officers than of the men. The rank and file of the Mexican Army do not hesitate to speak of Ampudia and of other officers as cowards, and as being the first to run away in battle."[18]

Many American soldiers expressed amazement that they were able to penetrate so deeply into Mexico with so little resistance. They pointed to the many rocky, easily defended mountain passes through which they marched unmolested as evidence of a lack of Mexican fighting spirit. In the words of a Virginia volunteer, the absence of aggressive defense displayed "a degree of cowardice & a want of patriotism perfectly incomprehensible to the sons of the Old Dominion, and the fact has convinced me, or rather strengthened the conviction already entertained, that the Anglo-Saxon race posses[ses] more of the higher qualities which ennoble man than any other on the face of the earth."[19]

Just as the American successes fed their martial egos, the Mexican soldiers found it more and more difficult to maintain any semblance of confidence in themselves or in their leaders. Many of them began to believe that the invaders were indeed invincible:

Some say that the enemy soldiers are such huge, strong men that they can cut an opponent in two with a single swipe of their swords. It is also said that their horses are gigantic and very fast and that their muskets discharge shots which, once they leave the gun, divide into fifty pieces, each one fatal and well-aimed. Let us say nothing about their artillery, which has inspired fear and terror in all our troops and is undeniable proof of our backwardness in military art.

The revolvers that the Texas Rangers and the dragoons carried also struck an unnatural fear into the hearts of some of the Mexicans who had not previously encountered this particular advance in weaponry. Those who had not actually seen one of these firearms sometimes mistakenly believed that the term "revolver" referred not to the gun's mechanism but to the behavior of the bullet it fired. They believed that such a bullet had the strange ability to "revolve in all directions after its victim, run around trees and turn corners, go into houses and climb up stairs, and hunt up folks generally." These types of fears quickly spread themselves throughout the retreating army, making it even more difficult to face the Americans again with any hope of success.[20]

After resting briefly, the American troops marched into Jalapa on April 19. The bulk of the army stopped there, but since armed Mexican resistance had practically vanished, General Worth's division traveled the thirty-five miles across the mountains to Perote, which it occupied three days later.

General Scott must have viewed the military situation in central Mexico with mixed emotions. His army had just defeated a large enemy force and driven it from the field in confusion. It did not really seem very likely that Santa Anna would be able to reorganize his army in time to prevent the Americans from marching straight into Mexico City. All this good news, however, was tempered by the fact that the twelve-month enlistments of most of the American volunteers were rapidly approaching expiration. Scott either had to reenlist his volunteers for the duration of the war, or wait for the creation, training, and transportation of entirely new regiments. It quickly became obvious that most of the volunteers viewed their military commitments as having been honorably fulfilled by their one-year's service, and they were ready to go home. Let someone else finish up the war! One volunteer colonel spoke for his entire regiment when he wrote, "Mr. Polk will be deceived in his calculations that the volunteers now in service will re-enlist for the war—not one out of 100 will re-enlist." The Alabama volunteers proposed to reenlist on terms that differed from those Scott offered. They agreed to stay with the army for three months, or until Mexico City was captured, but "Uncle Sam was strong enough to reject our compromise, and we began to think of home."[21]

Scott could have tried to advance as far as possible before the volunteers went home, but it was doubtful, under these circumstances, that they would have been very effective soldiers. With the end of their service drawing near they would not have been anxious to face the enemy when to do so might mean that they would never go home. Instead, the commanding general prudently decided to postpone his final move to Mexico City, send the volunteers home before the full onset of the yellow fever season, and wait for fresh reinforcements. The seven volunteer regiments left in early June, leaving Scott with an army of slightly more than seven thousand men.

The decision on the part of the volunteers not to extend their periods of enlistment is at variance with events in the Civil War that occurred under similar circumstances. In 1864, almost all of the Federal troops whose enlistments were up signed on until the end of the war. There are at least two possible explanations. The length of the respective wars must be considered. The Civil War had dragged on for almost three years already, and during that time many of the soldiers had grown to adulthood and formed very strong bonds with their comrades and with their regiments. These bonds would have been broken had the regiments disbanded and gone home. By this time, too, the Union had regained control of the Mississippi River and had driven the Confederates out of Missouri, Kentucky, most of Tennessee, and part of Louisiana. Troops who had been a part of all this wanted to stay and see the job finished. This same sort of reasoning should also apply to the volunteers in Mexico, but it apparently did not. It is possible that the volunteers did not consider the war aims of 1847 to be nearly as critical as those in 1864. If, by some stroke of fate, the Mexicans had rallied and forced Scott and Taylor north of the Rio Grande in 1847 the American loss would have been a loss of anticipated gains only. United States territory would still be the same as it was before the war. The stakes were much higher in the Civil War. Had Confederate forces pushed Sherman and Grant north of the Mason-Dixon line in 1864, it would have meant the end of the Union and the establishment of two separate republics where there had been only one.

In February 1847, Congress finally passed legislation permitting the creation of ten new temporary regular army regiments that would exist only until the end of the war. But recruiting was slow for these new regiments and for additional volunteer units already authorized. Now, almost a full year into the war, it was obvious to all that the martial glory so eagerly sought by the early volunteers could only be acquired at a great cost of pain, suffering, and death. Young men at home saw that thousands of their fellows had succumbed to disease in Mexico, many without ever having had a chance to make names for themselves on the field of battle. Men who had not been needed in the army back in May, but who had rushed to enlist and organize military companies in case the need arose, now had second thoughts. In several instances, full companies that had volunteered at the outbreak of war deserted almost en masse rather than face mustering several months later.

Those who finally did come forward to fill these new regiments were to serve for the duration of the war, whether it lasted another four months or another four years. Since the earlier volunteers had only enlisted for twelve months (some for as few as three months very early in the war), authorities faced a difficult challenge in trying to enroll troops for the war. A contemporary recruiting poster addressed prospective enlistees on three fronts—pride, patriotism, and pocketbook. First, it appealed to their self-image as upstanding citizens. In language similar to late twentieth-century recruiting ploys seeking "a few good men," this notice sought only those "of good character, and of respectable standing among their fellow citizens." Following that, the poster enjoined that "none need apply to enter the service, but those who are determined to serve honestly and faithfully, the period of their enlistment." It next displayed a pay schedule that showed an infantry private, in addition to his twelve-dollar enlistment bonus, receiving seven dollars per month for his services. Then, because Congress realized that in the face of growing lists of casualties from Mexico even more incentives were required to get men to sign up, the recruiting broadside also told civilians contemplating military service that they would each receive 160 acres of government land upon their honorable discharge. Even with all these inducements, recruiting was slow.[22]

While General Scott waited for more troops to arrive from the states he took advantage of the army he had. It was small in numbers, but it consisted almost entirely of regulars. These troops were, on the average, much better trained and more highly disciplined than the temporary citizen soldiers. Also, because it was small, this army was able to travel faster and subsist on less than a much larger force required. Scott therefore decided to move on to the city of Puebla and use that as a staging area for the final drive against the Mexican capital. By May 15, advance elements of Scott's army had reached that Mexican city of eighty thousand. Quite a few American soldiers, when they entered Puebla, described it as the most beautiful city they had ever seen. It was certainly a larger urban center than many of them had visited. One soldier, however, has left a bizarre impression. He wrote that the elevation of Puebla above sea level was so great that

> when people first arrive in the city they begin to expand on account of rareified air, and their clothing though loose before, soon becomes so tight as to be uncomfortable. It at first frightened our soldiers, for they thought they were about to be attacked by some terrible disease, as the change brought on a slight diarrhoea and much bloating and wind.[23]

In spite of such dire predictions, there were no reported cases of soldiers falling victim to such attacks of spontaneous expansion, and the army settled down to await reinforcements.

In early August 1847, over five thousand fresh American troops reached Scott, and he wasted no time in putting them to work. On August 7, even while some of his reinforcements were still on the road from Veracruz, he began sending his army—one division at a time— toward Mexico City.

The road to the Mexican capital wound through the mountains in such a way that the Americans' first view of the Valley of Mexico came upon them quite suddenly. Almost all were awed by the scene, and many of them waxed almost poetic in their descriptions. An Indianan wrote, "The high mountains on the left rose in silent and awful grandeur, pushing their great white cones up against the blue sky, and seeming to rise from a sea of green vegetation as luxuriant as it was beautiful." As the army descended into the valley, however, the natural beauties observed from the mountains seemed—at least to some soldiers—to change as if it had all been a mirage. "The lakes became marshes," wrote a disenchanted regular, "the fields are not cultivated, the villages are mud, and the inhabitants wretched-looking Indian peons, in rags and splendid misery."[24]

As the Americans neared the city from the east General Scott considered several possible routes for his final approach. He finally settled on the road along the southern shores of Lakes Chalco and Xochimilco, but only after his engineers assured him that the causeway could bear the weight of his artillery and baggage wagons. The army, which had paused on its march from Puebla, began to move again on August 15.

Five days later a portion of the American army attacked and overwhelmed an enemy position slightly southwest of Mexico City. The fighting was fast and furious. In less than twenty minutes it was all over. The Americans captured, according to one participant, "more prisoners than it was easy to know what to do with," including four generals. And, while losing only sixty killed and wounded, the Americans killed seven hundred of the enemy. Skewing the outcome of this fight even more was the fact that the Mexicans also gave up seven hundred pack mules and twenty-two cannons, including two American guns that they had captured at Buena Vista. The results of this battle, called by the Americans the Battle of Contreras and by the Mexicans the Battle of Padierna, brought General Scott another step closer to Mexico City.[25]

Santa Anna was still not willing to concede the capital of his country to the North American invaders, however, and he ordered the bulk of his army to the crossroads village of Churubusco. Churubusco lay on the road from San Antonio to Mexico City, just south of the junction with the road from Mexicalcingo. Seven cannons and fifteen to eighteen hundred men fortified a convent there. Three other Mexican regiments guarded a bridge over the Churubusco River, and the rest of Santa Anna's force remained in reserve north of the river.

General Scott must have been very happy as his troops moved through the tall cornfields toward the bridge at Churubusco. His army had already been victorious once this day and was soon to win another battle. Perhaps Santa Anna's troops were so dispirited that these would be the last battles of the war. It might have been such optimistic thinking that caused the attack to be made without adequate knowledge of the strength of the enemy works. Had the engineer officers been allowed to conduct their usual reconnaissance, they would have determined that the terrain around the convent did not lend itself to an easy approach by infantry. They might also have learned that these Mexican defenders should not be taken lightly. Time after time they beat back the American attackers before finally retreating.

American attention then focused on the convent. The defenders, including two companies of American deserters, the San Patricios, had abandoned their outer works and were now all in the convent building. At one point, two American officers led fifteen men against a point of the Mexican defenses held by the San Patricios. They did not recognize these deserters for what they were but thought they were friendly troops who had already gained a lodgement there. When instead the San Patricios fired, they killed or wounded all but one of the men in this party. Scott's forces continued moving in, however, and it became apparent that further Mexican resistance was futile. Still the San Patricios refused to give up, even tearing down surrender flags that went up around them. Those among them who had deserted the U.S. Army knew that they would face execution if they surrendered and preferred to die fighting than at the end of a rope. But they were too few to matter, and the Mexicans finally surrendered. Scott's men added seven more cannons to their growing collection of Mexican ordnance at the convent. They also captured three generals and over twelve hundred men, eighty-five of them San Patricios. One soldier summed up the general American attitude when he wrote to his cousin about the deserters: "We esteemed this capture as one of the best results of the day, for now examples would be made of the perjured villains for the benefit of the wavering."[26]

August 20, 1847, was an important day for the American army. It had fought and won two battles against entrenched enemies. But all of this was not without a price. General Scott lost fully 12 percent of his army in killed and wounded, about one thousand men. Still, it was invigorating to be so successful so close to the enemy capital.

The next day, acting upon hints that the Mexicans desired peace, General Scott offered them a short truce so that serious negotiations might commence. Nicholas Trist, an emissary from the U.S. State Department, had joined Scott's army back in May, hoping for just such an opportunity to present Mexican officials with a peace treaty. He began meeting with Mexican negotiators on August 27 but was unable to make much progress, and on September 6, Scott finally renounced the truce.

The American commander gathered some of his subordinates together that same evening and began to discuss what the American army's next move would be to capture Mexico City. Making any decision more difficult was the report of a large mass of Mexican cavalry southwest of the city, near Chapultepec Castle. These troops were ostensibly on hand to protect El Molino del Rey, where workmen were said to be busily melting down church bells and casting them into cannons—a report that later proved groundless.

The Mexican position at El Molino del Rey was extremely strong. Two infantry brigades manned the stone mill buildings, just a thousand yards west of Chapultepec Castle. Fifteen hundred troops defended another large building, Casa Mata, five hundred yards farther west. Yet another Mexican brigade, backed by seven cannons, occupied a dry drainage ditch running between the mill and Casa Mata. Finally, should the Americans still be bold enough to attack, Maj. Gen. Juan Alvarez poised his four thousand cavalrymen about a mile west of Casa Mata, ready to help out wherever the need proved greatest.

Scott nevertheless scheduled an attack for early on the morning of September 8, 1847. General Worth, who would direct the attack, began assembling his men at 3 A.M. Engineer officers went forward to reconnoiter the enemy position. The men in this branch of service had performed superbly up until then, so when they reported to Worth that the Mexicans had abandoned the mill buildings, he had no reason to doubt them. After only a light artillery preparation, the attack began just before 6 A.M.

As the attack unfolded, it quickly became obvious that the Mexicans had not abandoned the mill. The hail of metal that greeted the Americans was deadly. One survivor later wrote, "It seemed to me that the whole of my regiment fell at the first fire." Only three of the fourteen officers in one battalion emerged unscathed. The advance sputtered to a halt and the Mexicans, thus encouraged, continued to pour a lethal fire into the ranks of blue-clad infantry in their front. So enthusiastic did the defenders become that a Mexican regiment from nearby Chapultepec, acting completely without orders, launched a counterattack that almost totally destroyed one attacking battalion.[27]

The situation on the other end of the battle line was also critical. While artillery provided covering fire, the infantry advanced upon the Mexican works, but as the attackers drew nearer and nearer to the enemy the gunners had to cease firing for fear of hitting their own men. This respite allowed Mexican infantrymen to emerge from their fortifications and drive the Americans back. Three successive commanders of one American brigade fell, killed or wounded, and finally the survivors had seen enough. They broke for the rear and the safety of their artillery. When these field pieces again went into action they forced the enemy infantry back to the Casa Mata and, shortly, compelled the Mexican commander there to abandon his position altogether. While all this was going on, General Alvarez made a half-hearted attempt to get his cavalry into action, but American dragoons and well-directed artillery fire kept his men virtually out of the battle.

The action on the right was what finally decided the battle's outcome. The brigade there, although badly broken up into small disjointed units, kept pressing forward. General Worth committed some of his reserve force, and the troops were finally able to fight their way into the complex of mill buildings. The combat then degenerated into a room-to-room contest, somewhat reminiscent of the latter stages of the Battle of Monterrey, until the Mexicans were driven out and forced back toward Chapultepec.

The fighting lasted about two hours and when it was over, General Scott viewed the results with mixed emotions. His men had captured three more Mexican cannons and several hundred prisoners, but he had also lost 116 killed and 665 wounded. Among the Mexican defenders not listed as a prisoner was another member of the San Patricio Battalion. An American soldier recognized him among the prisoners as being a deserter. Then, "to save the trouble of a court martial," the soldier tossed his former comrade "into the mill flume and he was crushed to pieces by the wheel!" The "victory" at Molino del Rey had cost the American army one-quarter of its strength. The brigade that had fought to take Casa Mata suffered such losses that it almost ceased to exist as an effective combat unit. Half its officers and a third of its men were on the casualty list.[28]

The savagery of the Mexican defense demonstrated that Scott's army would have to face more fighting before they entered Mexico City. General Scott favored an attack against Chapultepec and then on into the city through the western gates (*garitas*). He conferred with his generals on September 11 and found that there was no consensus with regard to direction of approach. Some agreed with his suggestion to aim for the San Cosmé and Belén gates, and the others favored avoiding what promised to be a bloody struggle for Chapultepec and targeting the San Antonio Gate. In spite of the disagreement, Scott's mind was made up, and he began to plan accordingly.

The next day, under cover of a diversion on the American right, near Piedad, American artillerymen busily planted their guns in five different locations from which to batter Chapultepec. Scott only hoped that Santa Anna would not discover these moves in time to counter them effectively. Santa Anna discounted the artillery fire falling on Chapultepec and instead fell for the ruse. He ordered troops and cannons from Chapultepec and from the vicinity of the Belén Gate to march to Piedad. He also heard rumors of American activity near the southeast corner of the city and sent other men there. By the morning of September 13, when he discovered the real target, he was unable to get his soldiers through the American artillery barrage and back into Chapultepec.

General Scott had hoped that cannon fire alone would be enough to dislodge Chapultepec's defenders, because an infantry attack would be very difficult. The castle, which housed a military college, sat atop a two-hundred-foot hill and appeared to be strongly built. Stone walls protected the grounds on the south and east, as did a bricked-up aqueduct on the north. The swampy ground on the west contained some outworks and led to the ruins of El Molino del Rey. Mexican engineers had further prepared that side by burying quantities of gunpowder in the area. Long canvas hoses filled with powder led up the hill to the main works and served as fuses for the primitive land mines.

In spite of all these difficulties, the American infantry began its advance at 8 A.M. on September 13, following a two-and-a-half hour artillery bombardment. West of the castle, five regular army infantry regiments swept forward in a three-pronged attack. They got into the compound with relative ease and soon drove the enemy up the hill and into the castle itself. The attack in this quarter then lost speed because scaling ladders had not arrived, and the men could not get into the Mexican works without them. While they waited they continued to play their muskets along the castle parapets. They also had time to find and sever the powder trains to most of the mines.

Meanwhile, Gen. John Quitman's volunteer division advanced up the road from Tacubaya toward the southeast corner of the castle grounds, but this assault faltered in the face of Mexican artillery fire. Fortunately the American generals had contingency plans, and when they saw their initial efforts sputtering, they quickly committed reinforcements. Through an accident of good timing, each of the two reserve brigades and the tardy scaling ladders reached the base of the castle walls at about the same time.

The fresh troops injected renewed spirit into their comrades and up the ladders they went. As they pushed forward, one officer felt his face splashed with a warm sticky liquid that could only have been his own blood. He waited for the accompanying pain to overwhelm him, and when this did not happen he realized that it was not blood that he felt, but the juice from a nearby maguey plant that had been shredded by cannon fire. Many others, of course, were not this lucky and never lived to see what was behind the walls of Chapultepec, but their places were so rapidly filled that the defenders quickly gave way. About an hour and a half after the attack began, a lieutenant of New York volunteers accepted Gen. Nicolás Bravo's surrender.[29]

The loss of Chapultepec was a serious blow to Mexican resistance. Their success at Molino del Rey had buoyed their hopes, but those hopes began to fade after the loss of the castle. Santa Anna reportedly remarked that even if he planted his cannons in hell itself the "damned Yankees" would find a way to capture them. One of his subordinates commented sadly that "God is a Yankee."[30]

It was still early in the day. Wishing to take advantage of the American jubilation and the Mexican demoralization, General Quitman took his division down the causeway toward Belén Gate. This move was supposed to be a feint while General Worth made the main attack at San Cosmé Gate. A Mexican artillery battery hindered Quitman's advance briefly, and then the Americans pressed on without further interruption.

As bad as circumstances were for the Mexicans, they had not entirely given up hope. They gamely defended Belén Gate until they exhausted their artillery ammunition. Then they retired a few hundred yards into the city to a large tobacco factory, the Ciudadela, which they had converted into a barracks. The Americans entering the gate thus met serious musket fire from there. Artillerymen tried to use the abandoned Mexican guns on the Ciudadela but they, too, soon ran out of ammunition, and the fighting at Belén Gate bogged down into heavy sniping.

Worth's attack on San Cosmé Gate did not begin until late in the afternoon. His men had already fought off a Mexican cavalry attack, and they cleared some other minor resistance before arriving at the gate. The fact that there was any defense of the San Cosmé Gate was a tribute to the spirit of the Mexican soldiers. Santa Anna had not thought it likely that Scott would attack that far north and had made only minimal efforts at fortifying there. Still, when Worth headed that way from Chapultepec, the Mexicans, many of them refugees from that morning's fighting, hurried to do what they could to keep the Americans out.

The hastily thrown up Mexican defenses successfully held the Americans at bay for a while. When the attackers were unable to advance down the road they found another way. Using the protection of an aqueduct on the south side of the road, they leapfrogged forward. North of the road they burrowed through adjacent buildings just as they had done at Monterrey.

South of the road Lt. Ulysses Grant learned that the steeple of the San Cosmé Church overlooked the Mexican position and was large enough to accommodate a small cannon. He went to the door of the church and, with the rudimentary Spanish at his command, asked the priest's permission to enter. The priest was understandably reluctant, but Grant assured him that his consent was a mere formality since he intended to enter the church anyway. At this, the priest reluctantly "opened the door, though he did not look as if it gave him special pleasure to do so." Lieutenant Grant, along with another officer and a small party of regular infantrymen, manhandled a small mountain howitzer up into the tower. On the other side of the road a navy lieutenant named Raphael Semmes did the same thing. Just as the fire from these guns began to tell on the Mexican artillerists at the gate, a detachment of U.S. Marines somehow worked its way to the roof of a three-story building behind them and swept them from their guns with musket fire.[31]

American troops now were inside Mexico City, but nobody could say how long they would be able to stay there. Santa Anna still had approximately twelve thousand men in the city, many more than were available to General Scott. There was also the specter of a long guerrilla fight with the civilian populace. If it came to such a protracted campaign of attrition, the invaders could hold little hope for success. Happily for the Americans, the civil authorities convinced Santa Anna to leave the city and regroup his army elsewhere. Consequently, Mexican forces conceded their capital to the invaders and slipped away during the night to Guadalupe Hidalgo. Early on the morning of September 14, 1847, American forces under General Worth entered and took possession of Mexico City.

The conquerors marched through silent, almost deserted streets. As the head of the column neared one of the main plazas, Lt. Col. John Garland rode forward to talk to General Worth. The troops waited while the two men conversed. Suddenly, from a nearby house, a shot rang out and Colonel Garland slumped over, severely wounded. Other shots followed, but the American response was quick and decisive. As several infantrymen began returning fire, some of their comrades unlimbered a field piece and began sending rounds into the suspect house. After three or four cannon shots, the house was sufficiently battered to allow American troops to enter and capture the four snipers inside. This event was the first of its type in the Mexican capital, but not the last. For the next several days there was sporadic sniping, but it eventually abated in the face of determined response by American infantry and artillery.

Throughout the fighting in Mexico, soldiers found it difficult to describe to the family and friends at home just what it was like to take part in a battle. Many men employed a weather analogy to characterize their combat. Violent weather was something that everyone had experienced, so it was natural for the soldiers to tell how "bullets flew thick as rain around me," or how "the balls whistled through the air like hail in a storm." One man, writing of one of General Scott's battles in central Mexico, found it difficult to describe how terrible the experience was for him: "Imagine the most violent hail storm you ever saw, attended constantly with the loudest claps of thunder your ears ever heard and you can form but a faint idea of this battle."[32]

Of course, a hailstorm of lead inflicted much greater damage than one of nature's tempests. The observation of human slaughter had varying effects on the survivors. It caused some to lose any prebattle anxieties in an almost maniacal rage. "I expected to be very much frightened," said a Mississippian, "but when I saw our men, and some of them my immediate friends shot down by my side with the entrails torn out, heads, arms, and legs shot off, a kind of madness took possession of me, a perfect carelessness of consequences indescribable in fact, my whole mind being occupied by the one desire, viz. to revenge them and kill as many of the yellow skinned devils as I could." Following the Battle of Buena Vista, another soldier, employing the popular phrase of the day, told his brother, "I came to Mexico to see the 'Elephant.' I have seen him & am perfectly willing now to see him again." These were unusual sentiments.[33]

Most soldiers, even though they might become hardened to the terrible destruction of war, did not yearn for more. One soldier expressed the predominant sentiment when he wrote, "never can I forget the carnage, the groans of the wounded & dying proceeded from every direction and the horribly mutilated bodies would have moved the heart of any man less familiar with the horrors of battle than ourselves. it is almost incredible how a man can accustom himself to such sights, and look with indifference on the most agonizing spectacle." This soldier, who had been as eager as anyone to get into combat, also stated, "I have now seen as much of war as I desired and am willing, for the first time, to return to the United States and convert our 'spears into reaping hooks.' " Another man, one who had fought all the way from Palo Alto to Mexico City, decided that he had seen " 'processions of elephants,' " and he was "prepared to retire to some quiet spot in my own native land and spend the rest of my days in peace and quietness."[34]

Lt. Ulysses S. Grant shared this viewpoint when, after taking part in the opening battles of the war, he confided to his fiancée that there was "no great sport in having bullets flying" all around him. As a professional soldier he knew that battles were a necessary part of war, and "wherever there are battles a great many must suffer, and for the sake of the little glory gained I do not care to see it." A southern volunteer assured his uncle that "soldiering *ain't* what it is cracked up to be and the singing of Bullets & Grape & canister is any thing but comfortable. Glory & all that is nothing but Fudge."[35]

During the heat of battle the soldiers did not have time to reflect upon the gravity of their situations. But when the shooting stopped they were able to see the destruction all around them. After the Battle of Contreras, an American soldier described his shock regarding the carnage surrounding him:

The battlefield was such a sight as I had never seen before, and which I would have been satisfied never to see again. The ground was covered with gore from the wounds of the dying and dead which lay thick upon the field. The sight was horrible—enough to chill the hardest heart. Some had a leg, a foot, an arm or hand mangled to pieces and were lying upon the cold, muddy ground shivering with cold, begging for a bit of bread or a drink of water.[36]

An American doctor, who had certainly been witness to more dead and wounded than most ordinary soldiers, still seemed taken aback by the awful destruction at Chapultepec. He and his colleagues worked on Mexican wounded as well as injured Americans, but he was particularly moved by the spectacle of the large numbers of enemy casualties littering the field when the fighting stopped:

Their mangled bodies lay heaped in masses; some among them indeed were not yet dead, but were gasping in the last agonies, with their dark faces upturned to the sun, writhing and struggling in death, like fish thrown on shore by the angler. Crushed heads, shattered limbs, torn up bodies, with brains, hearts, and lungs exposed, and eyes torn from their sockets, were among the horrible visions that first arrested attention."[37]

Those killed in battle, of course, had nothing further to fear. They were wrapped in their blankets and buried, quite often in common graves. But for the wounded, it was often a very long road to recovery, if indeed they recovered at all.

Since most of the battles in this war were of relatively short duration, Monterrey and Buena Vista being exceptions, the wounded usually received at least some attention fairly quickly. Army doctors moved over the battlefields as soon as the firing stopped, and in some cases while the battle still raged, and administered basic aid to the wounded. Unfortunately, some doctors were less dedicated than others. Immediately following one battle, a soldier hailed the surgeon of the Fourth U.S. Artillery Regiment seeking help for a sergeant who had had a leg torn off by Mexican artillery fire. "Does the Sergeant belong to the 4th Artil[lery]?" asked the doctor. When the soldier responded that his wounded comrade was an infantryman the doctor passed on by, hurrying to catch up with his regiment rather than tending the injured man.[38]

The army had no permanent hospital corps or ambulances, so the trip from the battlefield to the hastily erected hospitals often did additional harm to the seriously injured. Common soldiers went out onto the battlefields with litters to bring in the wounded, and quarter-masters provided regular army wagons to help. These wagons lacked springs and a ride over the rough, uneven ground of a battlefield could be less than pleasant even for a man in good health. For many of the wounded it was pure torture.

Even when a wounded soldier reached a hospital the unsanitary conditions that usually greeted him did not ensure his recovery. Sometimes these hospitals were set up in tents, but the army usually commandeered nearby buildings for the purpose. Following the Battle of Cerro Gordo, the doctors established their hospital in several small cane buildings. These huts were bereft of any furniture, even bedding, and an observer noted that the wounded men "were ranged along on blankets, stretched on the bare earth. They lay in their ordinary clothing, in many instances stiff with blood. . . . Some were delirious and groaning with pain, some dying, some dead." At another, somewhat more permanent facility in Jalapa, the patients,

some of whom were wounded, and others wasted to skeletons with diarrhoea, and in the last stages of illness, lay on a thin piece of matting or a dirty doubled-up blanket, on the cold and hard brick floor. Many of them had on shirts which they had evidently worn for weeks, and . . . nearly all of them were infected with vermin. Their diet was bread and coffee, which few of them could eat.[39]

Compounding the effects of such filthy hospital conditions was the fact that doctors had little knowledge of antisepsis. They routinely moved from patient to patient, swabbing out the wounds with the same sponge that they had used all day. Infection was simply something regrettable, but expected. Because of such conditions many patients with flesh wounds often sickened and died.

Another problem was a dearth of qualified medical personnel. There never seemed to be enough doctors to care for all the sick and wounded, and hospital orderlies and cooks were merely soldiers on detail from combat units. Commanders were not likely to detach men they would need, so the hospital staff usually consisted of those who were misfits or who were themselves convalescent.

The wounded faced a variety of treatments, depending on the location and severity of their wounds. Many injuries were so traumatic as to require immediate amputation, but in these cases even the presence of a doctor was often of little comfort. The incidence of such injuries in civilian life was very small (Massachusetts General Hospital in Boston, for example, reported only 173 major amputations for the entire period from 1822 to 1850) so doctors were unaccustomed to amputating limbs. In fact, a surgeon in one of the newly formed regular army regiments performed the first amputation of his career following the Battle of Chapultepec. This lack of familiarity occasionally led to botched operations. A New Hampshire sergeant was severely wounded in the attack on Belén Gate at Mexico City and surgeons determined to amputate what remained of his badly mangled leg. They performed the procedure poorly, leaving two inches of thigh bone protruding from the stump. Doctors carried out a second operation, but it too was unsuccessful. When this soldier's commanding officer expressed a fear that he could not endure a third operation, the plucky soldier assured him that he could: "I want it taken off to-day, and, when they cut it off again, I hope they will cut it so that it will stay cut!"[40]

During the Battle of Monterrey a Mexican cannonball struck a soldier in both legs, near the ankles. His right leg was badly shattered, and one of the bones in his left was pulverized. The doctors wanted to amputate both legs immediately, "but the patient was a cross-grained Irishman," and he would not give his consent. He only allowed them to take the badly mangled right leg, but swore he would rather die than lose them both. The surgeons acquiesced. A few days later, the soldier decided that perhaps the doctors had been right, and asked them to take his left leg. Unfortunately, his condition had so rapidly deteriorated by that time that he did not survive.[41]

Military doctors during the Mexican War did not automatically amputate all wounded limbs. There were many cases in which the doctors tried to save the lives of soldiers without taking their arms or legs off in the process, and these decisions met with varied results. In one case, a Mexican musket ball struck a Texas Ranger in the leg, fracturing his kneecap. Doctors chose not to amputate the leg, and the man made a complete recovery. During the final battles around Mexico City, an American officer was wounded in the foot. The ball broke several small bones, and doctors cut it out while the man lay on the field. Within two hours of being wounded, this lieutenant was resting in a hospital. The attending physician treated the wound with poultices, and the patient steadily improved for a month. Then his condition suddenly worsened until a day—two months after being wounded—when a piece of leather, probably a portion of the man's shoe, worked its way out of the wound. His general health again improved, and he was sent home a few weeks later.[42]

The pain that wounded soldiers endured was often magnified by medical procedures. At Buena Vista a soldier was hit in the leg by a heavy Mexican musket ball. After the battle he lay in a hospital for almost six weeks with it still in his leg because doctors were not sure of the bullet's exact location. Finally, unable to stand it any longer, and fearful that he would die if the doctors allowed the bullet to remain in his leg, he convinced them that he knew where it was. He placed his finger where he thought the ball was and told the surgeon to cut it out. The pain must have been excruciating—there was no anesthetic. The patient later recalled that he watched the doctor's face intently as he probed the wound "and the moment he touched the ball I saw an expression of delight come over his countenance." This man made a full recovery and was extremely lucky to do so. The infection that followed such wounds often proved fatal.[43]

In addition to what would now be considered unsanitary habits of the surgeons, enemy bullets often carried such debris as pieces of the soldier's uniform into the wound. This foreign material also caused complications. Another soldier at Buena Vista suffered just such a wound in his arm. Five weeks after the battle he wrote his parents that the bullet and clothing fragments were still in his arm. "I live in hopes that the bullet may be located and removed and with it the pieces of clothing also, which I suppose will expedite the healing of the wound." Two weeks later, doctors removed the cloth fragments, but after another three weeks the bullet still remained and records are unclear whether it was ever removed. Nevertheless, this soldier survived the war.[44]

In spite of the number of cases in which doctors did not employ their amputating saws, there were many men not so fortunate. Since anesthesia was in its infancy during the Mexican War, most of those undergoing the loss of a limb, or indeed any surgical procedure, did so to the accompaniment of horrendous pain. In fact, it was because of the lack of an effective anesthesia that surgery was not a routine part of a doctor's practice. Some doctors were themselves almost overcome by having to witness the amount of pain that they necessarily inflicted upon their patients during the course of one of these rarely performed operations.

The search for an effective anesthetic agent had been going on for centuries. Dioscorides, in the first century a.d., prescribed the juice of the mandragora root for those who wished "to produce anesthesia while being cut or cauterized." During the last quarter of the eighteenth century various scientists uncovered the existence of nitrous oxide and its possible benefit as an anesthetic. In 1824, an American doctor experimented with carbon dioxide while operating on animals and noted its pain-reducing effect. In early 1842, a few other physicians began using sulphuric ether in selected cases, and in 1844 a Connecticut doctor employed nitrous oxide for tooth extraction. These early experimenters did not publicize their findings widely, so public acceptance waited for the first successful public demonstration of the surgical effects of ether, which took place in Boston in October 1846. Within a few weeks, a doctor performed a successful amputation on an etherized patient, and the use of this anesthetic rapidly began to gain acceptance.[45]

By the spring and summer of 1847, army doctors at Veracruz had begun to administer ether to their patients. They were seeing many more surgical cases than their civilian counterparts, and the witnessing of such suffering undoubtedly made them willing to grasp at the hope offered by anesthesia. In spite of this hope, after using sulphuric ether in several cases, the doctors at Veracruz discontinued its use. One of these army surgeons, while admitting that there were many causes of ill health in the port city, nevertheless thought that "the inhalation of ether . . . was as injurious as any other malign influence whatever." He also maintained that not only was ether unfavorable, but "it was decidedly pernicious," saying that anesthetics "poison the blood and depress the nervous system."[46]

Capt. Robert E. Lee probably best summed up the soldiers' attitudes toward battles when he said, "I think a little lead, properly taken, is good for a man. I am truly thankful however that I escaped all internal doses."[47]

Winfield Scott thus accomplished what few military men of his time would have dared to attempt. He had voluntarily cut himself loose from his base of support at Veracruz and marched his small army 250 miles into the very heart of the enemy's country and forced the surrender of its capital city. In fact, no less a soldier than England's Duke of Wellington, when he learned of this tactic, is said to have mourned, "Scott is lost—he cannot capture the city and he cannot fall back upon his base." Upon the successful completion of the campaign, however, the elderly victor of Waterloo reportedly exclaimed that Scott's "campaign was unsurpassed in military annals. He is the greatest living soldier." In less than twenty years another American general—William T. Sherman—would be just as successful when he marched his army from Atlanta to Savannah.[48]

The American soldiers who had worked so hard to achieve success must now wait for the political leaders of the two nations to hammer out a treaty before they could return to their homes.

CHAPTER 11

Peace at Last

Just as the British capture of Washington, D.C., in 1814 did not bring that war to a close, neither did the U.S. occupation of Mexico City effect an end to hostilities in 1847. At almost the same time that U.S. soldiers were triumphantly fighting their way past the city gates, Brig. Gen. Joaquin Rea and four thousand troops were beginning a twenty-eight-day siege of American forces in Puebla. Santa Anna himself arrived a week later to supervise matters. But in spite of the presence of the "Napoleon of the West" and the fact that the Americans were confined to three positions within the city, repeated Mexican attacks failed to bring victory. American reinforcements arrived from Veracruz on October 12 and lifted the siege. Organized Mexican resistance then ceased, giving way to occasional guerrilla raids.

Immediately after General Scott took control of Mexico City, he established martial law. He reissued to his troops the cautionary order that he had published prior to the capture of Veracruz. Under its provisions the soldiers were to respect private property and to comport themselves as gentlemen. Scott knew how important it was to pacify the inhabitants. To do otherwise was to invite destruction. His was a small army in the midst of a very large enemy city, far from any support. The civilian population of the city was alone large enough to bring disaster to his force, should it choose to do so, before any help could arrive. He therefore allowed Mexican civil courts to continue in operation for all cases involving only Mexicans. If Americans were involved, however, either as plaintiff or defendant, a military commission heard the case.[1]

Guerrilla attacks within the city ended rather quickly, but individual assassinations continued to be a problem. Quite a number of Scott's troops lost their lives in this manner. Even though American soldiers had long since learned to accept battle-related deaths, they never had tolerance for those Mexicans whom they considered murderers. Near the end of 1847, for instance, long after the surrender of Mexico City, a lone sniper ambushed an American military courier as he rode through a small deserted town near the capital. The shot was wide of the mark and the messenger kept on riding. He had only gone a few hundred yards when he met three American dragoons going in the opposite direction. Together the four men returned to the scene of the shooting and began to look for the assailant. They soon discovered a man hiding in a hedge and quickly convinced themselves that he was the gunman—he was carrying a musket that had recently been fired and it was again loaded and primed. Having thus established the Mexican's guilt, one of the dragoons said, "I think this is the best and shortest way to settle this affair," and shot the man in the chest with his own musket. Then, after administering a coup de grace with his pistol, the American suggested that they all retire to a nearby town for some brandy. He justified his act by saying that "the effect of sacrificing that treacherous *greaser* will be to stop these attempts in this neighbourhood; and I am quite satisfied that I have performed my duty properly . . . and probably saved the lives of some of Uncle Sam's soldiers."[2]

During the lull in the fighting between Churubusco and Molino del Rey, two military courts-martial convened to try the American deserters who had been recaptured at Churubusco. About a dozen of those taken were not deserters and were therefore treated as prisoners of war. Forty-three of the remainder faced trial at Tacubaya and the other twenty-nine at San Angel during the last week of August and the first week of September 1847. Sixty of the men pleaded guilty, eleven pleaded not guilty, and one man refused to enter a plea at all. He claimed that since he had never been officially sworn into the U.S. Army, and had never received any pay, that he could not be tried as a deserter.

Even though feelings against the accused deserters were very high among the American troops, the courts sought to assure that their trials were scrupulously fair. About half of the prisoners claimed that they were drunk when they had been seized by Mexicans, and that they had been forced into Mexican service on pain of death. This line of defense was done irreparable harm, however, when it came out that many other captured Americans had refused to join without suffering such a penalty.

At the end of the trials, the courts found all but two of the defendants guilty of desertion and sentenced them to die. They agreed with the captive who claimed never to have been properly mustered into service and released him. They judged a second prisoner to be mentally deficient, and therefore guilty only of being absent without leave.

Winfield Scott, as army commander, had to review and approve these death sentences, which caused him much anguish. He seemed almost to be looking for extenuating circumstances so that he would not have to approve the executions of these seventy soldiers. He pardoned five altogether, among them a sixty-year-old and two teenagers who had enlisted without parental consent, and commuted the sentences of fifteen others. The reduced sentences, however, were not light. They were to be whipped and branded.

The fifteen "lucky" San Patricios who escaped the hangman's noose nevertheless suffered their sentences on September 10, 1847, in the plaza at San Angel. Guards stripped them to the waist and then tied them securely to trees. Then, instead of having bandsmen ply the whip, experienced Mexican muleteers stepped forward to lay on the fifty lashes. Among those thus whipped and branded was John Riley. Most Americans thought Riley to have been a ringleader of sorts, since he had risen to officer rank in the Mexican service. The U.S. troops were particularly offended when, upon learning that Riley had deserted before the actual declaration of war, General Scott could not allow the death penalty to be imposed. General Twiggs, who was in charge of this phase of the punishment, therefore promised the muleteers large bonuses if Riley should happen to die under their whips. He did not, and a witness marveled that human beings could survive such a horrible whipping. "Their backs had the appearance of a pounded piece of raw beef, the blood oozing from every stripe as given."[3]

Having survived the first stage of their punishment, these deserters were still only part of the way through their sentence. Next, officials branded them with the letter *D*, for deserter. Branding was not an unusual punishment in the U.S. Army. It usually consisted of an indelible mark, or tattoo. In the case of the San Patricios, however, the brand was by a hot iron, like those used to mark cattle, and it was placed on their cheeks, where it would serve to tell all who saw these men that they were deserters.

John Riley paid a higher price than the other San Patricios. He was branded twice. Accounts vary. Some say that the soldier wielding the hot iron applied the brand upside down and he therefore had to try again. Another version, and one that seems just as plausible, is that as the iron contacted Riley's right cheek, he involuntarily flinched, causing the iron to move and blur the imprint. General Twiggs inspected the work and decided it was not adequate. Then, addressing the prisoner, he told him that "he was sentenced to be branded with the letter 'D', and that he would keep on branding him until he made a good plain 'D' if he had to burn his d——head off." In either case, a good, clear *D* soon appeared on his other cheek.[4]

The first part of September also saw the fifty condemned San Patricios meet their fates. American authorities hanged sixteen of them at San Angel on September 10, and four more the next day near Mixcoac. The remainder died on September 13, and their execution was one of some cruelty. Col. William S. Harney ordered a long scaffold erected and ordered the prisoners out early in the morning. Only twenty-nine of the thirty appeared, and Harney was furious. An investigation quickly revealed that one of the condemned prisoners had been badly wounded at Churubusco. The man had lost both legs and was dying without the aid of a noose, but Harney was adamant. He had orders to hang thirty men, and that is what he intended to do. The prisoners, their arms and legs bound, stood upon boards placed across the backs of wagons. Harney then ordered the injured man to be propped up so a noose could also be fitted around his neck.

By the time these difficulties could be corrected, the American assault on Chapultepec, two miles away, had begun. Adding a touch of grim irony, Colonel Harney told the San Patricios that they would watch the progress of the battle, and that as soon as the American flag was seen waving triumphantly over the parapets of the castle, they would "have seen the last of earth." And he was true to his word. Just as the stars and stripes appeared atop the Mexican works, the wagons all pulled forward, leaving the men to strangle at the ends of their ropes. When it was over, someone approached Colonel Harney to ask whether the bodies should be cut down. " 'No,' " he said, " 'I was ordered to have them hanged, and have no orders to *unhang* them.' "[5]

Until the United States and Mexico signed a formal treaty of peace, there was still the possibility of renewed warfare, but as time went on that became less and less likely. Instead, the men took on the roles of occupation troops in a foreign land. For most of them life became a search for amusement. And they did not have far to look. They seemed always able to find a fandango to attend, or a Mexican gambling house or drinking establishment to patronize. Nor were Mexican merchants the only ones to profit from the occupation troops. As in all cities previously occupied—Matamoros, Monterrey, Veracruz—entrepreneurs who followed the army established American-style hotels, restaurants, theaters, and newspapers.

As desperate as the soldiers were for news from home, whether letters or newspapers, it did not take long for some enterprising businessmen to begin publishing English-language newspapers in Mexico. Some such efforts were very crude and amateurish, and only lasted for a few issues, while others were quite professionally turned out and stayed in business for several months. Eventually, some of these newspapers became semiofficial organs of the American army in Mexico, publishing general orders and other important news.

Nevertheless, when one officer mentioned the existence of one of these newspapers to his wife, he assured her that he and his fellow officers did not place much credence in it as a source of information: "It will publish anything for money." And in spite of the respectability gained by publishing army orders, this officer was right. These newspapers had begun operations primarily for the reading enjoyment of the soldiers, and if all they printed were dry military orders and reports they would be missing out on a large market for lighter fare.[6]

In order to supply more entertaining reading, the newspapers turned to their readers for submissions. They asked the soldiers, for instance, to submit poems for consideration. Then, if the paper published them, the authors were rewarded with seeing their work in print, followed by their initials and their branch of service.

Desperation for items to print did not mean, however, that these newspapers printed everything their soldier readers submitted to them. Even when they chose not to run some of the poetry they received, they often made mention of the receipt of such material anyway. The tenor of these acknowledgments, like the tone of modern-day rejection slips from publishers, varied. For example, the editors of the Mexico City *North American* regretted, in December 1847, that they could not publish the poetry of a certain reader, whom they identified only by his initials: "We would gladly do any possible favor to him and the corps to which he is attached, but the publication of the rhymes in question would be no favor." A month later, the same paper, in a somewhat whimsical tone, wrote that a poem that it had recently received "is the best we have seen of the kind, but not liking that particular kind, we decline publishing it." These published rejections were sometimes much more blunt and to the point. Reflecting, perhaps, either a rash of substandard submissions or simply the fact that the editor was having a bad day, the following notice appeared in the *North American* in February 1848: "A. H. H. your rhymes are not readable, some of the words are nearly obliterated. The poem must have been written on the bottom of a camp kettle." In spite of such ego-deflating commentary, these newspapers continued to find avid readers for as long as American troops stayed in Mexico.[7]

The American newspapers in Mexico City quickly became organs for the U.S. Army. This quasiofficial backing also helped make the papers very popular among the soldiers. Not only could the soldiers read the latest official orders from army headquarters, but the editors did their best to keep their readers abreast of the peace negotiations. Part of the difficulties surrounding these talks was identifying the Mexican parties with whom to deal. No one seemed willing to take the responsibility of surrendering their country to the invaders. Playing upon this theme, the following ad appeared in one of the American newspapers in the Mexican capital:

Wanted immediately—A government in Mexico qualified to do general house-work, sign documents, or at least make its mark. Such a government, which can furnish satisfactory recommendations from its last place may procure a situation by addressing post paid James K. Polk, Washington, or by applying personally to General Winfield Scott, Hall of the Montezumas, second door below the grand plaza. N.B. No Protestant need apply.[8]

The American soldiers were not content to sit idly and read an occasional newspaper. Like occupation troops of other wars, they used their free time to see the sights, acquire souvenirs, and meet the local people. With the fighting over, there was less chance for martial trophies, but a lot of the married soldiers found time to buy mementos for their wives and children. Mexican coins were popular items because they were easy to obtain, yet conveyed the flavor of a foreign land. A North Carolina volunteer sent a dozen coins to one of his sons, some drawings to another, and two strings of beads to his daughter. Another volunteer told his mother that when he returned to Virginia he was going to bring several curiosities, "such as a full Mexican suit of clothes."[9]

Not all such attempts to find keepsakes met with success. Some of the soldiers, of more artistic bent, began to buy Aztec relics such as stone snakes, gods, and goddesses. Once this became the fashion, it did not take long for the local residents to begin a thriving trade in fakes.

There were other ways, too, in which the Mexicans were able to profit from the presence of the invaders. One such scam was for a citizen to approach a soldier with a five-dollar gold coin in his hand and five counterfeit silver dollars in his pocket. He would then ask for change, whereupon the American would take the gold piece and give the Mexican five silver dollars. The Mexican would then protest that the American had not given him enough silver. He wanted more than five pieces. By that time the soldier would become exasperated and demand his coins back. The Mexican would then happily make the refund, but with the counterfeit coins.[10]

Being far from home and having time on their hands, many soldiers sought out female companionship. Their lust overcame any initial feelings that Mexicans were greatly inferior to them. Not all Americans gave in to these primal urgings. Some resisted the allure of the Mexican women more stoutly than others. An Ohio volunteer officer, for example, wrote his wife that while he knew of some officers who chased after Mexican women, he and the officers of his company had nothing to do with them. A couple of weeks later he reassured her of his fidelity, not even committing "adultery of the mind." He and his friends spent their off-duty time playing cards or chess while their "brother officers are away in gambling houses and brothels."[11]

Lt. George Gordon Meade openly wrote to his wife about how he and two of his married friends, after hearing stories of the beautiful dark-eyed Mexican women, had tried to pass themselves off as single men "and enjoy our few days under the delusion." Although he never admitted any indiscretions in later letters, his wife surely must have wondered, particularly when his assurances of loyalty were couched in the following terms: "You must not be concerned about the pretty girls, for I will frankly confess as yet I have seen but one sufficiently good looking to stop me, and she evinced no disposition to cultivate my acquaintance."[12]

Not all of the liaisons between soldiers and Mexican women were illicit. When a body of troops remained in a given vicinity for a long time, quite a few real romances blossomed. There were several marriages between soldiers and local women, marriages that American newspapers in Mexico City referred to as "annexations." After one of these weddings in early 1848, an American editor wrote, "Hurrah for annexation! That's the way to do it! No more arguments on the policy of annexing Mexico but go to work and annex her daughters."[13]

Many Mexican men violently opposed such unions. In fact, they regarded as treasonous any Mexicans who held any sort of intercourse with the occupation forces. One tactic they used to dissuade their countrymen from befriending these soldiers and welcoming them into their homes was to say that the Church would excommunicate them for doing so. A touring Spanish theatrical company was cautioned that the Mexicans would boycott it if it performed for the Americans.[14]

Toward the end of American occupation in 1848, rumors began to circulate that any Mexican woman who had shown excessive favors toward the Americans would be severely punished. Lt. Ulysses Grant informed his fiancée that "some barbarities have been committed such as shaving the heads of females, and I believe in one or two cases they cut their ears off." Another soldier reported that guerrillas captured the Mexican wife of an American officer and gang raped her before they cut her ears off.[15]

Occupation troops in Mexico began to see an end to their service when American and Mexican diplomats finally hammered out a peace treaty on January 31, 1848. It then remained for both governments to ratify the instrument. In the meantime, military men from each side signed a "Military Convention for the Provisional Suspension of Hostilities" on February 29, 1848, and, for all practical purposes, the war was over. The U.S. Senate made a few changes in the treaty and then ratified it on March 10. Mexican officials took a little longer to mull it over, but they ratified the Treaty of Guadalupe Hidalgo on May 30, 1848.

Even before final Mexican approval, plans were under way to bring the American troops home. The first contingent of the main body left Mexico City on May 27, and within just over two weeks the capital was free of American soldiers. As the various bodies of troops headed toward the coast, they temporarily halted at Jalapa, out of the yellow fever zone, until their ships were ready to sail. They then marched rapidly into Veracruz and onto the ships. Most of the vessels then sailed for either New Orleans, Louisiana, or Pass Christian, Mississippi. From there, the regular army troops moved on to their next duty assignments. The volunteers received their discharges and started for home.

For the regulars, the end of the war was not as momentous an occasion as it was for the volunteers. The regulars' lifestyle did not change much. There were no welcome-home celebrations for them. They were still in the army. They still had to obey orders. The volunteers, on the other hand, were welcomed back to their communities as conquering heroes. The difference is easy to understand. Most of the regulars had enlisted in eastern cities. Many of them came from the lower rungs of society, and many were immigrants. Upon enlistment, they had been assigned to various regiments based upon manpower needs at the time. All of these factors, plus the fact that the regular units did not return to any sort of home base, meant that there was no great outpouring of affection for them by the general populace.

Homecoming for the volunteers was quite different. These troops tended to come from higher levels of society. Many, indeed, were prominent in their communities. The members of the various volunteer companies usually all came from the same counties, and their families knew one another. The volunteers had all gone into the service at the same time, and for a specified term. Therefore they were all coming home at the same time also. Finally, with the prevailing sentiment against the need for a professional, standing army, the people looked upon the accomplishments of the amateur soldiers as further proof of their argument, and feted them accordingly. A speaker welcoming back the Second and Third Indiana Volunteers took the occasion to take another swipe at the standing army of the United States: "Citizen soldiers, you are the living evidence of the wisdom of our fathers, who instead of encouraging large standing armies for our defence, which they regarded as dangerous to our liberties, they place you before the nation as the bulwarks of our civil liberties and *well* have you sustained their opinions."[16]

The welcome-home celebrations did not wait for the end of the war. Since the early volunteers returned in mid-1847, the festivities commenced then. So anxious were the citizens to have their loved ones back that most of the returning warriors were feted more than once. There would usually be a major celebration in whatever city served as the point of return for the regiment. In Illinois, for instance, the volunteers came up the Mississippi River from New Orleans and landed at Alton, where some five thousand people turned out to welcome them home. North Carolinians received a similar reception at Wilmington. Then, as the regiments broke up and the men reached their home towns, either by companies or individually, the festivities began anew.

There was something of a pattern to these occasions. There was a parade, featuring a brass band, perhaps a local militia company, and the veterans themselves. Sometimes the citizens of the community joined in, and the entire procession then marched to a nearby spot for a grand picnic. When the revelers reached the picnic grounds, some prominent local speaker typically welcomed the soldiers back to their home state, "the honour of which you have so nobly, so gallantly and so valiantly sustained." There followed a recounting of the brave deeds performed and the hardships endured. These speakers also heaped lavish praise upon the volunteers who had not seen any enemy action. A North Carolina newspaper, for example, reminded its readers that the local volunteers "deserve the gratitude and thanks of the State just as much as if they had been in every battle from Vera Cruz to the City of Mexico. They were anxious to be *there*, but fortune did not favor them." [17]

After the speeches, everyone sat down to eat. Most of the volunteers had not seen so much food since they had left their home states a year earlier. In Memphis, the tables were lined up end to end for almost a quarter of a mile, while in Lexington, Kentucky, the tables covered over two acres and the people ate in shifts, women first. The veterans of the North Carolina regiment were undoubtedly typical in their assault upon the assortment of eatables. A local newspaper noted that they "did ample justice to the luxuries under which the table groaned." Sometimes these parties lasted all day and into the night. And an Ohio soldier felt moved to remark, "Such a reception is worth a year's campaign." The men were truly glad to be home. [18]

Many returning veterans used their temporary hero's status as springboards to other things. The fact of military service undoubtedly won votes for veterans choosing to run for elective office. Indeed, General Taylor became president of the United States in 1849. And in 1852, Franklin Pierce, who had served as a general of volunteers, defeated General Scott for that same office. Across the nation, many veterans found themselves elected to local and state offices, or to Congress.

By the time the young soldiers of 1846–1848 began to reach their middle years, the nation was torn asunder by another war, a civil war. Exactly how many men returned to uniform for this war is impossible to know, but a great number of high-ranking officers on each side were veterans of the Mexican campaigns. The highest-ranking officer in each army, Robert E. Lee and Ulysses S. Grant, had each served in Mexico, and served with distinction. Generals Meade, McClellan, Bragg, D. H. Hill, and Thomas "Stonewall" Jackson all had Mexican campaign experience. And Confederate President Jefferson Davis had led the First Mississippi Rifles in the earlier conflict. In addition, a large number of company grade officers during the Mexican War led regiments in the later conflict, and former enlisted volunteers became company commanders.

Immediately following this second, more bitter conflict, Mexican War veterans in California began to organize under the direction of

Alexander Kenaday, who hoped to raise enough money to prevent county hospitals from sending the bodies of indigent veterans to medical schools. In 1874, delegates from thirty-three states met in the nation's capital and founded the National Association of Mexican War Veterans. The stated reason for the organization was to promote camaraderie and good fellowship among the surviving soldiers, but Kenaday and others worked tirelessly for government pensions for their comrades. It had taken until 1871 for the veterans of the War of 1812 to get pensions, and Kenaday asked the government to provide eight dollars per month to all Mexican War veterans with over sixty days' service. Congress finally granted this pension in 1887, but with reservations. Only those men who were either over the age of sixty-two or were no longer able to do physical labor could qualify. A further restriction kept any Mexican War veterans who had later served in the Confederacy from receiving government benefits. There were occasional increases in these pensions until, by 1903, the few surviving soldiers from the war with Mexico received the grand sum of twelve dollars per month (with the exception of former Confederates).[19]

CHAPTER 12

Epilogue

The American soldiers who fought in Mexico were like American soldiers in other wars in many ways. And in many ways they differed. The soldiers of the 1840s went off to war with a feeling of personal and national invincibility that was not often expressed in earlier conflicts but that American soldiers embraced avidly for the next hundred years. The soldiers of these later wars also shared a supreme confidence in their abilities to vanquish any enemy.

Those who volunteered for military service against Mexico took part in a very different kind of war than had faced their predecessors in uniform. It was a relatively short conflict in which American armies were universally victorious in major battles. It was also, from the beginning, a war of conquest against an ethnically dissimilar enemy. None of these factors by themselves are unique to the Mexican War, but taken together they set this war apart from all others and caused the experiences of those who took part in it to be unlike what American soldiers in most other wars encountered.

Lasting for approximately sixteen months, from the opening shots at Palo Alto until the capture of the enemy capital, the Mexican War was longer than the Spanish-American War, about the same length as American involvement in World War I, and shorter than all except the Persian Gulf War. This brevity worked to the benefit of the individual soldiers' perceptions of their roles in the war since it kept antiwar sentiment among American civilians to a minimum. This is not to say that there was no opposition to this war, only that the fighting did not drag on interminably and allow this resistance to fester and grow. Although there was a certain amount of political contrariness, particularly among the Whigs, the war ended before it reached the lengths to which the Federalists went during the War of 1812, or the Peace Democrats—or Copperheads—during the Civil War. The war with Mexico also produced very little in the way of organized popular protest. Even though the people on the home front undoubtedly grieved for their loved ones who died in the fighting or in their sick beds, it was all over before these emotions could be galvanized into widespread antiwar sentiments. Longer conflicts, such as the Civil War and the Vietnam War, did give rise to large segments of the population actively demonstrating against them.

Closely associated with the shortness of the Mexican War was the overwhelming success that United States forces enjoyed in battle. Every one of the major encounters with Mexican troops resulted in American victory. (The only other wars with such records were the Persian Gulf War, our shortest war, the Spanish American War and —according to some historians—the Vietnam War, our longest.) This unbroken string of triumphs made the war much more palatable to both the American public and the soldiers. It was still difficult to accept the loss of a son or brother in battle, but knowing that he died in a winning effort engendered a certain sense of pride and, no doubt, alleviated some of the emotional pain. The triumphant progress of the war also made it difficult for any sort of a popular antiwar movement to get started.[1]

The combination of a war that was both short in duration and of unparalleled success militarily meant that the supply of willing enlistees was sufficient to carry on the war. In spite of the fact that General Scott had to postpone his campaign to capture Mexico City until fresh volunteers arrived to replace those whose enlistments had expired, the government was able to raise these troops without resorting to conscription.

This facet of the war lends itself quite easily to historical speculation. For example, what would have happened if the Mexicans defending Monterrey had been able to hold out against Taylor's army, forcing him to invest the city in a long-term siege? Or what if Santa Anna had defeated Taylor at Buena Vista? What would have been the effect if Mexican troops had been able to raise the siege of Veracruz, or if they had defeated Scott's army at Cerro Gordo? Each of these scenarios would have resulted, at the very least, in much heavier American casualties, and would have undermined popular backing of the war. This loss of support might then have translated itself into smaller and smaller numbers of men willing to risk their lives by going into the army. This in turn would have meant that the only way to prosecute the war with any hope of success would be with some sort of forced enlistment of soldiers.

Conscription, or the draft, was a fixture of every other American war, except the war with Spain and the Persian Gulf War, and was often the focus of antiwar sentiment in the public. During the Civil War bloody antidraft riots swept New York City in the summer of 1863, and southerners, whose draft laws had gone into effect a year earlier, complained about its loopholes allowing wealthy planters to avoid service. World War I saw over three hundred thousand draft resisters; and the use of draftees to fight in Vietnam was one of the key elements of the antiwar movement of the 1960s and 1970s. It seems reasonable to assume, therefore, that had a military draft been necessary to prosecute the Mexican War, it would have had an adverse effect on civilian sentiment for the war.

At least as important as the impact on the public, conscription would have weakened morale among the troops. As was evidenced by events during the Civil War, those men who had to be forced into service bore a certain stigma that the regulars and volunteers found repulsive. In Mexico the antagonism between regulars and volunteers —and even among volunteers from different states—proved disruptive of good order in some instances. If the progress of the war had been such that conscription became necessary, the addition of this third category of soldier would have intensified this rivalry even further.

The short, successful war with Mexico also affected how the American troops maintained such a low opinion of their enemy. The war did not last long enough for them to develop anything akin to admiration of the Mexican soldiers' valor. In longer wars, such as the Civil War, Americans in uniform have exhibited a grudging respect for the fighting abilities of their enemies, but only after this respect had been earned by battlefield successes. Rarely did an American soldier in Mexico ever express any admiration for the bravery of Santa Anna's troops.

The Mexican War was a war of conquest. The United States has increased its landholdings as the result of warfare more than once, a fact to which the American Indians can readily attest. The war with Mexico, however, represents the only time that the nation went to war with another "civilized" nation with the express purpose of gaining territory from that country. Even the American occupation of the Philippines in 1898, although certainly the goal of many businessmen in this country, had not been one of President McKinley's initial war aims.

The fact that this was an offensive war, waged to gain control of large tracts of land adjacent to the United States, undoubtedly affected how the volunteers viewed themselves as active participants in this war. To some it almost must have seemed as if they were taking part in a holy crusade bent on liberating vast stretches of territory from the Mexican "infidels." A Tennessean was one of many volunteers who commented upon the richness of the lands along the Rio Grande River, and he matter-of-factly noted that "it will rival the coast of Louisiana in the cultivation of Sugar and Cotton whenever the direction of American enterprise shall tend to this country."[2]

Even if the soldiers did not consciously make such comparisons, some surely must have considered the possibilities of starting new lives for themselves in the newly acquired lands. One large group of soldiers that definitely considered the effects of opening up new areas for American settlement in the West was the Mormon Battalion. One of the main selling points that army officers used to get the Mormons to enlist was the fact that California—as yet only sparsely settled and therefore not hostile to their unconventional beliefs—offered them a rich new land in which to build their communities.

The fact that the volunteers of 1846 and 1847 were to take part in a foreign war was also an important factor. Although earlier American soldiers, in the wars against Great Britain, had left their home neighborhoods and sometimes had traveled considerable distances to fight, they had, for the most part, remained within the United States. The war with Mexico offered a chance for young Americans to go to a foreign country, a country that many of them regarded as strange and romantic. In an age when most Americans probably never left their home county, much less their state, this war offered a chance to visit the exotic lands of the tropics. Although few volunteers openly admitted that they enlisted for this reason, many of them had read the travel books of William H. Prescott and Madame Calderon de la Barca and wished to experience the sights and sounds therein described. The attraction of service in a foreign land did not again provide young men with the incentive to enlist until the war with Spain in 1898, but from that time onward recruiters have actively played upon the lure of faraway lands to gain enlistees.[3]

During both the American Revolution and the War of 1812, American soldiers faced an enemy not ethnically different from themselves. Racist feelings colored relations with warring Indian tribes, but in the war against Mexico the soldiers gave full voice to their intense racial animosity toward the enemy. Soldiers during the Civil War, particularly during the early stages, certainly exhibited a similar hostility toward the other side, but this hatred seems based more upon perceived cultural differences than any racial aspects. By the twentieth century, heightened feelings of racism were no longer a mere byproduct of foreign wars but an active tool to gain popular support for these wars. In 1917, George Creel's Committee on Public Information went to great lengths to label Germans as subhuman brutes. The same pattern repeated itself in World War II but then, with two enemies, the main target of racist epithets shifted to the Japanese. Editorial cartoons, recruiting posters, and Hollywood movies all portrayed the Japanese soldiers as short, bandylegged men with thick eyeglasses and prominent front teeth.

Finally, on a less noble note, it is interesting to see how the army behaved toward enemy civilians. In spite of official American policy in Mexico requiring that any and all goods taken by the soldiers be paid for, such was not always the case. Hungry soldiers often raided orange groves or corn fields for something to eat when government rations were insufficient or nonexistent. Likewise, they used fence rails for firewood with impunity. Worse, however, was the treatment meted out by some of the volunteers, notably those from Texas, to Mexican civilians. The number of citizens who were beaten, robbed, or murdered will never be known, but each such incident was a black mark on the record of the American army in Mexico. Still, however, this army was probably no worse than average with regard to such behavior in comparison with other nineteenth-century armies. In fact, one Mexican official, while decrying the excesses that American occupation forces did commit—he was astonished at their appetites for both food and liquor—nevertheless believed that their behavior consisted of "mingled barbarism and restraint."[4]

In Mexico there was no need to wage all-out war, as General Sherman did in Georgia in 1864. Conventional methods were very successful. And it was probably this success that went a long way toward preventing the type of destruction of civilian property that ensued during the Civil War. The American troops had not become embittered by a long, costly war. They had, after all, won every battle they fought. The absence of this bitterness probably saved a lot of Mexican property from the torch.

American soldiery during the Mexican War was not very different from the volunteer soldiers throughout American history. They believed themselves to be invincible in battle, and they complained about the food, their superiors, the weather, and the character of the enemy they faced. They viewed the enemy as being on a lower plane, and they therefore found it easier to hate and to kill in far-off Mexico.

Notes

Preface

1. Bell I. Wiley, *The Life of Johnny Reb* (New York: Bobbs-Merrill, 1943) and *The Life of Billy Yank* (New York: Bobbs-Merrill, 1951, 1952); James I. Robertson, Jr., *Soldiers Blue and Gray* (Columbia: University of South Carolina Press, 1988); Gerald F. Linderman, *Embattled Courage: The Experience of Combat in the American Civil War* (New York: Free Press, 1987); Reid Mitchell, *Civil War Soldiers: Their Expectations and Their Experiences* (New York: Viking Penguin, 1988); Joseph Allan Frank and George A. Reaves, *"Seeing the Elephant": Raw Recruits at the Battle of Shiloh* (Westport, Conn., and London: Greenwood Press, 1989); Joseph T. Glatthaar, *Forged in Battle: The Civil War Alliance of Black Soldiers and White Officers* (New York: Free Press, 1990).

2. James Kirby Martin and Mark Edward Lender, *A Respectable Army: The Military Origins of the Republic, 1763–1789* (Arlington Heights, Ill.: Harlan Davidson, 1982); Charles Royster, *A Revolutionary People at War: The Continental Army and American Character, 1775–1783* (Chapel Hill: University of North Carolina Press, 1979); J. C. A. Stagg, "Enlisted Men in the United States Army, 1812–1815: A Survey," *William and Mary Quarterly*, 3d ser., 43, no. 4 (October 1986): 615–45; Edward M. Coffman, *The Old Army: A Portrait of the American Army in Peacetime, 1784–1898* (New York and Oxford: Oxford University Press, 1986); Lee Kennett, *G.I.: The American Soldier in World War II* (New York: Scribner's, 1987); Norman Longmate, *The G.I.s: The Americans in Britain, 1942–1945* (New York: Scribner's, 1975).

1. "War Exists by the Act of Mexico Herself"

1. George Meade, comp., *The Life and Letters of George Gordon Meade*, 2 vols. (New York: Scribner's, 1913), 1: 47–48.

2. James K. Polk to the Senate and House of Representatives, May 11, 1846, in James D. Richardson, ed., *A Compilation of the Messages and Papers of the Presidents, 1789–1897* (Washington, D.C.; Government Printing Office, 1897), 4: 442.

3. "An Act providing for the prosecution of the existing war between the United States and the Republic of Mexico," approved May 13, 1846, in John F. Callan, ed., *The Military Laws of the United States, relating to the Army, Volunteers, Militia, and to Bounty Lands and Pensions, from the Foundation of the Government to the Year 1863* (Philadelphia: George W. Childs, 1863), 367.

4. H. [D. H. Hill], "The Battles of the Rio Grande," *Southern Quarterly Review*, n.s., 2, no. 4 (November 1850): 437; H. [D. H. Hill], "Taylor's Battles in Mexico," *Harper's New Monthly Magazine* 11, no. 62 (1855): 172.

5. Barna Upton, "Our First Foreign War," ed. William F. Goetzmann, *American Heritage* 17, no. 4 (1966): 89.

6. E. K. Smith to his sister, n.d., Smith-Kirby-Webster-Black-Danner Family Collection, MHI.

7. George A. McCall, *Letters From the Frontiers: Written during a Period of Thirty Years' Service in the Army of the United States* (Philadelphia: J. B. Lippincott, 1868), 452; James Duncan to W. G. Belknap, May 12, 1846, James Duncan Collection, USMA; Upton, 89.

8. Richard H. Coolidge, comp., *Statistical Report on the Sickness and Mortality in the Army of the United States, Compiled from the Records of the Surgeon General's Office, Embracing a Period of Sixteen Years, from January, 1839 to January, 1855* (Washington, D.C.: A. O. P. Nicholson, 1856), 611; K. Jack Bauer, *The Mexican War, 1846–1848* (New York: Macmillan, 1974), 57.

9. Upton, 89.

10. George Deas, "Reminiscences of the Campaign on the Rio Grande," *Dawson's Historical Magazine* 17, no. 2 (1870): 102; W. S. Henry, *Campaign Sketches of the War with Mexico* (New York: Harper and Brothers, 1847; repr. New York: Arno Press, 1973), 158.

11. Henry, 97.

12. Bauer, 62.

13. Coolidge, 611; Bauer, 62.

14. Sumner C. Brooks to his mother, Mrs. Charlotte Sargent, July 3, 1846, Sumner C. Brooks Collection, Yale; James Duncan to W. G. Belknap, May 12, 1846, James Duncan Collection, USMA; [Ramon Alcaraz, et al.], *The Other Side; or, Notes for the History of the War between Mexico and the United States*, trans. Albert C. Ramsey (New York: John Wiley, 1850), 53.

15. Bauer, 62.

16. Robert Hazlitt to Mary Hazlitt, July 28, 1846, Robert Hazlitt Collection, USMA.

17. H. [D. H. Hill], "The Battles of the Rio Grande," 444.

2. To the Colors

1. Emory Upton, *The Military Policy of the United States* (1904; repr. New York: Greenwood Press, 1968), 196, 200.

2. Walter Millis, *Arms and Men: A Study of American Military History* (New York: G. P. Putnam's, 1956), 51; "An Act providing for the prosecution of the existing war between the United States and the Republic of Mexico," approved May 13, 1846, in John F. Callan, ed., *The Military Laws of the United States, relating to the Army, Volunteers, Militia, and to Bounty Lands and Pensions, from the Foundation of the Government to the Year 1863* (Philadelphia: George W. Childs, 1863), 367–69, 374.

3. Paul T. Smith, "Militia of the United States from 1846 to 1860," *Indiana Magazine of History* (March 1919): 26–29. "Report of the Adjutant General of the Indiana Militia to the Governor, December 4, 1846," in Oran Perry, comp., *Indiana in the Mexican War* (Indianapolis: William B. Burford, 1908), 110; Dunbar Rowland, *Military History of Mississippi, 1803–1898* (repr. ed. Spartanburg, S.C.: Reprint Company, 1978), 15; Steven B. Michael, "Ohio and the Mexican War: Public Response to the 1846–1848 Crisis" (Ph.D. diss., Ohio State University, 1985), 10; Federal Writer's Project, *Military History of Kentucky* (Frankfort, Ky.: Works Progress Administration, 1939), 123–24.

4. K. Jack Bauer, *The Mexican War* (New York: Macmillan, 1974), 71.

5. James Wylie Gettys, Jr., " 'To Conquer a Peace': South Carolina and the Mexican War" (Ph.D. diss., University of South Carolina, 1974), 178–79; Theophilus Parvin to Mrs. Ann E. Harrison, June 17, 1846, Theophilus Parvin Papers, Ind H.

6. Barna Upton, "Our First Foreign War," ed. William F. Goetzmann, *American Heritage* 17, no. 4 (1966): 93; George Meade, comp., *The Life and Letters of George Gordon Meade*, 2 vols. (New York: Scribner's, 1913), 1: 154.

7. DeWitt Clinton Loudon diary, June 3, 1846, DeWitt Clinton Loudon Collection, Ohio; Robert W. Johannsen, *To the Halls of the Montezumas: The Mexican War in the American Imagination* (New York: Oxford University Press, 1985), 11; WPA, *Kentucky*, 124; Justin H. Smith, *The War with Mexico*, 2 vols. (New York: Macmillan, 1919; repr. Gloucester, Mass.: Peter Smith, 1963), 1: 195; Claude M. Fuess, *The Life of Caleb Cushing*, 2 vols. (New York: Harcourt, Brace, 1923), 2: 34–35.

8. Frankfort *Commonwealth*, June 8, 1846, cited in WPA, *Kentucky*, 126–27.

9. George F. Holmes to his mother, May 27, 1846, John Warfield Johnston papers, Duke.

10. Sydenham Moore diary, June 4, 1846, Sydenham Moore Collection, Ala; Johannsen, 27; Turner J. Fakes, Jr., "Memphis and the Mexican War," *West Tennessee Historical Society Papers* 2 (1948): 119; Rowland, 19, 28; Thomas

H. Kreneck, "The Lone Star Volunteers: A History of Texas Participation in the Mexican War" (M.A. thesis, University of Houston, 1973), 50–51.

11. "An Act providing for the prosecution of the existing war between the United States and the Republic of Mexico," approved May 13, 1846, in Callan, 367; Sydenham Moore diary, June 1846, Sydenham Moore Collection, Ala; Justin H. Smith, 1: 351.

12. Lee Alphonso Wallace, Jr., "North Carolina in the War with Mexico" (M.A. thesis, University of North Carolina, 1950), 37.

13. J. Jacob Oswandel, *Notes of the Mexican War, 1846–47–48* (Philadelphia, 1885), 18; Samuel E. Chamberlain, *My Confession: The Recollections of a Rogue* (1956; repr. Lincoln and London: University of Nebraska Press, 1987), 31; Marcus Cunliffe, *Soldiers and Civilians: The Martial Spirit in America, 1775–1865* (Boston and Toronto: Little, Brown, 1968), 172.

14. Arkansas *Democrat*, July 10, 1846; "Presentation of Flag to Forty-Sixth Indiana Regiment Mexican War," Cass County Collection, Ind L.

15. Arkansas *Democrat*, July 10, 1846.

16. DeWitt Clinton Loudon diary, June 6, 1846, DeWitt Clinton Loudon Collection, Ohio; Sydenham Moore diary, May 26, 1846, Sydenham Moore Collection, Ala.

17. "An Act supplemental to an Act entitled 'An Act providing for the prosecution of the existing war between the United States and the Republic of Mexico,' and for other purposes," approved June 18, 1846, in Callan, 374; Perry, 115; Ernest M. Lander, Jr., "The Palmetto Regiment Goes to Mexico," *Proceedings of the South Carolina Historical Association* (1973): 85; George Cassel Bittle, "In the Defense of Florida: The Organized Florida Militia from 1821 to 1920" (Ph.D. diss., Florida State University, 1965), 185; Fuess, 2: 38.

18. *General Regulations for the Army of the United States, 1847* (Washington, D.C., 1847), 140.

19. Thomas Henderson, *Hints on the Medical Examination of Recruits for the Army and on the Discharge of Soldiers from the Service on Surgeon's Certificate* (1840; rev. ed. by Richard H. Coolidge, Philadelphia: J. B. Lippincott, 1856), 79–80.

20. Ibid., 87–90.

21. Robert R. Ritchie to Thomas Ritchie, June 18–19, 1847, Ritchie-Harrison Collection, WM; *Indiana Sentinel*, June 27, 1846, cited in Perry, 70.

22. Zo. S. Cook, "Mexican War Reminiscences," *Alabama Historical Quarterly* 19 (1957): 438–39.

23. Leo E. Oliva, "Missouri Volunteers on the Santa Fe Trail, 1847–1848," *Trail Guide* 15, no. 3 (September 1970): 4; Thomas L. Karnes, "Gilpin's Volunteers on the Santa Fe Trail," *Kansas Historical Quarterly* 30, no. 1 (Spring 1964): 5–6.

24. *The Female Volunteer; or, The Life and Wonderful Adventures of Miss Eliza Allen, a Young Lady of Eastport, Maine,* cited by Robert W. Johannsen in *To The*

Halls of the Montezumas: The Mexican War in the American Imagination (New York and Oxford: Oxford University Press, 1985), 137; Indiana *Democrat*, June 22, 1846, cited by Perry, 65.

25. Henderson, 32.

26. Ibid., 32–33.

27. *General Regulations of the Army of the United States, 1841* (Washington, D.C., 1841), 122.

28. Frederick P. Todd, *American Military Equipage, 1851–1872* (Providence, R.I.: Company of Military Historians, 1974), 43; S. F. Nunnelee to Dr. W. S. Wyman, June 14, 1906, in "Alabama in Mexico War," *Alabama Historical Quarterly* 19 (1957): 417; Joseph Davis Howell to his mother, September 25, 1846, William Burr Howell and Family Collection, Miss.

29. *Standard*, July 1, 1846, cited by Lee Alphonso Wallace, Jr., 40; *General Regulations for the Army, 1835* (Washington, D.C., 1835), 209.

30. Benjamin A. Gould, *Investigations in the Military and Anthropological Statistics of American Soldiers* (New York, 1869), 34, 38, 86–88, cited by Bell Irvin Wiley in *The Life of Billy Yank: The Common Soldier of the Union* (New York: Bobbs-Merrill, 1951), 299, 302–3; published Mexican War muster rolls for one company of Virginia volunteers, one company of Arkansas volunteers, and all five Florida volunteer companies yields an average age of 25.68 years for 1,960 men. A random sampling of 388 men who enlisted in the regular army between 1846 and 1848 indicates that 74.5 percent of them fell within the twenty- to thirty-year-old age bracket. Virgil A. Lewis, *The Soldiery of West Virginia in the French and Indian War, Lord Dunmore's War, the Revolution, the Later Indian Wars, the Whiskey Insurrection, the Second War with England, the War with Mexico, and Addenda relating to West Virginians in the Civil War* (State of West Virginia; repr. ed. Baltimore: Genealogical Publishing, 1972), 188–89; "Capt. Stephen B. Enyart's Company: Arkansas Mounted Rifles," *Flashback* 5, no. 3 (1955): 17–19; State of Florida, Department of Military Affairs, *Compiled Muster and Service Records Florida Militia Volunteers, War with Mexico, 1846–1848*, Special Archives publication no. 9 (St. Augustine, Fla.: State Arsenal, n.d.); *Registers of Enlistments in the U.S. Army, 1798–1941, vol. 45, July 1846–May 1848; (National Archives Microfilm Publication M233), roll 22, Records of the Adjutant General's Office, 1780s-1917, Record Group 94*, National Archives, Washington, D.C.

31. Wiley, *Billy Yank*, 304; *Registers of Enlistments*.

32. Edward M. Coffman, *The Old Army: A Portrait of the American Army in Peacetime, 1784–1898* (New York and Oxford: Oxford University Press, 1986), 141. A random sample of 1,024 regular army recruits during the Mexican War reveals that 41.6 percent were foreigners. *Registers of Enlistments*.

33. Wiley, *Billy Yank*, 307–8.

34. Coffman, 144–45; John P. Brock to his sister Amanda J. Brock, April 24, 1847, Brock Collection, WM; *Northern Standard* (Clarksville, Texas), February 13, 1847.

35. Richard Reinhardt, " 'To a Distant and Perilous Service,' " *American Heritage* 30, no. 4 (June-July 1979): 68.

36. DeWitt Clinton Loudon to his father, Gen. James Loudon, June 3, 1846, DeWitt Clinton Loudon Collection, Ohio.

37. Portsmouth (Virginia) *New Era*, December 8, 1846, as cited by John Edward Buck, Jr., "Virginia and the Mexican War" (M.A. thesis, University of North Carolina at Chapel Hill, 1965), 42.

38. William A. Hall to his sister Lydia Marmion, June 10, 1846, Willard P. Hall Collection, Mo H; T. H. Towner to his father, February 12, 1847, Benjamin T. Towner Collection, Duke.

39. T. H. Towner to his father, April 14, 1847, Benjamin T. Towner Collection, Duke; J. Glenn Gray, *The Warriors: Reflections on Men in Battle* (New York: Harcourt Brace Jovanovich, 1959), 29; William Broyles, Jr., "Why Men Love War," *Esquire*, November 1984, 58.

40. *Northern Standard* (Clarksville, Texas), May 13, 1846, cited by Allan Robert Purcell in "The History of the Texas Militia, 1835–1903" (Ph.D. diss., University of Texas, 1981), 94; James E. Winston, "Kentucky and the Independence of Texas," *Southwestern Historical Quarterly* 16, no. 1 (July 1912): 28.

41. WPA, *Kentucky*, 122–23; James E. Winston, "Pennsylvania and the Independence of Texas," *Southwestern Historical Quarterly* 17, no. 3 (January 1914): 266–67; Jewel Davis Scarborough, "The Georgia Battalion in the Texas Revolution: A Critical Study," *Southwestern Historical Quarterly* 62, no. 4 (April 1960): 514; Claude Elliott, "Alabama and the Texas Revolution," *Southwestern Historical Quarterly* 50, no. 3 (January 1947): 327.

42. Wilbur G. Kurtz, Jr., "The First Regiment of Georgia Volunteers in the Mexican War," *Georgia Historical Quarterly* 27, no. 4 (December 1943): 307; T. E. Dansbee to his brother and sister, October 14, 1846, T. E. Dansbee Collection, Tenn; Albert Gallatin Cooper diary, October 20, 1846, Cooper Collection, Tenn; Wiley P. Hale to his mother, December 28, 1846, Wiley P. Hale Collection, Tenn; W. Austine to his cousin, April 23, 1847, William Austine Collection, UNC; Charles J. Sellon to Marilla Woods, September 6, 1846, Charles J. Sellon Collection, Ill; Henry Farno to his wife, September 21, 1846, Henry Farno Collection, LSU.

3. Off to War

1. "Report of the Adjutant General in reply to Resolution of the House of Representatives dated July 31, 1848," cited in Marvin A. Kreidberg and Merton G. Henry, *History of Military Mobilization in the United States Army, 1775–1945* (Westport, Conn.: Greenwood Press, 1955), 78.

2. Captain Maynardier, Ordnance Office, to Adjutant General, June 13, 1846; and Col. George Talcott, Ordnance Office, to Gen. John E. Wool, June 5, 1846, *Letters Received by the Office of the Adjutant General (main series), 1822–*

*1860 (National Archives Microfilm Publication M567), rolls 321 and 329, respec-
tively, Records of the Adjutant General's Office, 1780s-1917, Record Group 94, National Archives, Washington, D.C.*

3. Federal Writer's Project, *Military History of Kentucky* (Frankfort, Ky.:
Works Progress Administration, 1939), 128; Zo. S. Cook, "Mexican War
Reminiscences," *Alabama Historical Quarterly* 19 (1957): 437–38.

4. Cook, 438.

5. "Adjutant General's Report for 1845," in *Documents Including Messages
and Other Communications Made to the 44th General Assembly of the State of Ohio*
(Columbus: C. Scott and Co., 1846) 10, pt. 1: 456–57; Paul T. Smith, "Militia
in the United States from 1846 to 1860," *Indiana Magazine of History* (March
1919): 37.

6. "War Department Annual Report," 1840, 58; 1844, 296; 1845, 403;
1846, 147; 1847, 684; 1848, 343, in *Annual Reports of the War Department, 1822–
1907 (National Archives Microfilm Publication M997), rolls 7, 8, and 9, National
Archives, Washington, D.C.*

7. G. Talcott to Col. J. B. Walbach, August 30, 1845, *Records of Various
Ordnance Boards, 1846–1868, Proceedings, March 1846–Sept. 1863, Jan.-Feb. 1868,
Textual Records of the Office of the Chief of Ordnance, Record Group 156, National
Archives, Washington, D.C.*; New Orleans *Times Democrat*, December 6, 1889,
cited by James T. McIntosh, ed., *The Papers of Jefferson Davis* (Baton Rouge:
Louisiana State University Press, 1981), 3: 17.

8. Claud E. Fuller, *The Rifled Musket* (New York: Bonanza Books, 1958),
3; "Records of the firings and opinions of The Board assembled at the Washington Arsenal for the Trial of Small Arms according to Special Orders No.
23 War Department, February 1st 1860," in Fuller, 55, 148; Jac Weller, "Civil
War Minie Rifles Prove Quite Accurate," *American Rifleman*, July 1971, 36–40;
Ulysses S. Grant, *Personal Memoirs of U.S. Grant*, 2 vols. (New York: Charles
L. Webster, 1885), 1: 95.

9. William B. Campbell, "Mexican War Letters of Col. William Bowen
Campbell, of Tennessee, Written to Governor David Campbell, of Virginia,
1846–1847," ed. St. George L. Sioussat, *Tennessee Historical Magazine* 1, no. 2
(1915): 139.

10. S. F. Nunnelee, "Alabama in Mexico War," *Alabama Historical Quarterly* 19 (1957): 420.

11. Samuel Cooper, *A Concise System of Instruction and Regulations for the
Militia and Volunteers of the United States* (Philadelphia: Robert P. DeSilver,
1836), 10, 24; William Gilham, *Manual of Instruction for Volunteers and Militia of
the United States* (Philadelphia: Charles DeSilver, 1861), 88; Gustavus W.
Smith, *Company "A," Corps. of Engineers, U.S.A., 1846–'48, in the Mexican War*
(Willets Point, N.Y.: Battalion Press, 1896), 8–9.

12. Dan Runyon to his father, Asa R. Runyon, October 4, 1847, Runyon
Family Collection, Filson.

13. John H. Towner Papers, Ind H; Wilbur G. Kurtz, Jr., "The First Regiment of Georgia Volunteers in the Mexican War," *Georgia Historical Quarterly* 27, no. 4 (December 1943): 313–14.

14. Richard Reinhardt, " 'To a Distant and Perilous Service,' " *American Heritage* 30, no. 4 (June-July 1979): 70; David B. Tower journal, November 4, 1847, Ill; Thomas D. Tennery, *The Mexican War Diary of Thomas D. Tennery*, ed. D. E. Livingston-Little (Norman: University of Oklahoma Press, 1970), 7; James Wylie Gettys, Jr., " 'To Conquer a Peace': South Carolina and the Mexican War" (Ph.D. diss., University of South Carolina, 1974), 215, 231; Thomas T. Summers to his brother, June 3, 1846, Thomas T. Summers Collection, Filson.

15. James L. McClaughlin to ?, July 7, 1846, McClaughlin Family Collection, Tenn; William B. Taliaferro diary, July 25, 1847, Va A; Augustus Ehinger diary, July 16, 1846, Augustus Ehinger Collection, Rice; John Campbell to his father, July 6, 1847, John Campbell Collection, U Va.

16. Daniel Runyon to his sister Mary, November 6, 1847, Runyon Family Collection, Filson; John Campbell to his father, July 14, 1847, John Campbell Collection, U Va.

17. William B. Taliaferro diary, July 29, 1847, Va A.

18. Daniel Runyon to his brother David, November 19, 1847, Runyon Family Collection, Filson; John Campbell to his father, July 6, 1847, U Va; F. M. G. to the *Brookville American*, August 21, 1846, cited in Oran Perry, comp., *Indiana in the Mexican War* (Indianapolis: William B. Burford, 1908), 83.

19. J. Jacob Oswandel, *Notes of the Mexican War 1846–47–48* (Philadelphia, 1885), 55; Nathaniel Eaves to C. D. Milton, February 14, 1847, Nathaniel Ridley Eaves Collection, USC; Franklin Smith diary, August 13, 1847, Miss; James Reilly, "An Artilleryman's Story," *Journal of the Military Service Institution of the United States* 33, no. 126 (1903): 440.

20. Joseph Evans, "Around Cape Horn with Colonel Stevenson's Regiment in 1846," *Quarterly of the Society of California Pioneers* 7, no. 4 (1930): 245–46; John M. Hollingsworth, "Journal of John McHenry Hollingsworth: A Lieutenant in Stevenson's Regiment in California," *California Historical Society Quarterly* 1, no. 3 (January 1923): 213.

21. Reinhardt, 74.

22. Evans, 247–49; Reinhardt, 75.

23. H. Dailey to his father, August 12, 1846, David W. Dailey Collection, Ind H; Madison Mills diary, March 24, 1846, Filson; John W. Lowe diary, October 30, 1847, John Williamson Lowe Collection, Dayton; Daniel Runyon to his brother David, November 19, 1847, Runyon Family Collection, Filson; Wiley P. Hale to his mother, July 26, 1846, Wiley P. Hale Collection, Tenn.

24. Sydenham Moore diary, June 29, 1846, Sydenham Moore Collection, Ala; Edward A. Giller to Marcus North, May 2, 1847, Edward A. Giller Collection, Ill; Albert Gallatin Cooper diary, November 17, 1846, Tenn; John Campbell to Arch, November 11, 1847, John Campbell Collection, U Va;

William E. P——to Frances Milroy, April 28, 1847, Mildred Knight Richardson Collection, Ind L; Henry S. Lane, "The Mexican War Journal of Henry S. Lane," ed. Graham A. Barringer, *Indiana Magazine of History* 53, no. 4 (1957): 417; Jacob Latture to his brother and sister, March 14, 1848, Jacob Latture Collection, Yale; John W. Lowe to his wife's father and mother, November 1, 1847, John Williamson Lowe Collection, Dayton.

4. *"Nearly All Who Take Sick Die"*

1. Richard H. Coolidge, comp., *Statistical Report on the Sickness and Mortality in the Army of the United States, Compiled from the Records of the Surgeon General's Office, Embracing a Period of Sixteen Years, from January, 1839 to January, 1855* (Washington, D.C.: A. O. P. Nicholson, 1856), 610; Mary C. Gillett, *The Army Medical Department, 1818–1865* (Washington, D.C.: Center of Military History, U.S. Army, 1987), 124.

2. James Mahon diary, September 9, 1846, James Mahon Collection, Ill; Sydenham Moore diary, July 25, 1846, Sydenham Moore Collection, Ala; John W. Lowe to his brother, November 18, 1847, John Williamson Lowe Collection, Dayton; James A. Ramage, "John Hunt Morgan and the Kentucky Cavalry Volunteers in the Mexican War," *Register of the Kentucky Historical Society* 81, no. 4 (Autumn 1983): 354.

3. Benjamin F. Cheatham diary, January 17, 1848, Benjamin F. Cheatham Collection, Tenn; Joshua Jackson diary, September 3, 1846, and September 8, 1846, Joshua Jackson Collection, Ill.

4. Sylvia R. Frey, *The British Soldier in America: A Social History of Military Life in the Revolutionary Period* (Austin: University of Texas Press, 1981), 28, 41; George Worthington Adams, *Doctors in Blue: The Medical History of the Union Army in the Civil War* (New York: Henry Schuman, 1952), 194–95; Robert Underwood Johnson and Clarence Clough Buell, eds., *Battles and Leaders of the Civil War*, 4 vols. (repr. ed. New York: Castle Books, 1956), 2: 603.

5. William G. Rothstein, *American Physicians in the Nineteenth Century: From Sects to Science* (Baltimore and London: Johns Hopkins University Press, 1972), 88–89; F. Campbell Stewart, "An Anniversary Address Delivered before the New York Medical and Surgical Society, on the 3d of January, 1846," in Gert H. Brieger, ed., *Medical America in the Nineteenth Century: Readings from the Literature* (Baltimore and London: Johns Hopkins University Press, 1972), 66.

6. Daniel Drake, "Selection and Preparatory Education of Pupils," in Brieger, 9.

7. Brieger, 4. At least one recent source states that doctors accompanying the volunteer regiments did not have to submit to these examinations. However, the fact that the Army Board of Medical Examiners invited sixty-three physicians to take the test before there had been an increase in the number of

surgeons allowed in the regular army indicates that these men were probably prospective surgeons for volunteer regiments. Gillett, 97.

8. P. M. Ashburn *A History of the Medical Department of the United States Army* (Boston and New York: Houghton Mifflin, 1929), 56–57.

9. Harvey E. Brown, comp., *The Medical Department of the United States Army from 1775 to 1873* (Washington, D.C.: Surgeon General's Office, 1873), 179–80, 182–83.

10. Brown, 200; John S. Haller, Jr., *American Medicine in Transition, 1840–1910* (Urbana, Chicago, and London: University of Illinois Press, 1981), 213.

11. Brown, 189; John B. Porter, "Medical and Surgical Notes of Campaigns in the War with Mexico, during the Years 1845, 1846, 1847, and 1848," *American Journal of the Medical Sciences* 26 (October 1853): 332.

12. Ashburn, 57–58.

13. Coolidge, 610.

14. R. H. Milroy to James W. Milroy, October 18, 1846, Mildred Knight Richardson Collection, Ind L; Thomas N. Love to Mrs. Cannon, September ?, 1847, Tenn.

15. John W. Lowe to O. T. Fishback, November 1, 1847, John Williamson Lowe Collection, Dayton; Harvey Neville diary, Chi.

16. John F. Bouldin to his brother James, May 3, 1847, James O. Bouldin Collection, Duke; Miles Morris diary, December 26, 1846, Ill.

17. Charles Royster, *A Revolutionary People at War: The Continental Army and American Character, 1775–1783* (New York and London: W. W. Norton, 1981), 100; Bell Irvin Wiley, *The Life of Johnny Reb* (New York: Bobbs-Merrill, 1943), 253; Gillett, 8–9.

18. Gillett, 3–4; Rothstein, 42–43.

19. J. A. Hingeston, "The Neglect of the Use of Bleeding in the Treatment of Some of the Milder Ailments," *Association Medical Journal* 1 (1854): 266, cited in Haller, 49.

20. Rothstein, 46–47; T. L. Papin, "Venesection, Its Use and Abuse," *St. Louis Medical and Surgical Journal* 17 (1859): 230, cited in Haller, 49.

21. John B. Porter, "Medical and Surgical Notes of Campaigns in the War with Mexico, during the Years 1845, 1846, 1847, and 1848," *American Journal of the Medical Sciences* 25 (January 1853): 38–39.

22. Nathaniel Chapman, "Remarks on the Chronic Fluxes of the Bowels," in Brieger, 111–12.

23. *General Regulations for the Army of the United States, 1847* (Washington, D.C., 1847), 28–29; Report of Dr. R. S. Satterlee, July 5, 1847, in Brown, 187.

24. Charles H. Lesser, ed., *The Sinews of Independence: Monthly Strength Reports of the Continental Army* (Chicago and London: University of Chicago Press, 1976), xxx-xxxi; Bell Irvin Wiley, *The Life of Billy Yank* (New York: Bobbs-Merrill, 1952), 124; Paul E. Steiner, *Disease in the Civil War: Natural*

Biological Warfare in 1861–1865 (Springfield, Ill.: Charles C. Thomas, 1968), 13.

25. Richard McSherry, "A Mexican Campaign Sketch," *New Eclectic* 3 (1868): 329; George M. Burton to his brother, October 8, 1847, George M. Burton Collection, Ill; Ulysses S. Grant to Julia Dent, February 25, 1847, cited in Roger G. Miller, "Yellow Jack at Vera Cruz," *Prologue* 10 (Spring 1978): 47.

26. Miller, 44.

27. Ibid., 44–45; Gillett, 10; E. H. Barton, "Means of Preserving Health at Vera Cruz," *Boston Medical and Surgical Journal* 36, no. 24 (1847): 484; Daniel Runyon to his father, May 20, 1848, Runyon Family Collection, Filson.

28. Miller, 50.

29. John B. Porter, "Medical and Surgical Notes of Campaigns in the War with Mexico, during the Years 1845, 1846, 1847, and 1848," *American Journal of the Medical Sciences* 26 (October 1853): 312–16; Miller, 50; Rothstein, 50; Louis C. Duncan, "Medical History of General Scott's Campaign to the City of Mexico in 1847," *Military Surgeon* 47, no. 4 (1920): 445.

30. Coolidge, 605; James L. McCloughlin to his father, James Mc-Cloughlin, Sr., September 5, 1846, McCloughlin Family Collection, Tenn.

5. *"Reptiles in the Path of Progressive Democracy"*

1. Reginald Horsman, *Race and Manifest Destiny: The Origins of American Racial Anglo-Saxonism* (Cambridge, Mass., and London: Harvard University Press, 1981), 87, 92–93, 219.

2. D. D. Mitchell to Judge R. Wash, October 17, 1846, T. C. Link Collection, Mo H.

3. Sydenham Moore diary, January 11, 1847, Sydenham Moore Collection, Ala; Robert Hagan diary, March 10, 1848, Robert Hagan Collection, UT; Henry Smith Lane to Samuel Stone, November 5, 1846, Henry Smith Lane Collection, Filson; Wiley P. Hale to his mother, July 26, 1846, Wiley P. Hale Collection, Tenn; W. S. Henry, *Campaign Sketches of the War with Mexico* (New York: Harper and Brothers, 1847; repr. ed. New York: Arno Press, 1973), 120–21; Frank Hardy to his brother Horace, October 31, 1846, Frank Hardy Collection, Ohio.

4. Horsman, 229; John Moragne to his sister Mary E. Dervis, January 24, 1847, Mary Elizabeth Moragne Collection, USC; Henry Smith Lane to Samuel Stone, November 5, 1846, Henry Smith Lane Collection, Filson.

5. Henry Smith Lane to Samuel Stone, November 5, 1846, Henry Smith Lane Collection, Filson; James H. Hammond to John Y. Mason, January 13, 1846, in James Wylie Gettys, Jr., " 'To Conquer a Peace': South Carolina and the Mexican War" (Ph.D. diss., University of South Carolina, 1974), 372; John Cantey to his cousin, March 6, 1848, John Cantey Collection, Duke.

6. Sam Houston, *Writings of Sam Houston*, 8 vols., eds. Amelia W. Williams and Eugene C. Barker (Austin: University of Texas Press, 1938–1943), 5: 34–35, cited by Horsman, 243; Sydenham Moore diary, January 11, 1847, Sydenham Moore Collection, Ala; Horsman, 236.

7. Arnoldo De Leon, *They Called Them Greasers: Anglo Attitudes toward Mexicans in Texas, 1821–1900* (Austin: University of Texas Press, 1983), 4–5; David J. Weber, " 'Scarce more than apes': Historical Roots of Anglo American Stereotypes of Mexicans in the Border Region," in David J. Weber, ed., *New Spain's Far Northern Frontier: Essays on Spain in the American West, 1540–1821* (Albuquerque: University of New Mexico Press, 1979), 299.

8. De Leon, 36; Weber, 302; Winthrop D. Jordan, *White over Black: American Attitudes toward the Negro, 1550–1812* (Chapel Hill: University of North Carolina Press, 1968); Robert F. Berkhofer, Jr., *The White Man's Indian: Images of the American Indian from Columbus to the Present* (New York: Knopf, 1978).

9. Frances Calderon de la Barca, *Life in Mexico* (1843; repr. ed. New York: Dutton, 1970), 45; Andrew White to George W. Chase, May 30, 1846, George W. Chase Collection, LSU; Lewis Dunnels to Christian Cook [Koch], September 19, 1846, Christian D. Koch and Family Collection, LSU; Charles H. Brough to his wife, August 12, 1847, Charles H. Brough Collection, Ohio; Col. D. D. Mitchell to Judge R. Wash, October 17, 1846, T. C. Link Collection, Mo H.

10. E. Kirby-Smith to his sister Mrs. T. K. Smith, April 7, 1847, Edmund Kirby-Smith Collection, UNC; Stephen Franklin Nunnelee, "Incidents of a Campaign, &c—1846" (unpublished typescript), March 29, 1847, Ala; John W. Lowe to his wife, May 5, 1848, John Williamson Lowe Collection, Dayton; Charles H. Brough to his wife, February 22, 1848, Charles H. Brough Collection, Ohio.

11. John W. Lowe to Pinckney Fishback, March 9, 1848, John Williamson Lowe Collection, Dayton.

12. William B. Taliaferro diary, November 16, 1847, William B. Taliaferro Collection, Va A; Romeyn B. Ayres journal, Romeyn B. Ayres Collection, UNC; Levi White to his wife, October 10, 1846, Levi White Collection, Filson; Samuel E. Chamberlain, *My Confession: The Recollections of a Rogue* (1956; repr. Lincoln and London: University of Nebraska Press, 1987), 76.

13. Samuel Steele to William Keller, December 6, 1847, Samuel Steele Collection, Ind H; Romeyn B. Ayres journal, Romeyn B. Ayres Collection, UNC; Johann Karl Schneider to C. Schneider, November 24, 1847, trans. Dr. Wolfgang Fleischauer, Johann Karl Schneider Collection, Ohio.

14. T. H. Towner to his mother, March 16, 1847, July 21, 1847, Benjamin T. Towner Collection, Duke; DeWitt Clinton Loudon diary, October 9, 1846, DeWitt Clinton Loudon Collection, Ohio; Thomas D. Tennery, *The Mexican War Diary of Thomas D. Tennery*, ed. D. E. Livingston-Little (Norman: Univer-

sity of Oklahoma Press, 1970), 27–28; Sydenham Moore diary, December 27, 1846, Sydenham Moore Collection, Ala.

15. J. S. Arthur to David W. Daily, December 1, 1846, David W. Dailey Collection, Ind H; DeWitt Clinton Loudon diary, November 3, 1846, DeWitt Clinton Loudon Collection, Ohio; Daniel H. Hill diary, September 6, 1846, in Gettys, 344–50.

16. John W. Lowe to Pinckney Fishback, March 9, 1848, John Williamson Lowe Collection, Dayton.

17. Henry Smith Turner, "Letters about Mexican War," *Glimpses of the Past* 2, no. 2 (1934–1935): 8, 27.

18. R. H. Milroy to his sister Mrs. Abby A. Grimes, May 9, 1847, Mildred Knight Richardson Collection, Ind L; Chamberlain, 58.

19. Frank Hardy to his brother Horace, October 31, 1846; Frank Hardy Collection, Ohio; Will Wallace to his father, November 6, 1846, Wallace-Dickey Collection, Ill.

20. J. A. Merrifield to Dr. Samuel M. Bemis, March 9, 1847, Bemis Family Collection, Va H; Edmund Kirby-Smith to ?, May 20, 1846, Edmund Kirby-Smith Collection, UNC; Mexico City *Daily American Star*, February 26, 1848, cited by Robert Louis Bodson in "A Description of the United States Occupation of Mexico as Reported by American Newspapers Published in Vera Cruz, Puebla, and Mexico City, September 14, 1847, to July 31, 1848" (Ed.D. diss., Ball State University, 1971), 180–81.

21. Will Wallace to his father, November 6, 1846, Wallace-Dickey Collection, Ill; Milledge L. Bonham to Sophie Bonham, March 18, 1848, cited by Gettys, 365.

22. Jonathan R. McClanahan to his sister Mrs. James R. Taylor, August 15, 1846, McClanahan-Taylor Collection, UNC; Carr White to his sister Margaret A. White, December 6, 1846, Carr B. White Collection, Ohio; Robert Hagan diary, October 1, 1847, Robert Hagan Collection, UT; Pierce Mason Butler to his daughter, April 4, 1847, cited by Gettys, 365.

23. Wiley P. Hale to his mother, August 17, 1846, and December 28, 1846, Wiley P. Hale Collection, Tenn; G. Loomis to his niece Charity, February 23, 1848, G. Loomis Collection, LSU; Will Wallace to his sister Miss Helen M. Indson, November 16, 1846, Wallace-Dickey Collection, Ill.

24. Claude M. Fuess, *The Life of Caleb Cushing*, 2 vols. (New York: Harcourt, Brace, 1923), 2: 39; DeWitt Clinton Loudon diary, January 23, 1847, DeWitt Clinton Loudon Collection, Ohio; Bodson, 79; John Campbell to Alick, August 22, 1847, John Campbell Collection, U Va.

25. E. G. Henry to his sisters Rachel and Sarah, May 22, 1847, Bryce Family Collection, USC; Thomas T. Summers to his brothers, November 15, 1846, Thomas T. Summers Collection, Filson; William Austine to his cousin, February 28, 1847, William Austine Collection, UNC.

26. T. H. Towner to his father, April 14, 1847, Benjamin T. Towner

Collection, Duke; E. G. Henry to his sisters Rachel and Sarah, May 22, 1847, Bryce Family Collection, USC; John P. Brock to his sister Amanda J. Brock, April 24, 1847, John P. Brock Collection, WM; Charles H. Brough to his wife, January 5, 1848, Charles H. Brough Collection, Ohio; [?] to William Henry Grimes, December 14, 1847, William Henry Grimes Collection, Duke; J. A. Merrifield to Dr. Samuel M. Bemis, March 9, 1847, Bemis Family Collection, Va H; John F. Bouldin to his brother James, May 3, 1847, James O. Bouldin Collection, Duke.

27. Will Wallace to his sister Miss Helen M. Indson, November 16, 1846, Wallace-Dickey Collection, Ill.

28. W. S. Henry, *Campaign Sketches of the War with Mexico* (New York: Harper and Brothers, 1847; repr. ed. New York: Arno Press, 1973), 157–58.

29. Dayton W. Canaday, "Voice of the Volunteer of 1847," *Journal of the Illinois State Historical Society* 44, no. 3 (1951): 208.

30. Weber, 296.

31. Charles H. Brough to his wife, July 30, 1847, Charles H. Brough Collection, Ohio; N. J. T. Dana to his wife, February 14, 1847, in *Monterrey Is Ours: The Mexican War Letters of Lieutenant Dana, 1845–1847*, ed. Robert H. Ferrell (Lexington: University Press of Kentucky, 1990), 180–81; George M. Burton to a cousin, January 7, 1847 [1848], George M. Burton Collection, Ill; Levi White to his wife, October 10, 1846, Levi White Collection, Filson; Samuel V. Fulkerson journal, January 11, 1848, Samuel V. Fulkerson Collection, UT; T. H. Towner to his mother, March 28, 1848, Benjamin T. Towner Collection, Duke.

·32. Daniel Runyon to his sister Marie, April 21, 1848, Runyon Family Collection, Filson; DeWitt Clinton Loudon to Q. P. Elliott, August 9, 1846, DeWitt Clinton Loudon Collection, Ohio; W. Austine to his cousin, April 23, 1847, William Austine Collection, UNC.

6. *"All the Varieties of a Soldier's Life"*

1. George W. Clutter to his wife, Sarah M. Clutter, August 8, 1847, George Washington Clutter Collection, Yale; Charles R. Case to Daniel F. Case, June 13, 1847, Charles R. Case Collection, Yale.

2. Franklin Smith diary, October 13, 1846, Franklin Smith Collection, Miss.

3. William Seaton Henry, *Campaign Sketches of the War with Mexico* (New York: Harper and Brothers, 1847; repr. New York: Arno Press, 1973), 163; Lieutenant LeClerc to his parents, February 12, 1847, in *Danville* (Pennsylvania) *Intelligencer*, May 7, 1847, transcribed by Randy Hackenburg, Randy Hackenburg Collection, MHI; Edmund B. Alexander to his wife, February 9, 1847, Edmund B. Alexander Collection, USMA.

4. George A. McCall to "My dear M," July 2, 1846, in George A. McCall, *Letters from the Frontiers: Written during a Period of Thirty Years' Service*

in the Army of the United States (Philadelphia: J. B. Lippincott, 1868), 456; Theodore Laidley to his father, John Laidley, January 19, 1847, Theodore Laidley Collection, SMU.

5. J. R. McClanahan to his sister, October 25, 1846, McClanahan-Taylor Collection, UNC; Henry, 159.

6. George G. Meade to his wife, November 3, 1845, in George Gordon Meade, *The Life and Letters of George Gordon Meade*, 2 vols. (New York: Scribner's, 1913), 1: 35; Augustus Ehinger diary, May 17, 1847, Augustus Ehinger Collection, Rice.

7. Thomas G. Driss (?) to his cousin, February 26, 1848, Mexican War Collection, UTA.

8. DeWitt Clinton Loudon diary, November 27, 1846, DeWitt Clinton Loudon Collection, Ohio; Henry Edwards journal, July 8, 1846, Henry Edwards Collection, Ind H; *General Regulations for the Army of the United States, 1847* (Washington, D.C., 1847), 29.

9. A. G. Blanchard, *Diary and Biography of Capt. A. G. Blanchard Second Louisiana Infantry Volunteers Mexican War, May 2nd, 1846 to July 25, 1848*, June 25, 1846, LSU; Albert G. Brackett, *General Lane's Brigade in Central Mexico* (Cincinnati: H. W. Derby; New York: J. C. Derby, 1854), 293, 294.

10. Samuel C. Reid, Jr., *The Scouting Expeditions of McCulloch's Texas Rangers* (1847; repr. ed. Freeport, N.Y.: Books for Libraries Press, 1970), 15–16.

11. K. Jack Bauer, *The Mexican War, 1846–1848* (New York: Macmillan, 1974), 248; T. H. Towner to his father, June 8, 1847, Benjamin T. Towner Collection, Duke; George W. Hartman, *A Private's Own Journal: Giving an Account of the Battles in Mexico, under Gen'l Scott* (Greencastle, Pa.: E. Robinson, 1849), 8.

12. *General Regulations of the Army of the United States, 1841* (Washington, D. C., 1841), 14—hereafter *Army Regulations*; Samuel V. Fulkerson journal, March 4, 1848, Samuel V. Fulkerson Collection, UT.

13. Thomas D. Tennery, *The Mexican War Diary of Thomas D. Tennery*, ed. D. E. Livingston-Little (Norman: University of Oklahoma Press, 1970), 80.

14. Richard H. Coolidge, comp., *Statistical Report on the Sickness and Mortality in the Army of the United States, Compiled from the Records of the Surgeon General's Office, Embracing a Period of Sixteen Years, from January, 1839 to January, 1855* (Washington, D.C., A. O. P. Nicholson, 1856), 610.

15. R. H. Milroy to his sister Mrs. Abby A. Grimes, May 9, 1847, Mildred Knight Richardson Collection, Ind L.; J. M. Cook to William H. Leeves, October 12, 1847, J. M. Cook Collection, Yale; Milton Jamieson, *Journal and Notes of a Campaign in Mexico: Containing a History of Company C, of the Second Regiment of Ohio Volunteers* (Cincinnati, 1849), 37.

16. Ulysses S. Grant to Julia Dent, February 5, 1846, in Ulysses S. Grant, *The Papers of Ulysses S. Grant*, ed. John Y. Simon (Carbondale: Southern Illinois University Press, 1967), 1: 71; John T. Quinn to Joseph W. Templeton, April 3, 1848, Templeton Family Collection, USC.

17. Sydenham Moore diary, July 21, 1846, Sydenham Moore Collection, Ala.

18. John N. Dunlap journal, June 1, 1847, John N. Dunlap Collection, U Mo; J. R. McClanahan to his sister, October 25, 1846, McClanahan-Taylor Collection, UNC; Charles H. Heyer, "A Mexican War Letter," *Magazine of History* 17, no. 6 (1913): 239.

19. J. K. Johnson to his brother, May 12, 1847, and Thomas Barkley to William S. Shulse in same letter, Joseph K. Johnson Collection, U Mo; Charles J. Sellon to Marilla Woods, September 6, 1846, Charles J. Sellon Collection, Ill; Robert Hagan diary, July 3, 1847, Robert Hagan Collection, UT.

20. T. H. Towner to his father, April 23, 1847, Benjamin T. Towner Collection, Duke; Lewis Dunnels to Christian Cook [Koch], September 19, 1846, LSU; Adolph Engelmann, "The Second Illinois in the Mexican War: Mexican War Letters of Adolph Engelmann, 1846–1847," trans. and ed. Otto B. Engelmann, *Journal of the Illinois State Historical Society* 26, no. 4 (1934): 438.

21. Wiley P. Hale to his mother, October 3, 1846, Wiley P. Hale Collection, Tenn; William T. H. Brooks to ?, May 12, 1846, William T. H. Brooks Collection, MHI; William P. Rogers to his wife, October 8, 1846 and William P. Rogers to his brother Mat, March 20, 1847, John Thomas Bolton Collection, UT.

22. T. E. Dansbee to Maj. E. H. Spencer, October 14, 1846, T. E. Dansbee Collection, Tenn; Albert Gallatin Cooper diary, November 10, 1846, A. G. Cooper Collection, Tenn; W. M. Gardner to his sister Rose, November 22, 1847, William M. Gardner Collection, UNC.

23. Thomas N. Love to Mrs. Cannon, September 1847, Thomas N. Love Collection, Tenn; John W. Lowe to his brother, November 18, 1847, John Williamson Lowe Collection, Dayton; Jamieson, 70.

24. B. F. Perry to J. J. Perry, July 14, 1846, B. F. Perry Collection, Ill.

25. Sydenham Moore diary, September 16, 1846 and September 2, 1846, Sydenham Moore Collection, Ala; Samuel L. Milroy to James W. Milroy, October 18, 1846, Mildred Knight Richardson Collection, Ind L.

26. Simon Doyle to his father, Edward Doyle, November 26, 1847, James and Simon Doyle Collection, Yale; George M. Burton to his brother Joseph, November 26, 1847, George M. Burton Collection, Ill.

27. Thomas N. Love to Mrs. Cannon, September 1847, Thomas N. Love Collection, Tenn.

28. R. W. Burt to his parents, November 11, 1846, R. W. Burt Collection, U Mo.

29. Sydenham Moore diary, November 11, 1846, Sydenham Moore Collection, Ala.

30. Augustus Ehinger diary, December 16, 1846, Augustus Ehinger Collection, Rice.

31. Ibid.

32. Ibid.; William P. Tomlinson to John G. Spencer, February 15, 1848, William P. Tomlinson Collection, Yale.

33. Grady McWhiney, *Braxton Bragg and Confederate Defeat* (New York and London: Columbia University Press, 1969), 97–98.

34. Samuel E. Chamberlain, *My Confession: The Recollections of a Rogue* (1956; repr. Lincoln and London: University of Nebraska Press, 1987), 131.

35. *Army Regulations*, 261.

36. Richard E. Cochran to his parents, September 4, 1845, Mexican War Letters, UT; Frank Clarke to his sister Caroline M. Clarke October 10, 1845, Frank Clarke Collection, Yale; G. H. Crosman to General Dearborn, August 7, 1845, Mexican War Letters, UT.

37. Lindorf Ozburn to his wife, Liza M., July 10, 1847, Lindorf Ozburn Collection, Ill; Frank S. Edwards, *A Campaign in New Mexico* (Philadelphia: Carey and Hart, 1847; repr. Ann Arbor, Mich.: University Microfilms, 1966), 29.

38. Philip St. George Cooke, *The Conquest of New Mexico and California: An Historical and Personal Narrative* (New York: G. P. Putnam's Sons, 1878; repr. New York: Arno Press, 1976): 186, 192, 194; George Rutledge Gibson, *Journal of a Soldier under Kearny and Doniphan*, ed. Ralph P. Bieber (Glendale, Calif.: Arthur H. Clarke, 1935; repr. Philadelphia: Porcupine Press, 1974), 184.

39. Richard M. Creagh to Thomas Lewis Jefferson, September 21, 1846, Richard M. Creagh Collection, Filson; Stephen Franklin Nunnelee, "Incidents of a Campaign, &c—1846," June 20, 1846, S. F. Nunnelee Collection, Ala.

40. James Mahon to his wife, September 18, 1846, James Mahon Collection, Ill; John C. Getsinger to his wife, June 28, 1847, Getsinger Family Collection, E Car; Romulus E. Culver to his wife, Mary Ann Culver, November 1, 1846, Romulus E. Culver Collection, U Mo.

41. W. M. Albin to George B. Claver, January 15, 1846 [1847], W. M. Albin Collection, Yale.

42. Edwards, 62; Henry, 165.

43. *Army Regulations*, 36; DeWitt Clinton Loudon to his cousin J. A. Loudon, January 14, 1847, DeWitt Clinton Loudon Collection, Ohio; J. McDougal to *Indiana Democrat*, published August 28, 1846, in Oran Perry, comp., *Indiana in the Mexican War* (Indianapolis: William B. Burford, 1908), 86.

44. *Army Regulations*, 36.

45. Richard M. Creagh to his brother-in-law Thomas Lewis Jefferson, September 2, 1847, Richard M. Creagh Collection, Filson; Henry Edwards journal, Henry Edwards Collection, Ind H; S. F. Nunnelee, "Alabama in Mexico War," *Alabama Historical Quarterly* 19 (1957): 420.

46. Cooke, 24; Will Wallace to his sister Miss Helen M. Indson, November 16, 1846, Wallace-Dickey Collection, Ill.

47. John F. Bouldin to his brother James Bouldin, May 3, 1847, James O. Bouldin Collection, Duke; Zo. S. Cook, "Mexican War Reminiscences," *Alabama Historical Quarterly* 19 (1957): 442.

48. Gibson, 197; Jamieson, 82–83.

49. John P. Bloom, "New Mexico Viewed by Anglo-Americans, 1846–1849," *New Mexico Historical Review* 34, no. 3 (July 1959): 180.

50. Mexico City *North American*, January 8, 1848, in Robert Louis Bodson, "A Description of the United States Occupation of Mexico as Reported by American Newspapers Published in Vera Cruz, Puebla, and Mexico City, September 14, 1847, to July 31, 1848" (Ed.D. diss., Ball State University, 1971), 178.

51. John W. Stout to W. H. H. Terrell, September 3, 1847, William Henry Harrison Terrell Collection, Ind H; DeWitt Clinton Loudon diary, August 15, 1846, DeWitt Clinton Loudon Collection, Ohio; Joshua Jackson diary, October 15, 1846, Joshua Jackson Collection, Ill.

52. Stephen Franklin Nunnelee, "Incidents of a Campaign, &c—1846," November 9, 1846, S. F. Nunnelee Collection, Ala; George B. McClellan, *The Mexican War Diary of George B. McClellan*, ed. William Starr Myers (Princeton, N.J.: Princeton University Press, 1917), 57.

53. W. J. Rorabaugh, *The Alcoholic Republic: An American Tradition* (Oxford, New York, Toronto, Melbourne: Oxford University Press, 1979), 10; Dan Runyon to his father, October 9, 1847, Runyon Family Collection, Filson; R. R. Ritchie to his father, May 20, 1848, Ritchie-Harrison Collection, WM.

54. Ulysses S. Grant to Julia Dent, February 7, 1846, in Grant, 73.

55. Joshua Jackson diary, January 11, 1847, Joshua Jackson Collection, Ill.

56. Sydenham Moore diary, December 25, 1846, Sydenham Moore Collection, Ala; McClellan, 37–38.

57. Edwards, 135.

58. Frances Calderon de la Barca, *Life in Mexico* (1843; repr. New York: Dutton, 1970), 43.

59. Thomas E. Breckenridge memoirs, Thomas E. Breckenridge Collection, U Mo.

60. Engelmann, 366.

61. Brackett, 166.

62. Rorabaugh, 70–71.

63. E. W. H. Beck, "Case of Excision of the Whole of the Genital Organs," *Missouri Medical and Surgical Journal* 3 (1847–1848): 160.

64. Gibson, 149; Jamieson, 10.

65. Gibson, 236; Edwards, 59.

66. Chamberlain, 241–42.

67. John N. Dunlap journal, March 18, 1847, John N. Dunlap Collection, U Mo.

68. Levi White to his wife, October 10, 1846, Levi White Collection, Filson; Reid, 57–58.

69. Frank Hardy to his brother Horace, September 4, 1846, Frank Hardy Collection, Ohio; Thomas T. Summers to his brothers, November 15, 1846, Thomas T. Summers Collection, Filson.

70. John N. Dunlap journal, April 15, 1847 and June 3, 1847, John N. Dunlap Collection, U Mo.

71. John B. Porter, "Medical and Surgical Notes of Campaigns in the War with Mexico, during the Years 1845, 1846, 1847, and 1848," *American Journal of the Medical Sciences* 25 (January 1853): 40–41.

7. *"Keeping Down Unruly Spirits"*

1. Thomas G. Driss to his cousin, January 31, 1848, Mexican War Collection, UTA; DeWitt Clinton Loudon diary, August 27, 1846, DeWitt Clinton Loudon Collection, Ohio.

2. Alexander Macomb, *The Practice of Courts Martial* (New York: Samuel Colman, 1840), 77–78; Tennery, Thomas D., *The Mexican War Diary of Thomas D. Tennery*, ed. D.E. Livingston-Little (Norman: University of Oklahoma Press. 1970), 88.

3. Macomb, 47.

4. "Articles of War," *General Regulations for the Army of the United States, 1841* (Washington, D. C., 1841), Appendix, 1–24—hereafter *Army Regulations, 1841;* T. H. Towner to his father, December 29, 1847, Benjamin T. Towner Collection, Duke; John C. Getsinger to his wife, December 31, 1847, Getsinger Family Collection, E Car; Samuel E. Chamberlain, *My Confession: The Recollections of a Rogue* (1956; repr. ed. Lincoln and London: University of Nebraska Press, 1987), 224–25.

5. George Croghan, *Army Life on the Western Frontier*, ed. Francis Paul Prucha (Norman: University of Oklahoma Press, 1958), 120; John O'Brien, *A Treatise on American Military Laws, and the Practice of Courts Martial, with Suggestions for Their Improvement* (Philadelphia: Lea & Blanchard, 1846), 487; Macomb, 122–24.

6. Two contemporary accounts of this penalty vary with regard to details. One says that only half of the man's head was shaved, the other says that the *D* was tattooed on his hands. Harvey Neville diary, January 9, 1847, Chi; Augustus Ehinger diary, January 4, 1847, Rice.

7. Richard H. Coolidge, comp., *Statistical Report on the Sickness and Mortality in the Army of the United States, Compiled from the Records of the Surgeon General's Office, Embracing a Period of Sixteen Years, from January, 1839 to January, 1855* (Washington, D.C.: A. O. P. Nicholson, 1856); Charles Royster, *A Revolutionary People at War: The Continental Army and American Character, 1775–1783* (New York and London: W. W. Norton, 1981), 71; Bell Irvin Wiley, *The Life of Johnny Reb: The Common Soldier of the Confederacy* (New York: Bobbs-Merrill, 1943), 144.

8. Edward M. Coffman, *The Old Army: A Portrait of the American Army in*

Peacetime, 1784–1898 (New York and Oxford: Oxford University Press, 1986), 193.

9. John F. Meginnis journal, March 31, 1846 and April 3, 1846, John F. Meginnis Collection, UTA; George G. Meade to his wife, April 7, 1846, in George Gordon Meade, *The Life and Letters of George Gordon Meade*, 2 vols. (New York: Scribner's, 1913), 1: 53–54; William Seaton Henry, *Campaign Sketches of the War with Mexico* (New York: Harper and Brothers, 1847; repr. New York: Arno Press, 1973), 73.

10. Henry, 73–74.

11. George G. Meade to his wife, April 7, 1846, in Meade, 1: 53–54.

12. W. Austine to his cousin, November 1, 1847, William Austine Collection, UNC; Henry, 188.

13. Henry, 240, 188.

14. Robert Ryal Miller credits the design of the flag to a whim of Irish-born John Riley, one of the deserters who attained high rank within the battalion. Robert Ryal Miller, *Shamrock and Sword: The Saint Patrick's Battalion in the U.S.-Mexican War* (Norman and London: University of Oklahoma Press, 1989), 33.

15. James Kirby Martin and Mark Edward Lender, *A Respectable Army: The Military Origins of the Republic, 1763–1789* (Arlington Heights, Ill.: Harlan Davidson, 1982), 129.

16. *Army Regulations*, 2 of appendix; George M. Burton to a cousin, January 7, 1847 [1848], George M. Burton Collection, Ill.

17. John W. Lowe to his brother, November 18, 1847, John Williamson Lowe Collection, Dayton; Royster, 237–38; Romeyn B. Ayres journal, [September 1847], Romeyn B. Ayres Collection, UNC.

18. Lee A. Wallace, Jr., "The First Regiment of Virginia Volunteers, 1846–1848," *Virginia Magazine of History and Biography* 77, no. 1 (1969): 65–68; 30th Cong., 1st sess., Senate Executive Document 62, *Message from the President . . . Relative to an Alleged Mutiny at Buena Vista, about 15th August 1847*.

19. Edgefield (South Carolina) *Advertiser*, May 17, 1848, in James Wylie Gettys, Jr., " 'To Conquer a Peace': South Carolina and the Mexican War" (Ph.D. diss., University of South Carolina, 1974), 332–33; Greenville (South Carolina) *Mountaineer*, July 12, 1847, in ibid. 281–82; Miles Morris diary, August 23, 1846, Miles Morris Collection, Ill; Henry Edwards journal, November 1, 1846, Henry Edwards Collection, Ind H.

20. Milton Jamieson, *Journal and Notes of a Campaign in Mexico: Containing a History of Company C, of the Second Regiment of Ohio Volunteers* (Cincinnati, 1849), 98.

21. John Todd Roberts to R. Knott, January 5, 1846 [1847], John Todd Roberts Collection, Filson.

22. Wilbur G. Kurtz, Jr., "The First Regiment of Georgia Volunteers in the Mexican War," *Georgia Historical Quarterly* 27, no. 4 (1943): 301–23; D. E. Livingston-Little, "Mutiny during the Mexican War: An Incident on

the Rio Grande," *Journal of the West* 9, no. 3 (1970): 340–45; Royster, 141.

23. *A Discourse concerning Militias and Standing Armies* (London, 1686), 5, cited by Leonard J. Lerwill, *The Personnel Replacement System in the United States Army* (Washington, D.C., Department of the Army, 1954), 8; W. C. Ford, et al., eds., *Journals of the Continental Congress, 1774–1789* (Washington, D.C., 1905–1933), 27: 433, cited by Lerwill, 9.

24. John C. Fitzpatrick, ed., *The Writings of George Washington*, 39 vols. (Washington, D.C.: Government Printing Office, 1931–1944) 6: 110, cited by Allen Robert Purcell, "The History of the Texas Militia, 1835–1903" (Ph.D. diss., University of Texas, 1981), 10; Francis Collins, "Journal of Francis Collins: An Artillery Officer in the Mexican War," ed. Maria Clinton Collins, *Quarterly Publication of the Historical and Philosophical Society of Ohio* 10, nos. 2 and 3 (April and July 1915): 72.

25. S. F. Nunnelee, "Alabama in Mexico War," *Alabama Historical Quarterly* 19 (1957): 426; Meade, 1: 90–91; Philip St. George Cooke, *The Conquest of New Mexico and California: An Historical and Personal Narrative* (New York: G. P. Putnam's Sons, 1878; repr. New York: Arno Press, 1976), 62.

26. William P. Rogers, "The Diary and Letters of William P. Rogers, 1846–1862," ed. Eleanor Damon Pace, *Southwestern Historical Quarterly* 32, no. 4 (April 1929): 265.

27. Sydenham Moore diary, September 28, 1846, Sydenham Moore Collection, Ala.; George B. McClellan, *The Mexican War Diary of George B. McClellan*, ed. William Starr Myers (Princeton, N.J.: Princeton University Press, 1917), 16, December 5, 1846.

28. Clark Kennerly, "Recollections of Our War with Mexico: Memoirs of a Missouri Volunteer," Mexican War Papers, Mo H.

29. William P. Rogers to his wife, October 8, 1846, John Thomas Bolton Collection, UT; Anonymous to his mother, September 25, 1846, Tenn; Theodore Laidley to his father, John Laidley, October 24, 1847, Theodore Laidley Collection, SMU; Robert E. Lee to John Mackay, October 2, 1847, R. E. and G. W. C. Lee Collection, MHI.

30. Jamieson, 16; [George Ballentine], *Autobiography of an English Soldier in the United States Army* (New York: Stringer & Townshend, 1853), 43–44.

31. John F. Meginness journal, August 27, 1847, John F. Meginness Collection, UTA; Ulysses S. Grant to Julia Dent, July 25, 1846, in Ulysses S. Grant, *The Papers of Ulysses S. Grant*, ed. John Y. Simon (Carbondale: Southern Illinois University Press, 1967), 1: 102.

32. N. J. T. Dana, *Monterrey Is Ours!: The Mexican War Letters of Lieutenant Dana, 1845–1847*, ed. Robert H. Ferrell (Lexington: University Press of Kentucky, 1990), 181.

33. Rogers, 269.

34. *Proceedings of Military Commissions, Matamoros, Mexico, 1847–1848, Records of the Adjutant General's Office, Record Group 94, National Archives, Washington, D.C.*

35. J. Jacob Oswandel, *Notes of the Mexican War, 1846–47–48* (Philadelphia, 1885), 583–84; Daniel Runyon to his father, April 22, 1848 and May 20, 1848, Runyon Family Collection, Filson; George W. Hartman, *A Private's Own Journal* (Greencastle, Pa.: E. Robinson, 1849), 23, 25.

36. Augustus Ehinger diary, December 16, 1846, Augustus Ehinger Collection, Rice.

37. Meade, 1: 108.

38. John S. Ford, *Rip Ford's Texas*, ed. Stephen B. Oates (Austin, Texas, 1963), 93.

39. Samuel C. Reid, Jr., *The Scouting Expeditions of McCulloch's Texas Rangers* (1847; repr. Freeport, N.Y.: Books for Libraries Press, 1970), 53; Madison Mills diary, October 4, 5, 6, 1846, Madison Mills Collection, Filson; Zachary Taylor to R. C. Wood, June 30, 1846, in Zachary Taylor, *Letters of Zachary Taylor from the Battlefields of the Mexican War* (Rochester, N.Y.: William K. Bixby, 1908; repr. New York: Kraus Reprint, 1970), 22.

40. Peter Watson, *War on the Mind: The Military Uses and Abuses of Psychology* (New York: Basic Books, 1978), 243–45.

41. Ibid., 118.

8. The Volunteers Take the Field

1. T. H. Towner to his father, February 12, 1847, Benjamin T. Towner Collection, Duke.

2. B. F. Perry to J. J. Perry, July 14, 1846, B. F. Perry Collection, Ill.

3. Stephen Franklin Nunnelee, "Incidents of a Campaign, &c—1846," entry for June 1, 1846, Stephen Franklin Nunnelee Collection, Ala.

4. Memoir of D. M. Frost, D. M. Frost Papers, D. M. Frost Collection, Mo H; Edmund B. Alexander to his wife, March 6, 1847, Edmund B. Alexander Collection, USMA; Harvey Neville's diary, January 15, 1847, Chi.

5. Clark Kennerly, "Recollections of Our War with Mexico: Memoirs of a Missouri Volunteer," 1912, typescript in Mexican War Papers, Mo H; Will Wallace to George, March 1, 1847, Wallace-Dickey Collection, Ill; DeWitt Clinton Loudon to J. A. Loudon, January 14, 1847, DeWitt Clinton Loudon Collection, Ohio.

6. Milton Jamieson, *Journal and Notes of a Campaign in Mexico* (Cincinnati, 1849), 17–18; William P. Rogers to Mat [Rogers], March 20, 1847, William P. Rogers Collection, UT.

7. Thomas Claiborne reminiscences, UNC.

8. James D. Elderkin, *Biographical Sketches and Anecdotes of a Soldier of Three Wars* (Detroit, 1899), 67.

9. William B. Campbell, "Mexican War Letters of Col. William Bowen Campbell, of Tennessee, written to Governor David Campbell, of Virginia, 1846–1847," ed. St. George L. Sioussat, *Tennessee Historical Magazine* 1, no. 2 (1915): 141.

10. [J. B. Robinson], *Reminiscences of a Campaign in Mexico by a Member of "The Bloody-First"* (Nashville: John York, 1849), 166.

11. Manuel Balbontin, "The Siege of Monterey," trans. John Strother, *Journal of the Military Service Institution* 8 (1887): 339.

12. Campbell, 143; G. H. Nixon to his wife, Sarah, October 18, 1846, G. H. Nixon Collection, Tenn.

13. Carr B. White to his father, John D. White, September 27, 1846, Carr B. White Collection, Ohio.

14. Balbontin, "Monterey," 348.

15. Jefferson Davis to his brother Joseph E. Davis, September 25, 1846, in James T. McIntosh, ed., *The Papers of Jefferson Davis* (Baton Rouge: Louisiana State University Press, 1981), 3: 24; William P. Rogers, "The Diary and Letters of William P. Rogers, 1846–1862," ed. Eleanor Damon Pace, *Southwestern Historical Quarterly* 32, no. 4 (April 1929): 263; DeWitt Clinton Loudon diary, September 23, 1846, DeWitt Clinton Loudon Collection, Ohio.

16. E. Kirby-Smith to his mother, September 24, 1846, Edmund Kirby-Smith Collection, UNC; Ulysses S. Grant, *Personal Memoirs of U. S. Grant*, 2 vols. (New York: Charles L. Webster, 1885), 1: 95.

17. Robinson, 127; W. S. Henry, *Campaign Sketches of the War with Mexico* (New York: Harper and Brothers, 1847; repr. ed. New York: Arno Press, 1973), 219.

18. H. [D. H. Hill], "The Battles of the Rio Grande," *Southern Quarterly Review*, n.s., 2, no. 4 (November 1850): 462.

19. Levi White to Sarah White, September 12, 1846, Levi White Collection, Filson; T. B. Kinder to Dr. Dunlap, December 28, 1846, T. B. Kinder Collection, Ind H; J. S. Arthur to David W. Dailey, December 1, 1846, David W. Dailey Collection, Ind H.

20. Joseph Davis Howell to his mother, September 25, 1846, William Burr Howell and Family Collection, Miss; J. H. LaMotte to his wife, October 5, 1846, LaMotte-Coppinger Collection, Mo H; George Nauman, "A Lancastrian in the Mexican War," *Historical Papers and Addresses of the Lancaster County Historical Society* 12, no. 3 (1908): 122; Ulysses S. Grant, *The Papers of Ulysses S. Grant*, ed. John Y. Simon (Carbondale: Southern Illinois University Press, 1967) 1: 144.

21. James M. McCaffrey, *This Band of Heroes: Granbury's Texas Brigade C.S.A.* (Austin, Tex.: Eakin Press, 1985), 108.

22. Will Wallace to his sister Helen M. Indson, August 18–29, 1846, Wallace-Dickey Collection, Ill.

23. Adolph Engelmann, "The Second Illinois in the Mexican War: Mexican War Letters of Adolph Engelmann, 1846–1847," trans. and ed. Otto B. Engelmann, *Journal of the Illinois State Historical Society* 26, no. 4 (1934): 383; Will Wallace to his sister Helen M. Indson, August 18–29, 1846, Wallace-Dickey Collection, Ill.

24. Francis Baylies, "The March of the United States Troops, under the

Command of General John E. Wool, from San Antonio, Texas, to Saltillo, Mexico in the Year 1846," *Stryker's American Register and Magazine* 4 (July 1850): 299.

25. Ibid., 304, 306.

26. Manuel Balbontin, "The Battle of Angostura (Buena Vista)," trans. F. H. Hardie, *Journal of the United States Cavalry Association* 7, no. 25 (June 1894): 127.

27. Report of the Secretary of War in Senate Executive Document 1, 30th Cong., 1st sess., 98.

28. Will Wallace to George, March 1, 1847, Wallace-Dickey Collection, Ill; John J. Halsey to Edmund W. Halsey, March 21, 1847, John J. Halsey Collection, Filson.

29. J. A. Merrifield to Samuel M. Bemis, March 9, 1847, Bemis Family Collection, Va H.

30. There are several versions of the verbal exchange between Captain Bragg and General Taylor. One popular version has General Taylor calmly instructing Bragg to deliver "a little more grape, Captain Bragg." The wording used here seems more in keeping with what is known about General Taylor's personality.

31. Balbontin, "Angostura," 148; [Ramon Alcaraz, et al.], *The Other Side; or, Notes for the History of the War between Mexico and the United States*, trans. and ed. Albert C. Ramsey (New York: John Wiley, 1850), 137.

32. Will Wallace to George, March 1, 1847, Wallace-Dickey Collection, Ill.

33. William E. P——to Frances Milroy, April 28, 1847, Mildred Knight Richardson Collection, Ind L.

9. The Army of the West

1. John Steele, "Extracts from the Journal of John Steele," *Utah Historical Quarterly* 6, no. 1 (January 1933): 6–7.

2. Henry W. Bigler, "Extracts from the Journal of Henry W. Bigler," *Utah Historical Quarterly* 5, no. 2 (April 1932): 36.

3. Jacob S. Robinson, *A Journal of the Santa Fe Expedition under Colonel Doniphan* (Portsmouth, N.H.: Portsmouth *Journal* Press, 1848; repr. ed. Princeton: Princeton University Press, 1932, repr. ed. New York: Da Capo Press, 1972): 12–13.

4. Bigler, 42; Frank S. Edwards, *A Campaign in New Mexico with Colonel Doniphan* (Philadelphia: Carey and Hart, 1847; repr. ed. Ann Arbor, Mich.: University Microfilms, 1966), 34; William H. Richardson, "William H. Richardson's Journal of Doniphan's Expedition," ed. William B. McGroarty, *Missouri Historical Review* 22, no. 2 (1928): 222.

5. Steele, 8.

6. George Rutledge Gibson, *Journal of a Soldier under Kearny and Doniphan, 1846–1847*, ed. Ralph P. Bieber (Glendale, Calif.: Arthur H. Clarke, 1935; repr. ed. Philadelphia: Porcupine Press, 1974), 146.

7. Gibson, 186; Robinson, 24.

8. Henry S. Turner, "Letters about Mexican War," *Glimpses of the Past* 2, no. 2 (1934–1935): 8; Robinson, 24–25; Kimball Clark, "The Epic March of Doniphan's Missourians," *Missouri Historical Review* 80 (January 1986): 142.

9. Edwards, 51; Robert W. Whitworth, "From the Mississippi to the Pacific: An Englishman in the Mormon Battalion," *Arizona and the West* 7, no. 2 (1965): 144; Richardson, 234.

10. John F. Yurtinus, "The Battle of the Bulls," *Military History of Texas and the Southwest* 14, no. 2 (1978): 101.

11. Ibid., 101–5; Whitworth, 150.

12. Philip St. George Cooke, "Report of Lieut. Col. P. St. George Cooke of His March from Santa Fe, New Mexico, to San Diego, Upper California," ed. Hamilton Gardner, *Utah Historical Quarterly* 22, no. 1 (January 1954): 26.

13. Bigler, 49.

14. Whitworth, 151.

15. Ibid., 145–46, 154; Cooke, "Report," 32.

16. Nathaniel V. Jones, "The Journal of Nathaniel V. Jones, with the Mormon Battalion," *Utah Historical Quarterly* 4 (January 1931): 10; Whitworth, 152; Philip St. George Cooke, *The Conquest of New Mexico and California: An Historical and Personal Narrative* (New York: G. P. Putnam's Sons, 1878; repr. New York: Arno Press, 1976), 186; Anonymous, "The Mormon Battalion," *Historical Record* 8, nos. 7–8 (1889): 922.

17. B. H. Roberts, *The Mormon Battalion: Its History and Achievements* (Salt Lake City: Deseret News, 1919), 45–46.

18. Edwards, 76.

19. There are several versions of this encounter. The gist of all of them, however, is as presented here. C. H. Kribben, "Semi-Official Report of the Battle of Bracito," in Edwards, 170; Clark, 147; William H. Richardson, 22, no. 3 (1928): 346.

20. Edwards, 85.

21. Ponce de Leon to Luis Vidal, December 25, 1846, trans. F. M. Gallaher, *New Mexico Historical Review* 3, no. 4 (October 1928): 387–88; Gibson, 311; Edwards, 88; Edwards, 88; Gibson, 311; Cooke, *Conquest*, 121.

22. Gibson, 309.

23. Clark, 148.

24. Ibid., 151; William H. Richardson, 22, no. 4 (1928): 513.

25. Richardson, ibid., 511.

26. Edwards, 126–27.

27. Gibson, 351; Edwards, 117; Isaac George, *Heroes and Incidents of the Mexican War* (Greensburg, Pa.: Review, 1903; repr. ed. Hollywood, Calif.: Sun Dance Press, 1971), 97.

28. Edwards, 99.

29. Richardson, *Missouri Historical Review* 22, no. 4 (1928): 516–17.

10. To the Halls of the Montezumas

1. William B. Campbell, "Mexican War Letters of Col. William Bowen Campbell, of Tennessee, written to Governor David Campbell, of Virginia, 1846–1847," ed. St. George L. Sioussat, *Tennessee Historical Magazine* 1, no. 2 (1915): 149.

2. Clarksville (Texas) *Northern Standard*, December 12, 1846.

3. Robert Anderson, *An Artillery Officer in the Mexican War, 1846–7* (New York and London: G. P. Putnam's Sons, 1911), 21–22.

4. [George Ballentine], *Autobiography of an English Soldier in the United States Army* (New York: Stinger & Townshend, 1853), 146–47.

5. Ballentine, 145; J. Jacob Oswandel, *Notes of the Mexican War, 1846–47–48* (Philadelphia, 1885), 68.

6. Francis Collins, "Journal of Francis Collins: An Artillery Officer in the Mexican War," ed. Maria Clinton Collins, *Quarterly Publication of the Historical and Philosophical Society of Ohio* 10, nos. 2 and 3 (April and July 1915): 48; Gustavus W. Smith, *Company "A," Corps. of Engineers, U.S.A., 1846–'48, in the Mexican War* (Willets Point, N.Y.: Battalion Press, 1896), 19.

7. Clarence H. Frick to his brother Arthur W. Frick, March 28, 1847, Clarence Frick Collection, MHI.

8. Ballentine, 155.

9. Richard Coulter, "The Westmoreland Guards in the War with Mexico, 1846–1848," *Western Pennsylvania Historical Magazine* 24, no. 2 (June 1941): 110.

10. [Ramon Alcaraz, et al.], *The Other Side; or, Notes for the History of the War between Mexico and the United States* (New York: John Wiley, 1850), 184, 186.

11. Oswandel, 98–99; Anderson, 102.

12. Robert E. Lee to his wife, ca. March 24, 1847, cited in Philip Van Doren Stern, *Robert E. Lee: The Man and the Soldier* (New York: Bonanza Books, 1963), 78; Larkin Smith to his father, April 4, 1847, Larkin Smith Collection, U Va.

13. K. Jack Bauer, *The Mexican War: 1846–1848* (New York: Macmillan, 1974), 259.

14. Ballentine, 178–79.

15. Ibid., 180.

16. Noah Newton to Brown, April 25, 1847, Ritchie-Harrison Collection, WM; Barna Upton, "Our First Foreign War," ed. William F. Goetzmann, *American Heritage* 17, no. 4 (1966): 98.

17. Jose Fernando Ramirez to Francisco Elorriaga, April 25–May 13, 1847, in Jose Fernando Ramirez, *Mexico during the War with the United States*, trans.

Elliott B. Scherr, ed. Walter V. Scholes (Columbia: University of Missouri Press, 1950), 120.

18. [J. B. Robinson], *Reminiscences of a Campaign in Mexico by a Member of "The Bloody-First"* (Nashville: John York, 1849), 243; George Nauman, "A Lancastrian in the Mexican War," *Historical Papers and Addresses of the Lancaster County Historical Society* 12, no. 3 (1908): 122.

19. W. S. Henry, *Campaign Sketches of the War with Mexico* (New York: Harper and Brothers, 1847; repr. ed. New York: Arno Press, 1973), 70; Henry S. Lane, "The Mexican War Journal of Henry S. Lane," *Indiana Magazine of History* 53, no. 4 (1957): 395; T. H. Towner to his father, April 14, 1847, Benjamin T. Towner Collection, Duke.

20. Ramirez, 135; Isaac George, *Heroes and Incidents of the Mexican War* (Greensburg, Pa.: Review, 1903; repr. ed. Hollywood, Calif.: Sun Dance Press, 1971), 213.

21. Campbell, 160; S. F. Nunnelee, "Alabama in Mexico War," *Alabama Historical Quarterly* 19 (1957): 430.

22. Recruiting poster for Sixteenth U.S. Infantry Regiment, John Abram Hendricks Collection, UT.

23. John Williamson Lowe diary, December 3, 1847, John W. Lowe Collection, Dayton; Nathaniel Eaves to Messrs. C. D. Milton and Alexander, June 3, 1847, N. R. Eaves Collection, USC; James D. Elderkin, *Biographical Sketches and Anecdotes of a Soldier of Three Wars, as Written by Himself* (Detroit: Record Printing, 1899), 61–62.

24. Albert G. Brackett, *General Lane's Brigade in Central Mexico* (Cincinnati: H. W. Derby; New York: J. C. Derby, 1854), 281; Ballentine, 237.

25. Nauman, 124.

26. John D. Wilkins to his mother, August 24, 1847, John Darragh Wilkins Collection, Yale; W. Austine to his cousin, November 1, 1847, William Austine Collection, UNC.

27. William Chapman, "Letters from the Seat of War—Mexico," *Green Bay Historical Bulletin* 4, no. 4 (July–August 1928): 11.

28. George W. Kendall, "Mr. Kendall's Letters from the Army," September 9, 1847, *Littell's Living Age* 15, no. 183 (1847): 329.

29. Edmund B. Alexander to his wife, September 16, 1847, Edmund B. Alexander Collection, USMA.

30. Bauer, 318.

31. Ulysses S. Grant, *Personal Memoirs of U.S. Grant*, 2 vols. (New York: Charles L. Webster, 1885), 1: 158.

32. Will Wallace to George, March 1, 1847, Wallace-Dickey Collection, Ill; J. Rufus Smith to William M. Stakely, October 23, 1847, in Carolyn McKenzie, "Fighting Mexicans 100 Years Ago," in an unknown newspaper, probably Atlanta, ca. 1947, AH; Noah Newton to Brown, April 25, 1847, Ritchie-Harrison Collection, WM.

33. Joseph Davis Howell to his mother, September 25, 1846, William Burr

Howell and Family Collection, Miss; R. S. Dix to John Adams Dix, February 25, 1847, John Adams Dix Collection, Duke.

34. G. W. Rains to his brother, August 28, 1847, George Washington Rains Collection, UNC; Chapman, 19.

35. G. W. Rains to his brother, August 28, 1847, George Washington Rains Collection, UNC; Ulysses S. Grant to Julia Dent, May 11, 1846, in Ulysses S. Grant, *The Papers of Ulysses S. Grant*, ed. John Y. Simon (Carbondale: Southern Illinois University Press, 1967), 1: 86; ibid., August 14, 1846, 105; John L. P. Cantwell to Benjamin Lucas, October 27, 1847, John L. P. Cantwell Collection, UNC.

36. J. Rufus Smith to William M. Stakely, October 23, 1847, in McKenzie.

37. Richard McSherry, "A Mexican Campaign Sketch," *New Eclectic* 3 (1868): 335.

38. Josephus M. Steiner to Mary, March 9, 1847, Josephus Murray Steiner Collection, UT.

39. Louis C. Duncan, "Medical History of General Scott's Campaign to the City of Mexico in 1847," *Military Surgeon* 47, no. 4 (1920): 454; Ballentine, 207.

40. Robert Hagan diary, September 22, 1847, Robert Hagan Collection, UT; Chandler E. Potter, *The Military History of the State of New Hampshire, 1623–1861* (Baltimore: Genealogical Publishing, 1972), 351–52; William G. Rothstein, *American Physicians in the Nineteenth Century: From Sects to Science* (Baltimore and London: Johns Hopkins University Press, 1972), 249.

41. John B. Porter, "Medical and Surgical Notes of Campaigns in the War with Mexico, during the Years 1845, 1846, 1847, and 1848," *American Journal of the Medical Sciences* 23 (January 1852): 31.

42. Ibid., 33; Louis C. Duncan, "Medical History of General Scott's Campaign to the City of Mexico in 1847," *Military Surgeon* 47, no. 5 (1920): 602–3.

43. David Nevin, *The Mexican War* (Alexandria, Va.: Time-Life Books, 1978), 87.

44. Adolph Engelmann, "The Second Illinois in the Mexican War: Mexican War Letters of Adolph Engelmann, 1846–1847," trans. and ed. Otto B. Engelmann, *Journal of the Illinois State Historical Society* 26, no. 4 (1934): 442–52.

45. Emmet F. Horine, "Episodes in the History of Anesthesia," *Journal of the History of Medicine and Allied Sciences* 1 (October 1946): 521; Josiah Charles Trent, "Surgical Anesthesia, 1846–1946," *Journal of the History of Medicine and Allied Sciences* 1 (October 1946): 507–8.

46. John B. Porter, 33, 32, 30.

47. Robert E. Lee to John Mackay, October 2, 1847, R. E. and G. W. C. Lee Collection, MHI.

48. Otis A. Singletary, *The Mexican War* (Chicago and London: University of Chicago Press, 1960), 83; Bauer, 322.

11. Peace at Last

1. General Orders no. 284 and no. 287, in Senate Executive Document 1, 30th Cong., 1st sess., 386–87.

2. Anonymous, "A General's Orderly in Mexico," *United Service Magazine* (London) 78, no. 318 (1855): 83–84.

3. D. M. Frost memoirs, D. M. Frost Collection, Mo H; Amasa G. Clark, *Reminiscences of a Centenarian, as Told by Amasa Gleason Clark, Veteran of the Mexican War, to Cora Tope Clark*, ed. J. Marvin Hunter, Sr. (Bandera, Tex., 1930), 14, cited in Robert Ryal Miller, *Shamrock and Sword: The Saint Patrick's Battalion in the U.S.-Mexican War* (Norman and London: University of Oklahoma Press, 1989), 104.

4. Daniel M. Frost, "The Memoirs of Daniel M. Frost," ed. Mrs. Dana O. Jensen, *Missouri Historical Society Bulletin* 26, no. 3 (1970): 222.

5. Ibid., 222; W. Austine to his cousin, November 1, 1847, William Austine Collection, UNC.

6. Winslow F. Sanderson to his wife, May 7, 1847, Winslow F. Sanderson Collection, Rice.

7. Mexico City *North American*, December 10, 1847, January 22, 1848, February 5, 1848, as cited by Robert Louis Bodson, "A Description of the United States Occupation of Mexico as Reported by American Newspapers Published in Vera Cruz, Puebla, and Mexico City, September 14, 1847, to July 31, 1848" (Ed.D. diss., Ball State University, 1971), 31.

8. Mexico City *North American*, January 29, 1848, in Bodson, 233.

9. John C. Getsinger to his wife, February 17, 1848, Getsinger Family Collection, E Car; T. H. Towner to his mother, March 16, 1847, Benjamin T. Towner Collection, Duke.

10. Bodson, 183.

11. John W. Lowe to his wife, December 31, 1847, February 16, 1848, John Williamson Lowe Collection, Dayton.

12. George G. Meade to his wife, February 18, 1846, and May 19, 1846, in George Gordon Meade, *The Life and Letters of George Gordon Meade*, 2 vols. (New York: Scribner's, 1913), 1: 47, 86.

13. Samuel E. Chamberlain, *My Confession: The Recollections of a Rogue* (1956; repr. Lincoln and London: University of Nebraska Press, 1987), 67; Zo. S. Cook, "Mexican War Reminiscences," *Alabama Historical Quarterly* 19 (1957): 457; Mexico City *Daily American Star*, May 20, 1848, as cited by Bodson, 197–98.

14. Bodson, 174.

15. Ulysses S. Grant to Julia Dent, June 4, 1848, in Ulysses S. Grant, *The Papers of Ulysses S. Grant*, ed. John Y. Simon (Carbondale: Southern Illinois University Press, 1967), 1: 160–61; Anonymous, "Memories of Mexico," *Harper's New Monthly Magazine* 3 (June-November 1851): 464.

16. Milton Stapp diary, July 14, 1847, Milton Stapp Collection, Ind H.

17. Wilmington (North Carolina) *Journal*, July 7, 1848, in Lee Alphonso Wallace, "North Carolina in the War with Mexico" (M.A. thesis, University of North Carolina, 1950), 90–91.

18. Turner J. Fakes, Jr., "Memphis and the Mexican War," *West Tennessee Historical Society Papers* 2 (1948): 144; James A. Ramage, "John Hunt Morgan and the Kentucky Cavalry Volunteers in the Mexican War," *Register of the Kentucky Historical Society* 81, no. 4 (Autumn 1983): 362; Wilmington (North Carolina) *Journal*, August 11, 1848, in Wallace, 92; Steven Bruce Michael, "Ohio and the Mexican War: Public Response to the 1846–1848 Crisis" (Ph.D. diss., Ohio State University, 1985).

19. Wallace E. Davies, "The Mexican War Veterans as an Organized Group," *Mississippi Valley Historical Review* 35, no. 2 (September 1948): 222, 225–28.

12. Epilogue

1. Harry G. Summers, Jr., *On Strategy: A Critical Analysis of the Vietnam War* (New York: Dell, 1984), 21.

2. Wiley P. Hale to his mother, July 26, 1846, Wiley P. Hale Collection, Tenn.

3. William H. Prescott, *History of the Conquest of Mexico* (1843); Frances Calderon de la Barca, *Life in Mexico* (1843; repr. ed. New York: Dutton, 1970).

4. Jose Fernando Ramirez, *Mexico during the War with the United States*, trans. Elliott B. Scherr, ed. Walter V. Scholes (Columbia: University of Missouri Press, 1950), 161.

References

Manuscript Sources Consulted

ALABAMA DEPARTMENT OF ARCHIVES AND HISTORY

Matthew Power Blue
Sydenham Moore
Stephen Franklin Nunnelee
J. W. Triplet

ATLANTA HISTORICAL SOCIETY

John W. Fincher

AUBURN UNIVERSITY LIBRARY

Cox Family
  W. H. A. Cox
Robert S. Jemison
  E. Mims

CHICAGO HISTORICAL SOCIETY

Harvey Neville

DAYTON AND MONTGOMERY COUNTY PUBLIC LIBRARY

John Williamson Lowe

DUKE UNIVERSITY, SPECIAL COLLECTIONS DEPARTMENT,
WILLIAM R. PERKINS LIBRARY

Angus R. Blakey
James O. Bouldin
    John F. Bouldin
George Briggs
Archibald W. Burns
John Cantey
Nathaniel Comer
    Russell G. Comer
John Adams Dix
    R. S. Dix
Juliana (Paisley) Gilmer
William Allen Gordon
    George Crosman
    A. R. Hetzel
William Henry Grimes
John Warfield Johnston
    George Frederick Holmes
Abner M. Perrin
    Maxcy Gregg
    Abner M. Perrin
Scarborough Family
Josiah Townsend Smith
Benjamin T. Towner
    T. H. Towner
Robert & Newton D. Woody

EAST CAROLINA UNIVERSITY LIBRARY

Getsinger Family
    John C. Getsinger

FILSON CLUB, MANUSCRIPT DEPARTMENT, LOUISVILLE, KENTUCKY

Berry Family
John C. Breckinridge
Simon Bolivar Buckner
F. Cravens
Richard M. Creagh
William H. Daniel
Columbus Goodwin
John J. Halsey

Henry Smith Lane
Lillard Family
Walter J. McMurtry
Marshall Family
Richard A. Maupin
Madison Mills
Theodore O'Hara
Alfred Pirtle
Preston Family
John Todd Roberts
Runyon Family
D. W. Scott
Thomas T. Summers
Todd Family
Levi White

HOUSTON PUBLIC LIBRARY

R. J. Lawrence

ILLINOIS STATE HISTORICAL LIBRARY

William T. Barrett
Newton Bateman
James Berdan
George M. Burton
John M. Crockett
Lewis D. Erwin
John G. Fonda
Edward A. Giller
Thomas L. Harris
John P. Hatch
Joshua Jackson
John T. Jones
John A. McClernand
McMackin Family
James Mahon
W. L. Marcy
Miles Morris
Richard J. Oglesby
Lindorf Ozburn
B. F. Perry
James H. Ralston
Augustus K. Riggin

L. W. Ross
Robert C. Scott
Charles J. Sellon
David B. Tower
Lewis Varner
Wallace-Dickey
Isaac Watkinson

INDIANA HISTORICAL SOCIETY LIBRARY

Bartholomew County
David W. Dailey
John W. Dodd
Jacob Dunn
Henry Edwards
Willis A. Gorman
T. B. Kinder
Samuel Luckett
Charles Mayer
Samuel Merrill
Theophilus Parvin
Michael H. Reardon
Jacob Sickler
George Marion Smith
Milton Stapp
Samuel Steele
W. H. H. Terrell
John H. Towner

INDIANA STATE LIBRARY, MANUSCRIPT COLLECTION, INDIANA DIVISION

Calvin Benjamin
Cass County
John A. Graham
    John B. Avoline
    Alexander Wilson
Victor T. Hardin
Ezra Hayes
Mildred Knight Richardson
    Elias W. H. Beck
    R. H. Milroy
    Samuel L. Milroy
    William E. P——
Thomas Williams

LOUISIANA AND LOWER MISSISSIPPI VALLEY COLLECTIONS, LSU LIBRARIES

George W. Chase
Edward Eastman
Henry Farno
Christian D. Koch & Family
G. Loomis
Henry A. Lyons
Samuel J. Peters, Jr.
John C. Tibbetts
Benjamin Tureaud

MINNESOTA HISTORICAL SOCIETY

Hiram Wesley Catlin

MISSISSIPPI DEPARTMENT OF ARCHIVES AND HISTORY

James C. Browning
William Burr Howell & Family
Franklin Smith

MISSOURI HISTORICAL SOCIETY

D. C. Allen
Amoureux-Bolduc
Mary C. Clements
   Thomas B. Hudson
D. M. Frost
John P. Gaines
Hamilton R. Gamble
   James H. Birch, Jr.
Willard P. Hall
   William A. Hall
Lewis Jones
   W. H. Jones
James C. Lackland
   W. A. Beedy
Lamotte-Coppinger
   J. H. Lamotte
T. C. Link
   D. D. Mitchell
Lindenwood
Mexican War Envelope

M. B. Edwards
Ed. L. Hinton
Christian Kribben
T. L. Wooldridge
Mexican War Papers
    William Clark Kennerly
    C. Masten
    J. V. Masten
    W. W. Reynolds
    James V. A. Shields
Robert H. Miller
    William R. Franklin
    John T. Hughes
Sappington
Anson Sperry
Homer Stanford
John D. Stevenson
William L. Sublette

NATIONAL ARCHIVES

Annual Reports of the War Department, 1822–1907. (National Archives Microfilm Publication M997, roll 7 (1840–1844) and roll 8 (1845–1847).

Letters Received by the Office of the Adjutant General (main series), 1822–1860. National Archives Microfilm Publication M567, rolls 310, 312, 314, 320, 321, 323, 324, 328, 329, 333, 336, 344, 348, 395. Records of the Adjutant General's Office, Record Group 94.

Proceedings of Military Commissions, Matamoros, Mexico, 1847–1848. Records of the Adjutant General's Office, Record Group 94.

Records of Garrison Courts Martial, Tampico Department, Feb. 1–June 15, 1848. Records of the Adjutant General's Office, Record Group 94.

Records of Various Ordnance Boards, 1846–1868. Proceedings, March 1846–Sept. 1863, Jan.-Feb. 1868. Textual Records of the Office of the Chief of Ordnance, Record Group 156.

Registers of Enlistments in the U.S. Army, 1798–1914. Vol. 45, July 1846–May 1848, National Archives Microfilm Publication M233, roll 22. Records of the Adjutant General's Office, 1780s-1917, Record Group 94.

NEW HAMPSHIRE HISTORICAL SOCIETY

John Hatch George

OHIO HISTORICAL SOCIETY

Charles H. Brough
Frank A. Hardy
Stephen Hazelton
Nelson Huson
Edward A. King
DeWitt Clinton Loudon
Ohio Infantry
Johann Karl Schneider
James Thompson
Carr B. White

RICE UNIVERSITY

Augustus Ehinger
Winslow F. Sanderson

SOUTHERN METHODIST UNIVERSITY, DEGOLYER LIBRARY, DALLAS

Theodore Laidley

MRS. F. L. STUBBS

Samuel A. Kennedy

TENNESSEE STATE LIBRARY AND ARCHIVES

S. R. Anderson
Anonymous Letter
R. A. Bennett
Benjamin Franklin Cheatham
Albert Gallatin Cooper
T. E. Dansbee
Wiley P. Hale
Adolphus Heiman
Thomas N. Love
McClaughlin Family
    James L. McClaughlin
George Henry Nixon
Allen M. Short
John L. Temple
Samuel Anderson Weakley

U.S. ARMY MILITARY HISTORY INSTITUTE

Army of Mexico—First Division
William T. H. Brooks
Civil War Times Illustrated
Columbia County Historical Society
James Duncan
Clarence Frick
Stuart A. Goldman
James D. Graham
Randy Hackenburg
Curtis J. Herrick
Joseph Hooker
R. E. & G. W. C. Lee
Lewis Leigh
Norwick Civil War Round Table
John Olohlin
Smith-Kirby-Webster-Black-Danner Family
Steele-Boyd Family
Wiley Sword

U.S. MILITARY ACADEMY, OMAR N. BRADLEY LIBRARY

Alden Family
Edmund Brooke Alexander
Philip Norbourne Barbour
James Duncan
Robert Hazlitt
Jeremiah Mason Scarritt
Charles Seaforth Stewart

UNIVERSITY OF MICHIGAN, BENTLEY HISTORICAL LIBRARY

Michigan Historical Collections
   John Davis Pierce

UNIVERSITY OF NORTH CAROLINA AT CHAPEL HILL LIBRARY,
SOUTHERN HISTORICAL COLLECTION

William Austine
Romeyn B. Ayres
John L. P. Cantwell
Thomas Claiborne
Robert C. Foster

William M. Gardner
John J. Green
John Kimberly
Edmund Kirby-Smith
McClanahan-Taylor
    John R. McClanahan
    Nelson McClanahan
James S. McIntosh
Abraham C. Myers
George Washington Rains
William D. Valentine

UNIVERSITY OF SOUTH CAROLINA, SOUTH CAROLINIANA LIBRARY

John P. Barratt
Preston Smith Brooks
Bryce Family
    E. G. Henry
    Giles Henry
Nathaniel Ridley Eaves
    R. J. M. Dunnovant
    Nathaniel Ridley Eaves
Adley Hogan Gladden
Maxcy Gregg
Mary Elizabeth Moragne
    John Moragne
Noble Family
    P. Noble
E. G. Randolph
Templeton Family
    John T. Quinn
Townes Family
    N. H. Moragne
John Rogers Vinton

UNIVERSITY OF TEXAS ARCHIVES

William W. Arnett
William Pitt Ballinger
Hamilton P. Bee
Peter H. Bell
John Thomas Bolton
    William P. Rogers
Guy Morrison Bryan

Richard E. Cochran
Francis Collins
Martin Labor Crimmins
W. A. Droddy
Samuel V. Fulkerson
Robert Hagan
Charles T. Harlan
James Pinckney Henderson
John Abram Hendricks
   George Berry
   John M. Lord
Benjamin F. Hughes
James Hampton Kuykendall
Letters
   J. D. Affleck
   Crutcher-Shannon
   Dancy
   Eberstadt
   Grayson
   James Jones
William Alexander McClintock
Nathan Mitchell
George Washington Morgan
Josiah Pancoast
Recruiting Poster
William P. Rogers
Daniel Ruggles
Josephus M. Steiner
Henderson King Yoakum

UNIVERSITY OF TEXAS AT ARLINGTON LIBRARIES, SPECIAL COLLECTIONS DIVISION

John B. Butler
Edmund Kirby
John F. Meginness
Mexican War Collection
   Anonymous
   William ———
   Robert Armstrong
   E. T. Blamire
   W. L. Bliss
   G. W. Burton
   Guy Carleton
   John Quincy Carlin

H. S. Clan
Jefferson Davis
Thomas G. Driss [?]
Robert E. Lee
George W. Pickett
W. B. Thorpe
W. H. T. Walker
Trussell Family
Andrew J. Trussell

UNIVERSITY OF VIRGINIA LIBRARY

James D. Blanding
Brown-Hunter
Burwell Family
John Campbell
David I. McCord
James Wall Schureman
Singleton Family
Larkin Smith

VIRGINIA HISTORICAL SOCIETY

Benjamin H. D. Allen
Bemis Family
J. A. Merrifield
Mason Family
William Alexander Spark
Massie Family
George Columbus Palmore
Edward B. Shelton
Thornton Family
William Shover

VIRGINIA STATE LIBRARY AND ARCHIVES, PERSONAL PAPERS COLLECTION,
ARCHIVES BRANCH, RICHMOND, VIRGINIA

Harvy Black
Garnett Family
George Pickett
William B. Taliaferro

WESTERN HISTORICAL MANUSCRIPT COLLECTION, COLUMBIA, MISSOURI

James Austin
Thomas E. Breckenridge
Richard W. Burt
N. H. Clark
Colman-Hayter
Romulus Culver
J. N. Dunlap
William H. H. Gist
Spencer H. Givens
Odon Guitar
C. Harrison
Joseph K. Johnson
Waldo P. Johnson
C. William F. Jones
Abiel Leonard
Thomas Bryan Lester
Mexican War Veterans
Mrs. John G. Miller
Missouri Association of Mexican War Veterans
Betty J. Mussell
John Ralls
Benjamin Ladd Wiley

COLLEGE OF WILLIAM AND MARY, SWEM LIBRARY

John P. Brock
Ritchie-Harrison
    Noah Newton
    Robert R. Ritchie

YALE UNIVERSITY, BEINECKE LIBRARY

Western Americana Collection
    Augustus———
    Franklin———
    Wm. F. Adee
    W. M. Albin
    Thos. Ludwell Alexander
    M. L. Baker
    William G. Belknap
    B. Loring Bonner
    Edmund Bradford

Sumner C. Brooks
John Brown
Wellington C. Burnett
Charles R. Case
Frank Clarke
Charles C. Clement
George W. Clutter
J. M. Cook
James Crabb
George H. Crossman
Albion T. Crow
Caleb Cushing
Jefferson Davis
James and Simon Doyle
Jubal Early
Fleming Gardner
Robert Selden Garnett
John B. Grayson
Joseph A. Haskin
William Higgins
Jacob Z. Hoffer
R. W. Jones
Edmund Kirby
Edmund Kirby-Smith
Jacob Latture
Robert Morrison
Ebenezer W. Pomeroy
Joseph Rowe Smith
William P. Tomlinson
William Stephen Walker
John Darragh Wilkins
William T. Withers
David Wooster
Richard Yost

Primary Sources

BOOKS

[Alcaraz, Ramon, et al.] *The Other Side; or, Notes for the History of the War between Mexico and the United States.* Translated and edited by Albert C. Ramsey. New York: John Wiley, 1850.
Anderson, Robert. *An Artillery Officer in the Mexican War, 1846–7.* New York and London: G. P. Putnam's Sons, 1911.

[Ballentine, George]. *Autobiography of an English Soldier in the United States Army*. New York: Stringer & Townshend, 1853.

Beauregard, P. G. T. *With Beauregard in Mexico: The Mexican War Reminiscences of P. G. T. Beauregard*. Edited by T. Harry Williams. [Baton Rouge]: Louisiana State University Press, 1956.

Brackett, Albert G. *General Lane's Brigade in Central Mexico*. Cincinnati: H. W. Derby; New York: J. C. Derby, 1854.

Brown, Harvey E., comp. *The Medical Department of the United States Army from 1775 to 1873*. Washington, D.C.: Surgeon General's Office, 1873.

Calderon de la Barca, Frances. *Life in Mexico*. 1843. Reprint. New York: Dutton, 1970.

Callan, John F., ed., *The Military Laws of the United States, Relating to the Army, Volunteers, Militia, and to Bounty Lands and Pensions, from the Foundation of the Government to the Year 1863*. Philadelphia: George W. Childs, 1863.

Chamberlain, Samuel E. *My Confession: The Recollections of a Rogue*. 1956. Reprint. Lincoln and London: University of Nebraska Press, 1987.

Cooke, Philip St. George. *The Conquest of New Mexico and California: An Historical and Personal Narrative*. New York: G. P. Putnam's Sons, 1878. Reprint. New York: Arno Press, 1976.

Coolidge, Richard H., comp. *Statistical Report on the Sickness and Mortality in the Army of the United States, Compiled from the Records of the Surgeon General's Office, Embracing a Period of Sixteen Years, from January, 1839 to January, 1855*. Washington, D.C.: A. O. P. Nicholson, 1856.

Coulter, Richard, and Barclay, Thomas. *Volunteers: The Mexican War Journals of Private Richard Coulter and Sergeant Thomas Barclay, Company E, Second Pennsylvania Infantry*. Edited by Allan Peskin. Kent, Ohio: Kent State University Press, 1991.

Croghan, George. *Army Life on the Western Frontier*. Edited by Francis Paul Prucha. Norman: University of Oklahoma Press, 1958.

Dana, N. J. T. *Monterrey Is Ours!: The Mexican War Letters of Lieutenant Dana, 1845–1847*. Edited by Robert H. Ferrell. Lexington: University Press of Kentucky, 1990.

De Hart, William C. *Observations on Military Law, and the Constitution and Pratice of Courts Martial, with a Summary of the Law of Evidence, as Applicable to Military Trials: Adapted to the Laws, Regulations, and Customs of the Army and Navy of the United States*. New York: Wiley and Halsted, 1846, 1859.

Edwards, Frank S. *A Campaign in New Mexico*. Philadelphia: Carey and Hart, 1847. Reprint. Ann Arbor, Mich.: University Microfilms, 1966.

Elderkin, James D. *Biographical Sketches and Anecdotes of a Soldier of Three Wars, as Written by Himself*. Detroit: Record Printing, 1899.

Elliott, Isaac H. *Record of the Services of Illinois Soldiers in the Black Hawk War, 1831–32, and in the Mexican War, 1846–48*. Springfield: State of Illinois, 1908.

Gibson, George Rutledge. *Journal of a Soldier under Kearny and Doniphan, 1846–*

1847. Edited by Ralph P. Bieber. Glendale, Calif.: Arthur H. Clarke, 1935. Reprint. Philadelphia: Porcupine Press, 1974.

Grant, Ulysses S. *The Papers of Ulysses S. Grant, Vol. 1, 1837–1861.* Edited by John Y. Simon. Carbondale: Southern Illinois University Press, 1967.

Hartman, George W. *A Private's Own Journal: Giving an Account of the Battles in Mexico, under Gen'l. Scott.* Greencastle, Pa.: E. Robinson, 1849.

Henderson, Thomas. *Hints on the Medical Examination of Recruits for the Army and on the Discharge of Soldiers from the Service on Surgeon's Certificate.* 1840. Rev. ed. by Richard H. Coolidge. Philadelphia: J. B. Lippincott, 1856.

Henry, William Seaton. *Campaign Sketches of the War with Mexico.* New York: Harper and Brothers, 1847. Reprint. New York: Arno Press, 1973.

Jamieson, Milton. *Journal and Notes of a Campaign in Mexico: Containing a History of Company C, of the Second Regiment of Ohio Volunteers.* Cincinnati, 1849.

Lippitt, Francis J. *Reminiscences of Francis J. Lippitt.* Providence, R.I.: Preston and Rounds, 1902.

McAfee, Ward, and Robinson, J. Cordell, comps. *Origins of the Mexican War: A Documentary Source Book.* 2 vols. Salisbury, N.C.: Documentary Publications, 1982.

McCall, George A. *Letters from the Frontiers: Written during a Period of Thirty Years' Service in the Army of the United States.* Philadelphia: J. B. Lippincott, 1868.

McClellan, George B. *The Mexican War Diary of George B. McClellan.* Edited by William Starr Myers. Princeton, N.J.: Princeton University Press, 1917.

Macomb, Alexander. *The Practice of Courts Martial.* New York: Samuel Colman, 1840.

McSherry, Richard. *El Puchero; or, A Mixed Dish from Mexico.* Philadelphia: Lippincott, Grambo, 1850.

Meade, George Gordon. *The Life and Letters of George Gordon Meade.* 2 vols. New York: Scribner's, 1913.

O'Brien, John. *A Treatise on American Military Laws, and the Practice of Courts Martial, with Suggestions for Their Improvement.* Philadelphia: Lea & Blanchard, 1846.

Oswandel, J. Jacob. *Notes of the Mexican War, 1846–47–48.* Philadelphia, 1885.

Perry, Oran, comp. *Indiana in the Mexican War.* Indianapolis: William B. Burford, 1908.

Ramirez, Jose Fernando. *Mexico during the War with the United States.* Edited by Walter V. Scholes. Translated by Elliott B. Scherr. Columbia: University of Missouri Press, 1950.

Redington, Alfred. *Report of the Adjutant General of the Militia of Maine, May 12, 1846.* Augusta, Maine: William T. Johnson, 1846.

Reid, Samuel C., Jr. *The Scouting Expeditions of McCulloch's Texas Rangers.* 1847. Reprint. Freeport, N.Y.: Books for Libraries Press, 1970.

Roberts, B. H. *The Mormon Battalion: Its History and Achievements.* Salt Lake City: Deseret News, 1919.

Robinson, Jacob S. *A Journal of the Santa Fe Expedition under Colonel Doniphan.* Portsmouth, N.H.: Portsmouth *Journal* Press, 1848. Reprint. Princeton, N.J.: Princeton University Press, 1932. Reprint. N.Y.: Da Capo Press, 1972.

Smith, Gustavus W. *Company "A," Corps. of Engineers, U.S.A., 1846–'48, in the Mexican War.* Willets Point, N.Y.: Battalion Press, 1896.

Taylor, Zachary. *Letters of Zachary Taylor from the Battle-Fields of the Mexican War.* Rochester, N.Y.: William K. Bixby, 1908. Reprint. New York: Kraus Reprint, 1970.

Tennery, Thomas D. *The Mexican War Diary of Thomas D. Tennery.* Edited by D. E. Livingston-Little. Norman: University of Oklahoma Press, 1970.

U.S. Government. *General Regulations for the Army, 1835.* Washington, D.C., 1835.

———. *General Regulations for the Army of the United States, 1841.* Washington, D.C., 1841.

———. *General Regulations for the Army of the United States, 1847.* Washington, D.C., 1847.

PERIODICALS

Abbott, Jacob. "The Armory at Springfield." *Harper's New Monthly Magazine* 5, no. 26 (July 1852): 145–61.

Archer, J. J. "A Marylander in the Mexican War: Some Letters of J. J. Archer." Edited by C. A. Porter Hopkins. *Maryland Historical Magazine* 54, no. 4 (1959): 408–22.

Backus, Electus. "A Brief Sketch of the Battle of Monterey, with details of that portion of it, which took place at the eastern extremity of the city." *Historical Magazine* 10, no. 7 (July 1866): 207–13.

———. "Details of the Controversy between the Regulars and Volunteers, in relation to the part taken by each in the capture of Battery No. 1 and other works at the east end of the City of Monterey, on the 21st of September, 1846." *Historical Magazine* 10, no. 8 (August 1866): 255–57.

Bailey, Thomas. "Diary of the Mexican War." *Indiana Magazine of History* 14, no. 2 (1918): 134–47.

Balbotin, Manuel. "The Battle of Angostura (Buena Vista)." Translated by F. H. Hardie. *Journal of the United States Cavalry Association* 7, no. 25 (June 1894): 125–54.

Balboutin, Manuel. "The Siege of Monterey." Translated by John Strother. *Journal of the Military Service Institution* 8 (1887): 325–54.

Barton, E. H. "Means of Preserving Health at Vera Cruz." *Boston Medical and Surgical Journal* 36, no. 24 (1847): 484.

Baylies, Francis. "The March of the United States Troops, under the Command of General John E. Wool, from San Antonio, Texas, to Saltillo,

Mexico, in the Year 1846." *Stryker's American Register and Magazine* 4 (July 1850): 297–312.

Bigelow, Henry Jacob. "Insensibility during Surgical Operations Produced by Inhalation." *Boston Medical and Surgical Journal* 35, no. 16 (November 18, 1846): 311–17.

Bigler, Henry W. "Extracts from the Journal of Henry W. Bigler." *Utah Historical Quarterly* 5, no. 2 (April 1932): 34–64.

Bliss, Robert S. "The Journal of Robert S. Bliss, with the Mormon Battalion." *Utah Historical Quarterly* 4, no. 3 (July 1931): 67–96; 4, no. 4 (October 1931): 110–28.

Brydolph, Fabian. "An Iowan in the Mexican War." Edited by George S. May. *Iowa Journal of History* 3, no. 2 (1955): 167–74.

Campbell, William Bowen. "Mexican War Letters of Col. William Bowen Campbell, of Tennessee, Written to Governor David Campbell, of Virginia, 1846–1847." Edited by St. George L. Sioussat. *Tennessee Historical Magazine* 1, no. 2 (1915): 129–67.

Chapman, William. "Letters from the Seat of War—Mexico." *Green Bay Historical Bulletin* 4, no. 4 (July-August 1928): 1–24.

Clutter, George Washington. "George Washington Clutter in the Mexican War." Edited by Florence Johnson Scott. *Texas Military History* 4, no. 2 (1964): 119–31.

Coffey, Chesley Sheldon. "The Mexican War Letters of Chesley Sheldon Coffey." Edited by Mary Ellen Rowe. *Journal of Mississippi History* 44, no. 3 (August 1982): 235–52.

Collins, Francis. "Journal of Francis Collins: An Artillery Officer in the Mexican War." Edited by Maria Clinton Collins. *Quarterly Publication of the Historical and Philosophical Society of Ohio* 10, nos. 2 and 3 (April and July 1915): 37–109.

Cook, Zo. S. "Mexican War Reminiscences." *Alabama Historical Quarterly* 19 (1957): 435–65.

Cooke, P. St. George. "Report of Lieut. Col. P. St. George Cooke of His March from Santa Fe, New Mexico, to San Diego, Upper California." Edited by Hamilton Gardner. *Utah Historical Quarterly* 22, no. 1 (January 1954): 15–40.

Cox, Leander M. "Mexican War Journal of Leander M. Cox." Edited by Charles F. Hinds. *Register of the Kentucky Historical Society* 55, no. 1 (1957): 29–52; 55, no. 3 (1957): 213–36; 56, no. 1 (1958): 47–69.

Crockett, John M. "Letter of John M. Crockett, 1846." *Register of the Kentucky Historical Society* 52, no. 178 (January 1954): 305–9.

Deas, George. "Reminiscences of the Campaign on the Rio Grande." *Dawson's Historical Magazine* 17, no. 1 (January 1870): 19–22; 17, no. 2 (February 1870): 99–103; 17, no. 4 (April 1870): 236–38; 17, no. 5 (May 1870): 311–16.

Emory, William H. "New Mexico Diary—1846." Edited by Irving F. Hand. *New Mexico* 26, no. 10 (October 1948): 24, 47.

Engelmann, Adolph. "The Second Illinois in the Mexican War: Mexican War Letters of Adolph Engelmann, 1846–1847." Translated and edited by Otto B. Engelmann. *Journal of the Illinois State Historical Society* 26, no. 4 (1934): 357–452.

Evans, Joseph. "Around Cape Horn with Colonel Stevenson's Regiment in 1846." *Quarterly of the Society of California Pioneers* 7, no. 4 (1930): 244–54.

Frost, Daniel M. "The Memoirs of Daniel M. Frost." Edited by Dana O. Jensen. *Missouri Historical Society Bulletin* 26, no. 3 (1970): 200–26.

Gailland, P. C. "On Some Points of Hygiene, and Their Connection with the Propagation of Yellow Fever and Cholera." *Charleston Medical Journal and Review* 4 (1849): 280–95.

"A General's Orderly in Mexico." *United Service Magazine* (London) 78, no. 318 (1855): 78–85.

Gordon, George H. "The Battle of Contreras and Churubusco." *Papers of the Military Historical Society of Massachusetts* 13 (1913): 561–98.

———. "Battles of Molino del Rey and Chapultepec." *Papers of the Military Historical Society of Massachusetts* 13 (1913): 601–13.

Griffin, John S. "A Doctor Comes to California: The Diary of John S. Griffin, Assistant Surgeon with Kearny's Dragoons, 1846–47." Edited by George Walcott Ames, Jr. *California Historical Society Quarterly* 21, no. 3 (1942): 193–224; 21, no. 4 (1942): 333–57; 22, no. 1 (1943): 41–66.

Hamilton, Charles S. "Memoirs of the Mexican War." *Wisconsin Magazine of History* 14, no. 1 (1930): 63–92.

Herrick, W. B. "Remarks upon the Organization of the Medical Department of the Army, and the Effects of Marching and a Camp Life in Producing and Modifying Disease." *Illinois and Indiana Medical and Surgical Journal* 2, no. 3 (1847): 225–32.

Hess, John W. "John W. Hess, with the Mormon Battalion." *Utah Historical Quarterly* 4, no. 2 (1931): 47–55.

Heyer, Charles H. "A Mexican War Letter." *Magazine of History* 17, no. 6 (1913): 238–41.

H. [Hill, D. H.] "The Battles of the Rio Grande." *Southern Quarterly Review*, n.s., 2, no. 4 (November 1850): 427–63.

Holland, James K. "Diary of a Texan Volunteer in the Mexican War." *Southwestern Historical Quarterly* 30, no. 1 (July 1926): 1–33.

Hollingsworth, John McHenry. "Journal of John McHenry Hollingsworth: A Lieutenant in Stevenson's Regiment in California." *California Historical Society Quarterly* 1, no. 3 (January 1923): 207–70.

Jarvis, Nathan S. "An Army Surgeon's Notes of Frontier Service—Mexican War." *Journal of the Military Service Institution of the United States* 40, no. 147 (May 1907): 435–52; 41, no. 148 (June 1907): 90–105.

Johnson, William S. "Private Johnson Fights the Mexicans, 1847–1848." Edited by John Hammond Moore. *South Carolina Historical and Genealogical Magazine* 67, no. 4 (1966): 203–28.

Jones, Nathaniel V. "The Journal of Nathaniel V. Jones, with the Mormon Battalion." *Utah Historical Quarterly* 4 (January 1931): 6–23.

K., G. W. "Vera Cruz." *Littell's Living Age* 13, no. 157 (1847): 328–29.

Kendall, George W. "Mr. Kendall's Letters from the Army." *Littell's Living Age* 15, no. 183 (1847): 323–35.

King, John Nevin. "The Happy Soldier: The Mexican War Letters of John Nevin King." Edited by Walter B. Hendrickson. *Journal of the Illinois State Historical Society* 46, no. 1 (1953): 13–27; 46, no. 2 (1953): 151–70.

Lane, Henry S. "The Mexican War Journal of Henry S. Lane." Edited by Graham A. Barringer. *Indiana Magazine of History* 53, no. 4 (1957): 383–434.

Lane, W. B. "The United States Cavalry in the Mexican War." *Journal of the United States Cavalry Association* 3, no. 11 (December 1890): 388–408.

Long, Edwin Ramsey. "An Essay on Delerium Tremens." *Illinois and Indiana Medical and Surgical Journal* 1, no. 2 (June 1846): 97–107.

Lundie, Thomas Y. "Letters from Mexico: 1847–1848." Edited by James W. McKee. *Tennessee Historical Quarterly* 29, no. 2 (1970): 152–59.

McClintock, William A. "Journal of a Trip through Texas and Northern Mexico in 1846–1847." *Southwestern Historical Quarterly* 34, no. 1 (1930): 20–37; 34, no. 2 (1930): 141–58; 34, no. 3 (1931): 231–56.

McSherry, Richard. "A Mexican Campaign Sketch." *New Eclectic* 3 (1868): 327–36.

McWilliams, William Joseph. "A Westmoreland Guard in Mexico, 1847–1848: The Journal of William Joseph McWilliams," *Western Pennsylvania Historical Magazine* 52, no. 3 (July 1969): 213–40; 52, no. 4 (October 1969): 387–413.

Manigault, Arthur M. "A Letter from Vera Cruz in 1847." Edited by Robert A. Law. *Southwestern Historical Quarterly* 18, no. 2 (1914): 215–18.

"Memories of Mexico." *Harper's New Monthly Magazine* 3 (June-November 1851): 461–66.

Molina, Ignacio. "El Asalto al Castillo de Chapultepec: El Dia 13 Septiembre de 1847." *Revista Postiva Cientifica, Filosofica, Social y Politica; Organa del Positivismo*, no. 22 (1902): 444–64.

Morrison, George S. "Letter from Mexico by George S. Morrison, a Member of Capt. Albert Pike's Squadron." *Arkansas Historical Quarterly* 16, no. 4 (1957): 398–401.

Nauman, George. "A Lancastrian in the Mexican War." *Historical Papers and Addresses of the Lancaster County Historical Society* 12, no. 3 (1908): 109–29.

———. "In Command at Vera Cruz, 1847–1848." *Papers Read to Lancaster County Historical Society* 18, no. 6 (June 1914): 157–60.

Nunnelee, S. F. "Alabama in Mexico War." *Alabama Historical Quarterly* 19 (1957): 413–33.

Patton, A. "Recollections of Medical Service during the War with Mexico." *Indiana Journal of Medicine* 5, no. 4 (August 1874): 145–50.

Porter, John B. "Medical and Surgical Notes of Campaigns in the War with Mexico, during the Years 1845, 1846, 1847, and 1848." *American Journal of the Medical Sciences* 23 (January 1852): 13–37; 24 (July 1852): 13–30; 25 (January 1853): 25–42; 26 (October 1853): 297–333; 35 (April 1858): 347–52.

Proctor, Alfred N. "A Massachusetts Mechanic in Florida and Mexico—1847." Edited by Arthur W. Thompson. *Florida Historical Quarterly* 33, no. 2 (1954): 130–41.

Quesenbury, William. "William Quesenbury of Fayetteville Reports the Battle of Buena Vista, Mexico." *Flashback: Preserving the Past for the Future* 4, no. 2 (1954): 34–36.

Reilly, James. "An Artilleryman's Story." *Journal of the Military Service Institution of the United States* 33, no. 126 (1903): 438–47.

Richardson, William H. "William H. Richardson's Journal of Doniphan's Expedition." Edited by William B. McGroarty. *Missouri Historical Review* 22, no. 2 (1928): 193–236; 22, no. 3 (1928): 331–60; 22, no. 4 (1928): 511–42.

Rogers, William P. "The Diary and Letters of William P. Rogers, 1846–1862." Edited by Eleanor Damon Pace. *Southwestern Historical Quarterly* 32, no. 4 (April 1929): 259–99.

Scott, Winfield, and Harney, William S. "Scott and Harney—An Official Episode of the Mexican War." *Journal of the United States Cavalry Association* 9, no. 35 (December 1896): 316–27.

Skelly, James. "Diary of a Pennsylvania Volunteer in the Mexican War." Edited by James K. Greer. *Western Pennsylvania Historical Magazine* 12, no. 3 (1929): 147–54.

"Sketches of the Mexican War: The Texan Ranger." *Fraser's Magazine* 38, no. 7 (July 1848): 91–102.

Smith, Persifor F. "The Second Brigade, at Monterey." *Historical Magazine* 3, no. 1 (March 1874): 138–40.

Steele, John. "Extracts from the Journal of John Steele." *Utah Historical Quarterly* 6, no. 1 (January 1933): 2–28.

Sweeny, Thomas W. "Narrative of Army Service in the Mexican War and on the Plains, 1846–1853." *Journal of the Military Service Institution of the United States* 42, no. 151 (1908): 126–35.

Taliaferro, William Booth. "William Booth Taliaferro's Letters from Mexico, 1847–1848." Edited by Ludwell H. Johnson. *Virginia Magazine of History and Biography* 73, no. 4 (1965): 455–73.

"Taylor's Battles in Mexico." *Harper's New Monthly Magazine* 11, no. 62 (1855): 170–85.

Thomas, John. "A Mexican War Incident." Edited by Tom Feathers. *Flashback: Preserving the Past for the Future* 7, no. 3 (1957): 23–24.

Toll, Isaac D. "Michigan's Record in the War with Mexico." *Pioneer Society of Michigan Papers* 2 (1877): 171–77.

———. "Michigan Soldiers in Mexico." *Pioneer Society of Michigan Papers* 7 (1884): 112–21.

Turner, Henry Smith. "Letters about the Mexican War." *Glimpses of the Past* 2, no. 2 (1934–1935): 1–31.

Upton, Barna. "Our First Foreign War." Edited by William F. Goetzmann. *American Heritage* 17, no. 4 (1966): 18–27, 85–99.

Viall, Nelson. "Recollections of the Mexican War." *Rhode Island Historical Collections* 30, no. 3 (July 1937): 65–82.

Watson, Henry Bulls. "The Journal of Second Lt. Henry Bulls Watson." *Fortitudine* (Summer 1985): 3–8.

Weber, R. B., ed. "The Mexican War: Some Personal Correspondence." *Indiana Magazine of History* 65, no. 2 (1969): 133–39.

Whitworth, Robert W. "From the Mississippi to the Pacific: An Englishman in the Mormon Battalion." Edited by David B. Gracy II and Helen J. H. Rugeley. *Arizona and the West* 7, no. 2 (1965): 127–60.

Wynne, James. "Memoir of the Rev. Anthoy Rey, S. J." *United States Catholic Magazine* 6, no. 10 (1847): 543–52.

Wool, John E. "General John E. Wool's Memoranda of the Battle of Buena Vista." Edited by K. Jack Bauer. *Southwestern Historical Quarterly* 77, no. 1 (1973): 111–25.

Secondary Sources

BOOKS

Ashburn, P. M. *A History of the Medical Department of the United States Army.* Boston and New York: Houghton Mifflin, 1929.

Brieger, Gert H., ed. *Medical America in the Nineteenth Century: Readings from the Literature.* Baltimore and London: Johns Hopkins University Press, 1972.

Coffman, Edward M. *The Old Army: A Portrait of the American Army in Peacetime, 1784–1898.* New York and Oxford: Oxford University Press, 1986.

Cunliffe, Marcus. *Soldiers and Civilians: The Martial Spirit in America, 1775–1865.* Boston and Toronto: Little, Brown, 1968.

Cutler, Wayne; Eisenhower; John S. D.; Soto, Miguel E.; and Richmond, Douglas W. *Essays on the Mexican War.* Edited by Douglas W. Richmond. College Station: Texas A&M University Press, 1986.

De Leon, Arnoldo. *They Called Them Greasers: Anglo Attitudes toward Mexicans in Texas, 1821–1900.* Austin: University of Texas Press, 1983.

Dolph, Edward Arthur. *"Sound Off!": Soldier Songs from the Revolution to World War II.* New York and Toronto: Farrar & Rinehart, 1929, 1942.

Eisenhower, John S. D. *So Far from God: The U.S. War with Mexico, 1846–1848.* New York: Random House, 1989.

Faulk, Odie, and Stout, Joseph A., Jr. *The Mexican War: Changing Interpretations*. Chicago: Swallow Press, 1973.

Federal Writer's Project. *Military History of Kentucky*. Frankfort, Ky.: Works Progress Administration, 1939.

Frank, Joseph Allan, and Reaves, George A. *"Seeing the Elephant": Raw Recruits at the Battle of Shiloh*. New York: Greenwood Press, 1989.

Fuess, Claude M. *The Life of Caleb Cushing*. 2 vols. New York: Harcourt, Brace, 1923.

Fuller, Claud E. *The Rifled Musket*. New York: Bonanza Books, 1958.

Gillett, Mary C. *The Army Medical Department, 1818–1865*. Washington, D.C.: Center of Military History, U.S. Army, 1987.

Glasson, William H. *Federal Military Pensions in the United States*. New York: Oxford University Press, 1918.

Haller, John S., Jr. *American Medicine in Transition, 1840–1910*. Urbana, Chicago, London: University of Illinois Press, 1981.

Hicken, Victor. *The American Fighting Man*. New York: Macmillan, 1969.

Horsman, Reginald. *Race and Manifest Destiny: The Origins of American Racial Anglo-Saxonism*. Cambridge, Mass., and London: Harvard University Press, 1981.

Johannsen, Robert W. *To the Halls of the Montezumas: The Mexican War in the American Imagination*. New York and Oxford: Oxford University Press, 1985.

Katcher, Philip R. N. *The Mexican-American War, 1846–1848*. London: Osprey Publishing, 1976.

Kreidberg, Marvin A., and Henry, Merton G. *History of Military Mobilization in the United States Army, 1775–1945*. Westport, Conn.: Greenwood Press, 1955.

Lacour-Gayet, Robert. *Everyday Life in the United States before the Civil War, 1830–1860*. Translated by Mary Ilford. New York: Frederick Ungar, 1969.

Leach, Jack Franklin. *Conscription in the United States: Historical Background*. Rutland, Vt.: Charles E. Tuttle, 1952.

Lerwill, Leonard J. *The Personnel Replacement System in the United States Army*. Washington, D.C.: Department of the Army, 1954.

Lewis, Virgil A. *The Soldiery of West Virginia in the French and Indian War, Lord Dunmore's War, the Revolution, the Later Indian Wars, the Whiskey Insurrection, the Second War with England, the War with Mexico, and Addenda relating to West Virginians in the Civil War*. Reprint. Baltimore: Genealogical Publishing, 1972.

McWhiney, Grady. *Braxton Bragg and Confederate Defeat*. New York and London: Columbia University Press, 1969.

Miller, Robert Ryal. *Shamrock and Sword: The Saint Patrick's Battalion in the U.S.-Mexican War*. Norman and London: University of Oklahoma Press, 1989.

Morison, Samuel Eliot; Merk, Frederick; and Friedel, Frank. *Dissent in Three American Wars*. Cambridge, Mass.: Harvard University Press, 1970.

Nevin, David. *The Mexican War*. Alexandria, Va.: Time-Life Books, 1978.

Potter, Chandler E. *The Military History of the State of New Hampshire, 1623–1861*. Baltimore: Genealogical Publishing, 1972.

Prucha, Francis Paul. *The Sword of the Republic: The United States Army on the Frontier, 1783–1846*. Lincoln and London: University of Nebraska Press, 1969.

Risch, Erna. *Quartermaster Support of the Army: A History of the Corps, 1775–1939*. Washington, D.C.: Quartermaster Historian's Office, Office of the Quartermaster General, 1962.

Roberts, B. H. *The Mormon Battalion: Its History and Achievements*. Salt Lake City: Deseret News, 1919.

Rothstein, William G. *American Physicians in the Nineteenth Century: From Sects to Science*. Baltimore and London: Johns Hopkins University Press, 1972.

Rowland, Dunbar. *Military History of Mississippi, 1803–1898*. Reprint. Spartanburg, S.C.: Reprint Company, 1978.

Sandweiss, Martha A.; Stewart, Rick; and Huseman, Ben W. *Eyewitness to War: Prints and Daguerreotypes of the Mexican War, 1846–1848*. Fort Worth, Tex., and Washington, D.C.: Amon Carter Museum and Smithsonian Institution Press, 1989.

Schroeder, John H. *Mr. Polk's War: American Opposition and Dissent, 1846–1848*. Madison: University of Wisconsin Press, 1973.

Singletary, Otis A. *The Mexican War*. Chicago and London: University of Chicago Press, 1960.

Smith, George W., and Judah, Charles. *Chronicles of the Gringoes: The U.S. Army in the Mexican War, 1846–1848*. Albuquerque: University of New Mexico Press, 1968.

Smith, Merrit Roe. *Harpers Ferry Armory and the New Technology*. Ithaca, N.Y., and London: Cornell University Press, 1977.

Stouffer, Samuel L., et al. *The American Soldier*, Vol. 2, *Combat and Its Aftermath*. Princeton, N.J.: Princeton University Press, 1949.

Takaki, Ronald T. *Iron Cages: Race and Culture in Nineteenth-Century America*. New York: Alfred A. Knopf, 1979.

Upton, Emory. *The Military Policy of the United States*. 1904. Reprint. New York: Greenwood Press, 1968.

Watson, Peter. *War on the Mind: The Military Uses and Abuses of Psychology*. New York: Basic Books, 1978.

Weber, David J., ed. *New Spain's Far Northern Frontier: Essays on Spain in the American West, 1540–1821*. Albuquerque: University of New Mexico Press, 1979.

PERIODICALS

Anderson, John Q. "Soldier Lore of the War with Mexico." *Western Humanities Review* 11, no. 4 (1957): 321–30.

Armstrong, Andrew. "The Brazito Battlefield." *New Mexico Historical Review* 35, no. 1 (1960): 63–74.

Baker, B. Kimball. "The St. Patricks Fought for Their Skins, and Mexico." *Smithsonian* 8, no. 12 (1978): 94–101.

Bauer, K. Jack. "The Veracruz Expedition of 1847." *Military Affairs: Journal of the American Military Institute* 20, no. 3 (1956): 162–69.

Berg, Richard, and Balkoski, Joe. "Veracruz: U.S. Invasion of Mexico, 1847." *Strategy and Tactics*, no. 63 (1977): 4–18.

Blied, Benjamin J. "Catholic Aspects of the Mexican War, 1846–1848." *Social Justice Review* 40, no. 11 (March 1948): 367–71.

Bloom, John P. "New Mexico Viewed by Anglo-Americans, 1846–1849." *New Mexico Historical Review* 34, no. 3 (July 1959): 165–98.

Brack, Gene M. "Mexican Opinion, American Racism, and the War of 1846." *Western Historical Quarterly* 1, no. 2 (April 1970): 161–74.

Brent, Robert A. "Mississippi and the Mexican War." *Journal of Mississippi History* 31, no. 3 (August 1969): 202–14.

Brown, Walter Lee. "The Mexican War Experiences of Albert Pike and the 'Mounted Devils' of Arkansas." *Arkansas Historical Quarterly* 12, no. 4 (Winter 1953): 301–15.

Callahan, Donald, and Seinfeld, Richard. "Sons of Erin, Sons of Mexico." *Houston Chronicle*, March 17, 1983.

Campbell, Eugene E. "Authority Conflicts in the Mormon Battalion." *Brigham Young University Studies* 8, no. 2 (1968): 127–42.

Canaday, Dayton W. "Voice of the Volunteer of 1847." *Journal of the Illinois State Historical Society* 44, no. 3 (1951): 199–209.

Chin, Brian, and Langellier, J. Phillip. "General Stephen Watts Kearney [sic] and Officers of the First U.S. Dragoons, 1847." *Military Collector and Historian* 31, no. 2 (Summer 1979): 82–83.

Clark, Kimball. "The Epic March of Doniphan's Missourians." *Missouri Historical Review* 80 (January 1986): 134–55.

Coulter, Richard. "The Westmoreland Guards in the War with Mexico, 1846–1848." *Western Pennsylvania Historical Magazine* 24, no. 2 (1941): 101–26.

Crimmins, Martin L. "First Stages of the Mexican War: Initial Operations of the Army in 1846." *Army Ordnance* 15, no. 88 (1935): 222–25.

Cross, Fred W. "The First Regiment, Massachusetts Infantry in the Mexican War." *Citizens Service Journal*, July-August 1928, 9, 11, 13; September 1928, 10–11, 23; November 1928, 7–8.

Crowson, E. T. "Manifest Destiny, Mexico, and the Palmetto Boys." *South Carolina History Illustrated* 5, no. 1 (1972): 32–35, 66–69.

————. "West Virginians with General Taylor in Mexico." *West Virginia History* 35, no. 1 (1973): 56–65.

Davies, Wallace E. "The Mexican War Veterans as an Organized Group." *Mississippi Valley Historical Review* 35, no. 2 (September 1948): 221–38.

Davis, T. Frederick. "Florida's Part in the War with Mexico." *Florida Historical Quarterly* 20 (January 1942): 235–59.

Davis, William. "Victory at Monterrey." *American History Illustrated* 5, no. 5 (1970): 12–23.

Downey, Fairfax. "Tragic Story of the San Patricio Battalion." *American Heritage* 6, no. 4 (1955): 20–23.

Duncan, H. C. "Monroe County in the Mexican War." *Indiana Magazine of History* 12, no. 4 (December 1916): 287–98.

Duncan, Louis C. "A Medical History of General Zachary Taylor's Army of Occupation in Texas and Mexico, 1845–1847." *Military Surgeon: Journal of the Association of Military Surgeons of the United States* 48, no. 1 (1920): 76–104.

————. "Medical History of General Scott's Campaign to the City of Mexico in 1847." *Military Surgeon: Journal of the Association of Military Surgeons of the United States* 47, no. 4 (1920): 436–70; 47, no. 5 (1920): 596–609.

————. "The Days Gone By: A Volunteer Regiment in 1846–7." *Military Surgeon: Journal of the Association of Military Surgeons of the United States* 56, no. 5 (1929): 709–13.

Durham, Walter T. "Mexican War Letters to Wynnewood." *Tennessee Historical Quarterly* 32, no. 4 (Winter 1974): 389–409.

Evans, John R. "The Reading Artillerists in the Mexican War." *Historical Review of Berks County* 15 (October 1948): 130–41.

Fakes, Turner J., Jr. "Memphis and the Mexican War." *West Tennessee Historical Society Papers* 2 (1948): 119–44.

Finke, Detmar H. "The Organization and Uniforms of the San Patricio Units of the Mexican Army, 1846–1848." *Military Collector and Historian* 9 (Summer 1957): 36–38.

Fisher, George J. B. "Buena Vista—A Western Thermopylae." *Coast Artillery Journal* 72, no. 2 (1930): 141–50.

Franklin, William B. "The Battle of Buena Vista." *Papers of the Military Historical Society of Massachusetts* 13 (1913): 545–57.

Gardner, Hamilton. "The Command and Staff of the Mormon Battalion in the Mexican War." *Utah Historical Quarterly* 20, no. 4 (1952): 332–51.

Garrison, Fielding H. "Notes on the History of Military Medicine." *Military Surgeon: Journal of the Association of Military Surgeons of the United States* 50, no. 6 (1922): 691–718.

Haarmann, Albert W. "Uniform Notes on the Maryland Volunteer Militia, about 1846." *Military Collector and Historian* 36, no. 3 (Fall 1984): 113–15.

Hatch, Katherine. "Saint Patrick's Battalion: Unlikely Victims of a Mexican War." *Ireland of the Welcomes* 26, no. 2 (March-April 1977): 32–35.

Henderson, Alfred J. "A Morgan County Volunteer in the Mexican War." *Illinois Historical Society Quarterly* 41, no. 4 (December 1948): 383–401.

Higham, C. L. "Songs of the Mexican War: An Interpretation of Sources." *Journal of the West* 28, no. 3 (July 1989): 16–23.

Hinckley, Ted C. "American Anti-Catholicism during the Mexican War." *Pacific Historical Review* 31, no. 2 (1962): 121–37.

Hopkins, G. T. "The San Patricio Battalion in the Mexican War." *Journal of the United States Cavalry Association* 24, no. 98 (September 1913): 279–84.

Horine, Emmet F. "Episodes in the History of Anesthesia." *Journal of the History of Medicine and Allied Sciences* 1 (October 1946): 521–26.

Houston, Flora Belle. "The Mormon Battalion." *Historical Society of Southern California* 14, no. 3 (1928): 338–54.

Irey, Thomas R. "Soldiering, Suffering, and Dying in the Mexican War." *Journal of the West* 11, no. 2 (1972): 285–98.

Karnes, Thomas L. "Gilpin's Volunteers on the Santa Fe Trail." *Kansas Historical Quarterly* 30, no. 1 (Spring 1964): 1–14.

Kreneck, Thomas H. "The Neglected Regiment: East Texas Horsemen with Zachary Taylor." *East Texas Historical Society* 12, no. 2 (1974): 22–31.

Kurtz, Wilbur G., Jr. "The First Regiment of Georgia Volunteers in the Mexican War." *Georgia Historical Quarterly* 27, no. 4 (December 1943): 301–23.

Lander, Ernest M., Jr. "The Palmetto Regiment Goes to Mexico." *Proceedings of the South Carolina Historical Association* (1973): 83–93.

Lane, W. B. "The 'Regiment of Mounted Riflemen'; or, From Puebla to the City of Mexico." *United Service* 14, no. 4 (October 1895): 301–13.

Le Sueur, James W. "When the Mormon Battalion Came to Tucson." *Improvement Era* 49, no. 12 (1946): 791.

Livingston-Little, D. E. "Mutiny during the Mexican War: An Incident on the Rio Grande." *Journal of the West* 9, no. 3 (1970): 340–45.

Lyman, Amy Brown. "The Women of the Mormon Battalion." *Relief Society Magazine* 35, no. 7 (1948): 436–40.

McAfee, Michael. "The Assault on Mexico City, 13 September 1847." *Military Collector and Historian* 29, no. 2 (Summer 1977): 81–85.

McAnaney, William D. "Desertion in the United States Army." *Military Service Institution of the United States* 10 (September 1889): 450–78.

McCornack, Richard B. "The San Patricio Deserters in the Mexican War." *The Americas: A Quarterly Review of Inter-American Cultural History* 8, no. 2 (October 1951): 131–42.

McMaster, Fitzhugh. "Military Dress: The Uniform of the Militia of South Carolina, 1839–1849: Infantry." *Military Collector and Historian* 30, no. 4 (Winter 1978): 173–76.

———. "James Walker's Painting 'The Assault on Mexico City.'" *Military Collector and Historian* 31, no. 1 (Spring 1979): 28–29.

May, Robert E. "Invisible Men: Blacks and the U.S. Army in the Mexican War." *Historian: A Journal of History* 49, no. 4 (August 1987): 463–77.

Meehan, Thomas F. "Catholics in the War with Mexico." *Historical Records and Studies* 12 (June 1918): 39–65.

Michel, Peter J. "No Mere Holiday Affair: The Capture of Santa Fe in the Mexican-American War." *Gateway Heritage: Quarterly Journal of the Missouri Historical Society* 9 (Spring 1989): 12–25.

Miller, Roger G. "Yellow Jack at Vera Cruz." *Prologue* 10 (Spring 1978): 43–53.

"The Mormon Battalion." *Historical Record* 8, nos. 7–8 (1889): 905–38.

Myers, Lee. "Illinois Volunteers in New Mexico, 1847–1848." *New Mexico Historical Review* 47, no. 1 (1972): 5–31.

Oates, Stephen B. "The Texas Rangers in the Mexican War." *Texas Military History* 3, no. 2 (Summer 1963): 65–84.

———. "Los Diablos Tejanos." *American West* 2, no. 3 (1965): 41–50.

Oliva, Leo E. "Missouri Volunteers on the Santa Fe Trail, 1847–1848." *Trail Guide* 15, no. 2 (June 1970): 1–20; 15, no. 3 (September 1970): 1–20.

Payne, Darwin. "Camp Life in the Army of Occupation: Corpus Christi, July 1845 to March 1846." *Southwestern Historical Quarterly* 73, no. 3 (1970): 326–42.

Power, Wally. "The Enigma of the Patricios." *Eire-Ireland* 4, no. 4 (Winter 1969): 7–12.

Ramage, James A. "John Hunt Morgan and the Kentucky Cavalry Volunteers in the Mexican War." *Register of the Kentucky Historical Society* 81, no. 4 (Autumn 1983): 343–65.

Reilly, Tom. "Jane McManus Storms: Letters from the Mexican War, 1846–1848." *Southwestern Historical Quarterly* (July 1981): 21–44.

Reinhardt, Richard. " 'To a Distant and Perilous Service.' " *American Heritage* 30, no. 4 (June-July 1979): 64–77.

Santoni, Pedro. "A Fear of the People: The Civic Militia of Mexico in 1845." *Hispanic American Historical Review* 68, no. 2 (May 1988): 269–88.

Sapper, Neil. "Barbarism and Restraint: The Occupation of Mexico City." *Texas Military History* 8, no. 2 (1970): 97–110.

Schroeder, Theodore. "A Question of Mormon Patriotism." *American Historical Magazine* 1, no. 4 (July 1906): 279–91.

Shields, Elise Trigg. "The Storming of Chapultepec." *Confederate Veteran* 26, no. 9 (1918): 399–401.

Simmons, Edward. "Who Was First at Chapultepec?" *Fortitudine* 12 (Spring-Summer 1982): 3–6.

Smith, Edmund Banks. "Sixty Years After." *Journal of the Military Service Institution of the United States* 42, no. 151 (1908): 136–37.

Smith, Paul T. "Militia of the United States from 1846 to 1860." *Indiana Magazine of History*, March 1919, 20–41.

Spell, Lota M. "The Anglo-Saxon Press in Mexico, 1846–1848." *American Historical Review* 38 (October 1932): 20–31.

Spencer, Ivor. "Overseas War—in 1846!" *Military Affairs* 9, no. 4 (1945): 306–13.

Spurlin, Charles. "American Attitudes in the Mexican-American War." *Military History of Texas and the Southwest* 12, no. 2: 83–92.

———. "Mobilization of the Texas Militia for the Mexican War." Ibid. 15, no. 3: 25–44.

———. "Camp Life of the Texas Volunteer in the Mexican War." *Texana* 12, no. 3: 248–63.

Stearns, Morton E. "Pittsburgh in the Mexican War." *Western Pennsylvania Historical Magazine* 7, no. 4 (1924): 215–44.

Stinson, Byron. "They Went Over to the Enemy." *American History Illustrated* 3, no. 5 (1968): 30–33, 36.

Swan, Guy C.; McGraw, Kenneth S.; Wood, Edward K.; Walters, Ronald; Burchstead, John H. "Scott's Engineers." *Military Review* (March 1983): 61–69.

Trent, Josiah Charles. "Surgical Anesthesia, 1846–1946." *Journal of the History of Medicine and Allied Sciences* 1 (October 1946): 505–14.

Viola, Herman J. "Zachary Taylor and the Indiana Volunteers." *Southwestern Historical Quarterly* 72, no. 3 (1969): 335–46.

Wallace, Edward S. "Deserters in the Mexican War." *Hispanic American Historical Review* 15, no. 3 (1935): 374–83.

———. "The Great Western." *Westerners: New York Posse Brand Book* 5, no. 1 (1958): 58–59, 61–62, 66.

Wallace, Lee A., Jr. "Raising a Volunteer Regiment for Mexico, 1846–1847." *North Carolina Historical Review* 35, no. 1 (January 1958): 20–33.

———. "The First Regiment of Virginia Volunteers, 1846–1848." *Virginia Magazine of History and Biography* 77, no. 1 (1969): 46–77.

Walworth, Ellen Hardin. "The Battle of Buena Vista." *Magazine of American History* 3, no. 12 (December 1879): 705–38.

Weller, Jac. "Civil War Minie Rifles Prove Quite Accurate." *American Rifleman*, July 1971, 36–40.

Williams, Ora. "Forgetting Chapultepec." *Annals of Iowa* 28, no. 2 (October 1946): 81–92.

Willing, Wildurr. "The Engineers and the Mexican War." *Professional Memoirs* 7 (1915): 333–56.

Wood, Walter S. "The 130th Infantry, Illinois National Guard: A Military History, 1778–1919." *Journal of the Illinois State Historical Society* 30, no. 2 (1937): 192–255.

Yurtinus, John F. "The Battle of the Bulls." *Military History of Texas and the Southwest* 14, no. 2 (1978): 99–106.

———. "The Mormon Volunteers: The Recruitment and Service of a Unique Military Company." *Journal of San Diego History* 25, no. 3 (1979): 242–61.

————. "Images of Early California: Mormon Battalion Soldiers' Reflections during the War with Mexico." *Historical Society of Southern California Quarterly* (Spring 1981): 23–43.

Zais, Mitchell M. "Military History: Why Men Fight and Fight Well." *Army* 37, no. 12 (December 1987): 34–38.

Zobell, Albert L., Jr. "The Mormon Battalion in California." *Improvement Era* 54, no. 4 (1951): 242–43, 258, 260, 262, 264, 266.

Unpublished Sources

Bittle, George Cassel. "In the Defense of Florida: The Organized Florida Militia from 1821 to 1920." Ph.D. diss., Florida State University, 1965.

Bloom, John Porter. "With the American Army into Mexico." Ph.D. diss., Emory University, 1956.

Bodson, Robert Louis. "A Description of the United States Occupation of Mexico as Reported by American Newspapers Published in Vera Cruz, Puebla, and Mexico City, September 14, 1847, to July 31, 1848." Ed.D. diss., Ball State University, 1971.

Buck, John Edward, Jr. "Virginia and the Mexican War." M.A. thesis, University of North Carolina at Chapel Hill, 1965.

Evans, James Leroy. "The Indian Savage, the Mexican Bandit, the Chinese Heathen—Three Popular Stereotypes." Ph.D. diss., University of Texas, 1967.

Gamble, Richard Dalzell. "Garrison Life at Frontier Military Posts, 1838–1860." Ph.D. diss., University of Oklahoma, 1956.

Gettys, James Wylie, Jr. " 'To Conquer a Peace': South Carolina and the Mexican War." Ph.D. diss., University of South Carolina, 1974.

Hackenburg, Randy. "The Columbia Guards: Danville's Volunteer Infantry, 1817–1861." M.A. thesis, Bloomsburg State College, 1975.

Hughes, J. Patrick. "The Adjutant General's Office, 1821–1861: A Study in Administrative History." Ph.D. diss., Ohio State University, 1977.

Kreneck, Thomas H. "The Lone Star Volunteers: A History of Texas Participation in the Mexican War." M.A. thesis, University of Houston, 1973.

Lasswell, Lynda Jane. "The First Regiment of Mississippi Infantry in the Mexican War and Letters of Jefferson Davis concerning the War." M.A. thesis, Rice University, 1969.

McCartney, Samuel Bigger. "Illinois in the Mexican War." Ph.D. diss., Northwestern University, 1939.

McEniry, Blanche Marie. "American Catholics in the War with Mexico." Ph.D. diss., Catholic University of America, 1937.

Michael, Steven Bruce. "Ohio and the Mexican War: Public Response to the 1846–1848 Crisis." Ph.D. diss., Ohio State University, 1985.

Purcell, Allen Robert. "The History of the Texas Militia, 1835–1903." Ph.D. diss., University of Texas, 1981.

Wallace, Lee Alphonso, Jr. "North Carolina in the War with Mexico." M.A. thesis, University of North Carolina, 1950.

Whitfield, Henry J., Jr. "Alabama and the Mexican War." M.A. thesis, Alabama Polytechnic Institute, 1940.

Wynn, Dennis J. "The San Patricios and the United States-Mexican War of 1846–1848." Ph.D. diss., Loyola University of Chicago, 1982.

Index